Quiller Couch

A Portrait of 'Q.'

Quiller Couch

A Portrait of 'Q.'

A. L. Rowse

Methuen London

First published in Great Britain 1988
by Methuen London Ltd
11 New Fetter Lane, London EC4P 4EE
Copyright © 1987 A. L. Rowse

Printed in Great Britain
by Redwood Burn Ltd,
Trowbridge, Wilts

British Library Cataloguing in Publication Data

Rowse, A. L.
Quiller Couch: a portrait of 'Q'
1. Quiller – Couch, *Sir* Arthur—Biography
2. Authors, English—Biography
I. Title
828'809   PR5195

ISBN 0 413 17940 0

To
Daphne du Maurier
in common admiration
for our old mentor
and friend

Contents

Foreword

Many people have urged me to write this personal memoir of Q., since I am – along with Dame Daphne du Maurier – one of the few remaining to have known him well. Other tasks have postponed till now what I have recognised all along as a duty to the memory of the most famous Cornishman of his day, as well as a most admirable and enjoyable writer. But my belatedness has had the advantage that at last Q.'s correspondence has been made available to me by the kindness of his great-nephew, Mr Guy Symondson.

I am deeply indebted to him for this privilege. Q.'s letters have never been collected for publication, but he now turns out to have been an enchanting letter-writer. They add a whole dimension to our portrait of him, giving a picture of his many activities as public man, concerned all his life with education, his enjoyment of the sea and sailing from his base at Fowey, depicted in his novels as Troy Town.

To him writing was part of a whole, well-rounded life of action and public service. But we can now see how wide his circle of literary friendships was: not only his chief friends, the dramatist Barrie and Kenneth Grahame of *The Wind in the Willows*, but we have the bonus of letters from Hardy, Henry James, Robert Bridges, A. E. Housman and others too numerous to cite. Unexpectedly, Stanley Baldwin's letters reveal him as the attractive character he was in private life.

Q.'s long life ranges widely: from early days in Cornwall, where he kept his footing all his life; then to Oxford – the Oxford of Jowett, Matthew Arnold and Mark Pattison; literary life in the London of the eighties and nineties; finally the return to academic life at Cambridge. Of that we have a most enjoyable picture – though we must never forget Q.'s prime work, apt to be overlooked – as creator of the School of English Literature there.

A.L.R.

I

Introductory

When a distinguished writer dies his reputation is liable to go down into a trough of the waves, and to emerge again some time afterwards – especially if he has been over-popular in his lifetime. The most notorious case is that of Anthony Trollope, who was dismissed for a generation, if not two, after the appearance of his too honest (and admirable) Autobiography; and his reputation never stood higher than today.

Q. was very popular in his day, and no less prolific than Trollope. He spread himself even more widely: a score of tales and novels, a dozen collections of short stories, half-a-dozen or more volumes of lectures, essays, literary criticism. There were another half-dozen anthologies, including the most famous, *The Oxford Book of English Verse*, which set a fashion for so many others. He compiled editions innumerable, children's books, 'King's Treasuries' for schools; *The Cambridge Shorter Bible* for the general reader, followed by two further arrangements for children. He initiated *The Cambridge Shakespeare* and wrote Introductions to about a third of the plays. He wrote many Forewords and Prefaces to various works; and all his life he wrote verses, usually light verse, only a portion of which was collected into a fairly slim book of *Poems*.

Was it too much altogether? Q. was a very conscious artist, stylish in everything he wrote (and did); so that there is good work in all of it. Some of it was written for an immediate purpose, always a useful one, and need not detain us. But a good deal has lasting value: a handful of the tales and romances; many short stories, for he was at his best as a short-story writer; a good number of his essays and lectures, for he was a wise and sympathetic critic, with an astonishing width of reading; a few poems, and more of his lighter verse, always fun.

His writing, however, was but one half of the man. He led an exceptionally active, full, well-rounded life, public and private. I cannot think how he managed it all, and to write as well. For he wrote slowly and carefully, stylishly, with polished pen – sometimes perhaps too polished, particularly in his professorial dress (he dressed the part), for our more hurried, casual taste. He was unhurried; yet for thirty years he served on boards and committees for education in Cornwall, on the bench as J.P.; as chairman of the Harbour Commissioners and of the Yacht Club at Fowey, eventually serving a term as Mayor. For some thirty years he was a professor at Cambridge, and there a member again of too many boards, committees, clubs to specify. He was inveterately social, delighting in luncheon and dining clubs; he always had time for friends and guests, and numerous speaking engagements around the country as a man of letters, constantly in request.

He was a devoted family man, his personal life quite as full at Fowey – sailing, rowing, organising regattas in the harbour, celebrations of coronations, what not; gardening in the 'farm' across the river, where bombs in the Second German War nearly caught him out and shook him up towards the end. Earlier, he had been a good man on a horse – he never took to a motor-car or a typewriter; he wrote everything long-hand in that beautiful, scholarly script with his old much-mended pen.

What a man! – and a great dear, as all those who knew him could testify. What a happy, enjoyable life, full of service, duty, gaiety – save for one great grief: the death of his only son, who had fought all through the war of 1914–18 and come through safely, though wounded – to die shortly after, in the Occupation of Germany in 1919.

Things were never again the same for Q., though he bore up bravely, working harder than ever at his public tasks. Some gaiety had gone out of life – as with so many who knew *ce que c'était que la douceur de vivre* in the world before 1914. Though he did not specifically say so, he knew whom we have to blame it on, who were responsible for 1914: that fatal date for our civilisation, which ended a more humane Europe and set in motion the gathering violence and terrorism characteristic of the world today. Q. did not give up hope: he did not live to see the *fine fleur* that followed upon the Second German War.

*

Perhaps his work suffered from this dissipation of effort over so large an area. It was not from a failure of concentration on his part, but from circumstances which forced him to spread himself and undertake all that offered. Laurence Binyon, who knew him at Oxford, told me that earlier they all expected that he would write a great novel – at least one classic by which he would be known for good and all. This did not happen – we shall see partly why.

Q. was precocious. He began with more literary gift, more facility, even virtuosity, than many writers attain at the end of their days. One is reminded of Daudet in France, who had such an easy, sheer gift of writing; yet Flaubert, to whom writing came hard, who would devote a whole day to writing a sentence, and wrote so few books, in the end went beyond Daudet. Q. was a Daudet, not a Flaubert.

There was something else that entered into this. Q. believed that writing was only a part of life: life in the round came first. He told me once that, in his early prentice years in London, in the 1880s and '90s, literary life fell into two main schools. One was that of the aesthetes, who held not only to 'art for art's sake' but regarded their art, their writing, as all in all. The other school, to which Q. belonged – by nature no less than by conviction – was that of action, adventure, the romance of life itself.

The first included Pater, Wilde, Yeats, Arthur Symons (a fellow-Cornishman whose work Q. did not care for and certainly neglected) – and these he knew. But he himself belonged to the school of Stevenson, Kipling, Henley, Rider Haggard, joined later by the young John Buchan (who in turn admired Q.).

But what of those greater writers, Hardy and Henry James? Neither was confined to any school; however, with both of them, writing came first: they lived to write. Perhaps this is true of the greatest writers, who do little else but write. This is certainly true of Dickens as of Balzac, of Tolstoy and Dostoievsky, and fairly certainly of Shakespeare (apart from acting) and of Milton, save for his political digression, which went into his work, poetry as well as prose. Q. does not come into their class, gifted dedicated writer as he was.

There is perhaps a subtler reason beneath this. Take Hardy, whom Q. knew well. Hardy was at bottom a tragic writer – and the greatest works of Shakespeare, Tolstoy, Dostoievsky, are tragic. Q. flinched from the tragic view of life; he knew about it, and touched on it in some novels and short stories. But it was not his view of life; he resolutely turned his face to comedy. He could not put the tragedy in his own life, his only son's death from the war, as Kipling did with his only son's death – stoically writing one of the finest short stories ever written out of it: 'The Gardener'. An extremely sensitive man, Q. could hardly ever mention his boy; neither could Kipling, most vulnerable of men, yet he could transmute the grief into his writing.

A dark view of life was contrary to Q's code. This is evident in his choice of poems in *The Oxford Book of English Verse* – the chief defect of the book. Many finer, darker poems – the whole poetry of Swift, for example – are overlooked for lighter pieces, sometimes light triolets, *jeux d'esprit*, such as Q. fancied. Nor did he care for satire; any sort of cynicism went against the grain. His view of life was a noble and idealistic one – and he was a noble man, the greatest gentleman that I have ever known. Yet there is so much of the ignoble in life that calls for expression in literature along with the rest – think of Balzac or Dostoievsky! Q. could not contemplate it for long, allow his eyes to rest on it for the benefit of his work.

Similarly with sex. With him it is always love – delicately, gallantly, romantically treated; never sex, crude, raw sex. He had been at a public school – a singularly 'pure' school, as public schools went. (He must have known of the other side of their life.) He fell in love at seventeen or so with the girl who became his wife; married her without much to live on, wrote her every day that he was away from her side. And that was it – rather endearing, if inimitable.

I find his gallantry about women, their innocence etc, out of date – he should have lived into the era of Women's Lib. He was very shockable; how shocked he would have been by Simone de Beauvoir or Colette; he clearly thought not well of Virginia Woolf, nor did his Victorian-minded contemporary, G. M. Trevelyan ('nasty lot', he dismissed all Bloomsbury to me). They had an idealistic view of life. Perhaps that was naif of them.

Q. was a shy man. He one day said to me, with every expression of shyness, pushing the subject away from him with physical distaste: 'If anything goes wrong, er, in regard to sex . . . it is – you know – the end.' And that was all he ever said to me on the subject.

[4]

Yet he remained on friendly terms with Lord Alfred Douglas, and once invited him down to Fowey to stay. At this Lady Q. bridled: 'My dearr Arrthurr [Cornish r's], we can't have that man here with small children in the house.'

Though ill-treated women, the fair sex taken cruel advantage of, etc, come into his work – like Hetty Wesley or Lady Good-for-nothing – ladies like Lady Macbeth or Madam Golovlyov or the horrible daughter of Père Goriot, did not come into his line of vision. At least he did not care to reflect on them – a considerable limitation in his view of mankind, or womankind.

This inflexion, a certain Victorianism of mind, has led him to be much underestimated by writers who are nothing like so gifted, or so good as he was.

Q. *created* the school of English literature at Cambridge – which, he one day said to me shyly, 'in a manner of speaking, I invented'. Subsequently it became divided by the aggressive campaign led by F. R. Leavis. Something may fairly be said *for* Leavis: his revolt against the cult of Bloomsbury, for example; his insistence that literary taste, of the kind of Desmond McCarthy and Edmund Gosse, was a secondary matter compared with genius. But he exaggerated, and his relentless preaching got everything out of proportion; while his insistence that literary criticism was an end in itself, that it had an objective existence with its principles and rules, was largely a projection of his own personal predilections. Q. stood for everything that Leavis disapproved of: the Greek and Latin classics (like Housman or Bridges) – and Leavis had no languages to speak of, did not know English very well, at least couldn't write it. A former editor of the *Times Literary Supplement* commented that Leavis was neither 'high-brow, nor low-brow, nor middle-brow, but flat-brow, his prose the texture of coke'. Q. stood for a humane view of letters, a cultivated width of reading (Leavis was not widely read, even in English), above all for *style*, the love of the best in literature, and the practice of good writing. These principles Q. inculcated as professor, and to a much wider public through his books and anthologies: he appealed to the real Common Reader, not merely to the Bloomsbury, or Cambridge, reader. He was an Oxford humanist.

This was totally opposed to the Leavis-*Scrutiny* school. But it was

Q. who got Leavis his job. Q. persuaded his friend Sir Herbert Richmond, who was Master of Downing, to take Leavis on as tutor in English. Henceforth Downing was the base from which Leavis made war on the humanists. In literature there is room for everybody, even a Leavis; in the arts catholic sympathies, not partisan ones, are best.

When Q. became, effectively, the first Professor of English Literature at Cambridge all was to do; it fell to him to build up a School. He was no professional professor, and there was some opposition, not only within Cambridge but from the English Association. He took counsel with Sir Walter Raleigh at Oxford, who, with the historian Sir Charles Firth, had already built up a School of English Literature there. These had all been trained in the best standards of ancient Classics, and one of Q.'s ideas was to recruit from the Classics the best teachers he could for his new School.

For all his limitations, an extraordinary width of activities, normal and masculine (so unlike Henry James or Hardy), gave Q. a rich and varied equipment as writer of fiction. It is surprising how much he knew about all sorts and conditions of men. In his *Memories and Opinions* he relates this to his happy childhood.

> *Looking back, I count it happy fortune that cast a child's lot among these scenes and these people in a passage of time when so much that was homely, comely, and of mutual accord in village life, had come almost to the edge of disappearing. Yet I believe that those childish days held a lesson, at the time unconsciously imbibed and long latent, that, reviving in middle life, helped me to enjoy dealing with all sorts in local affairs, committee work, session work; to amuse many an hour, cheat impatience and master the desire to be at home attempting a fresh page of a book.*

For a writer Q. had much of Cornish folklore at the tip of his pen. He was perfect in Cornish dialect – as naturally Hardy was not (in *A Pair of Blue Eyes*, set on the coast of North Cornwall, the locals speak Dorset dialect). Though Q. was not a historian, he picked up historical material from his wide reading. I have been surprised at how much of the past in Cornwall he knew – stories of simple folk, fishermen and farmers, of village and town, parish and manor, stories of family and historic personages.

He had a practical knowledge of the sea, the handling of boats and ships, marine lore and all the technical terms that decorate his pages. He knew about the army, from the grander regiments involved in the wars of the eighteenth century down to the Looe Volunteers of the Napoleonic era. He came from a family of seamen and doctors on one side, and of yeomen farmers on the other – good upper middle-class stock, so that a wide spectrum of social life was open from the beginning to the novelist. To that he added his own intellectual qualities, of public school, university, literary life in London. In fact, though no mention was made of it, and he set no store by it – he was a clever man. His daughter knew that best.

All this added up to a remarkable equipment for the writer he was to be. He had also more specialised gifts: his senses were preternaturally acute. He could hear, as most people cannot, a bat's cry; he had the long sight of a seaman, a sharp nose for scents. His delicate ear thought the sound of running water the most beautiful music in the world. I note only one defect: he had no proper appreciation of cats.

Equally, the range of his writing was as wide, his standards in accord. They were of the highest – more than those even of a great gentleman, for he was a perfectionist, in life as in art. In both, courage, particularly courage in adversity, in women as in men, loyalty and generosity of spirit, were what he admired and put forward; he hated any kind of cruelty or meanness, vindictiveness or the spirit of revenge. He was a practising, as well as believing, Christian. He loved adventure and comradeship, was extremely sociable – especially so for a writer, had a great gift for friendship, which extended itself to the young, though for them it was also a challenge, to do well. At Cambridge he had a second youth; he threw himself into all sorts of activities, membership of clubs, both college and university (what a contrast to Housman, who was, however, a friend). I am astonished at the number of societies he belonged to, literary, dramatic, educational; or just for celebrating – he was a great one for festivities, commemorations, birthdays, keeping Christmas. He was always ready with a humorous speech, dressing up, adorned for the part; at Fowey on Regatta nights, in his seventies, in evening dress, cigar in mouth, he would ride a circus horse on the merry-go-round.

It all adds up to a boy's, or a youth's, spirited enjoyment of life, like

Kipling's; their genius came out of their perpetual youth, a certain naiveté. Q., like Kipling, was a moralist. How shocked he would have been by Gide's immoral cult of *l'acte gratuit*, if he had read of it! Besides the romance and tales of high adventure Q. liked best – *Sir John Constantine* was his favourite among his books – there was social comedy: the loves and foibles of maiden ladies, all treated with chivalrous delicacy along with the fun; the skittish and hoydenish; the local 'characters', eccentrics and loonies among the men. Oddly enough, *The Astonishing History of Troy Town*, with which Q. brought fame to Fowey as Troy, was not a favourite with him.

This early book had success with the public for its Barrie-like character, the Barrie of *Quality Street*. Barrie – more of a best-seller than Q. in his time – was a life-long friend. He too had a boy's view of life; so had Kenneth Grahame, whose *Wind in the Willows* was inspired by the Fowey river, another close friend. When *Troy Town* came out it was written down by Andrew Lang, who could rarely be generous about his contemporaries. Q. showed no resentment, and later reaped his reward, when Andrew Lang suggested the plot for *The Mayor of Troy*. Later, Q. dedicated one of his best books, *Hetty Wesley*, to Lang.

Hetty Wesley has never received its proper due. André Maurois got the credit for inventing the biographical novel – *Ariel, ou la Vie de Shelley*, etc – a biography variegated by fiction. Q. was some years before him – *Hetty Wesley* was published in 1903. It is documented from the sources of that remarkable family's history – deeply sympathetic to the strange story of this gifted girl's cruel treatment at their saintly hands.

This excellent book was given a bad reception by 'present-day "leaders of Wesleyan thought"', to use their phrase. They charged him with 'caricaturing' the sainted family. In a later Preface he answered them.

> *Now the trouble with my Wesleyan critics is not that they consent to discuss my book as 'caricaturing' . . . but that the language in which they condemn it proves that they have never so much as looked the facts in the face. Worse, it raises a suspicion that they do not face the facts because they do not dare.*

Q. always remained a Liberal; he one day said to me, 'The best thing is to be politically liberal, and socially conservative.' I accepted the second half of that, rather than the first: I agreed more with Kipling, of whom he said to me, 'I detest his opinions, but I worship his genius.' That shows how superior a critic he was – able to offset his personal bias by justice of mind, such as few critics have. Such a contrast to the Bloomsbury attitude, when a Raymond Mortimer could say of Kipling, 'I hate his guts.' They all prefer E. M. Forster's superficial view of India, which Indians resent as patronising; when its first President, Radakrishnan, said to me of *Kim*, 'After all, the best Western book ever written about India.'

True, Kipling had a strong dose of Nonconformist moralism; while Q. disliked the Nonconformist element in his own Liberal Party. That meant the pre-1914 political Nonconformity of such stalwarts as Hugh Price Hughes and the Baptist Dr Clifford, who held up elementary education out of envy of the Church of England. Q. was a good friend to Church schools in his thirty years of service on the County Education Committee.

What he cared for most was poetry. He had an extraordinarily retentive memory for verse – as so many Victorians had – in both English and Latin: quotations sprang readily to his mind. From his earliest days he had a gift for writing light verse, which they had more of a taste for than we have today.

At heart he would most like to have been a poet. He tells us that he would go off to bed – late, for he worked late – with verses sounding in his head, which by the morning he had forgotten. He could not afford to set aside the prose by which he earned the living for his family, to dedicate himself to poetry. Hardy had to wait many years before he could afford to give up novel-writing for poetry. With Q. it was not only circumstances that deflected him. Writing poetry is a vocation: one has to set apart one's inner life. Q. had a genuine vein of poetry; but it was not the essential thing in the inner man – he probably had too normal and happy a nature.

Family and School

Q. was half-Cornish, half-English. Though to the world he appeared as a Cornishman, wholly identified with Cornwall, for which he spoke, I have often thought that the English side was uppermost in him. He had none of the characteristics of the Celtic temperament. It is odd that most of those of Cornish stock who have made a name as writers are only half-Cornish. Matthew Arnold notably, though his temperament was recognisably that of a Celt.[1] So too the Brontës – Branwells of Penzance on their mother's side. Keats had Cornish blood and name. Hawker of Morwenstow was wholly Devonian; William Golding and Charles Causley, half-and-half, like Q.

The English side to Q. gave him equanimity, his control and balance; he lacked the *fougue* of the Celt, and he lacked passion – another reason why he did not excel as a poet. However, the mixture, in whatever the proportions, gave him his judicious character. We must add the class element: on both sides he came from good upper middle-class stock, with a public school background, public spirit and the sense of responsibility towards the society in which, after all, they enjoyed some position. Q. was born a gentleman (contrast Hardy, or D. H. Lawrence).

The Couches – the name is pronounced Cooch and means red and Q. was a red-head – produced a remarkable man in his grandfather, Jonathan Couch. He was the well-known doctor at Polperro, the tiny fishing haven between Fowey and Looe. He was London-trained and a good scholar, but his life-long passion was the scientific study of fishes, and he became the leading ichthyologist in the country, author of the standard *History of British Fishes* in four volumes.

Old Jonathan Couch, of whom his grandson gives a portrait in his *Memories and Opinions*, married a Quiller and theirs was the odd and

[1]   v. my *Matthew Arnold, Poet and Prophet*, ch. I.

huddled house, leaning over the stream in the heart of the little place, that now goes by his name. Quiller may have been a Breton name – it is not Cornish – and all the men of the family had been drowned, except one. This last one, on a cross-Channel trip, dreamed on his last night that he saw himself go through the bottom of his boat. Persuaded to take no notice of his dream, he was drowned on the way back, last of the Quillers. The celebrated art-connoisseur, Sir Hugh Lane, had Quiller blood: he was drowned when the Germans sank the *Lusitania*.

Jonathan Couch in his sixties married a girl of twenty as his third wife, and this led to a family split. The rest of the family took against him – except Q.'s father, also a doctor. Q. was proud of his grandfather's tribute to this son: 'Thomas is one of the best fellows that ever lived; you can trust him if all the rest of the world fails.' This may be said of Q. himself, for *loyalty* was of the essence of his character. He had many loyalties, especially to Cornwall, to Oxford and Cambridge, and to his friends.

Q. told me a comic episode that resulted from the family breach. He was going back to school, when the train was held up in a snowy cutting near Liskeard. He looked up from his book to find himself being eyed by a girl of his own age or rather younger. She said, 'Is your name Couch?' Q. replied that it was; to which the girl said, 'Then I must be your aunt' – and was. As Q. went up in the world and lived in style at Fowey, 'the uncrowned king' of the place, there was not much communication with the Couches left behind.

His social position and even his academic career were not achieved without set-backs. His father was the doctor at Bodmin and had a good practice. Well educated, he was a good naturalist and amateur painter; he contributed some of the plates to his father's great work. He put together Jonathan's *History of Polperro* and wrote a number of papers on Cornish antiquities, folklore and dialect. There were plenty of books in the house. One sees that writing was in the family.

Though Q.'s was an upper middle-class home, he knew Cornish dialect and renders it perfectly in his books. His speech had several old-fashioned West Country pronunciations: an 'ar' sound for 'or', for example, he would say 'starm' for 'storm', and he never elided his r's. This gave his speech a decided flavour.

[11]

In everything that he wrote or spoke he was above all *stylish*, always addicted to a well-turned phrase. When he raised some cash from his colleagues on the County Education Committee to enable me to try for a scholarship at Oxford, he made himself the 'conduit', and he hoped that I would not object to his service, etc. 'Object'? – I could not have got to Oxford without it, but I relished the word 'conduit'.

His father, the doctor, neglected to send out his bills, and his mother was hopelessly extravagant. In the end it led to serious difficulties for the whole family. The household lived in style beyond its means – and Q. always lived *up* to his, had his own vein of extravagance. He had little money-sense, nor did his books bring in a great deal; early on he had to sell even the copyrights, while some of the books were pirated in USA, before the international copyright agreement.

His mother was the only child of her Devonshire parents, who owned some property in the charming parish of Abbotskerswell near Newton Abbot. Q. waxes sentimental about his mother's looks, of Devon 'cream and roses'. He certainly didn't inherit them, he took after his grandfather: an extraordinary idiosyncratic appearance, like a weather-beaten old sailor; red face, markedly creased, heavy jowl, long upper lip, close-clipped moustache, small cocked head; the whole redeemed by brownish bright eyes, intelligent and kindly. He held himself like a countryman, long lanky stride. This appearance went oddly with a nature of exceptional sensitivity, a public man who was yet very shy, apt to put up his hands to his face from shyness. An entirely masculine nature, given to an out-of-doors life – rowing, sailing, riding a horse – he had a more than feminine sensibility. A strange combination, presenting itself as a very normal human being – but, within, fired by genius – no doubt about that.

As a boy he must have been an 'ugly urchin', as he says; and a very clever one. He was well taught at home, and by a couple of local lady-teachers; so that he arrived at his preparatory school in Devon 'far better grounded in Latin, French, Euclid and even arithmetic (my life-long abhorrence) than the boys of thirteen and fourteen in whose form the headmaster placed me'. A master said that he soaked up Greek and Latin like a sponge. Q. always regretted that he was not more of a scholar – in the sense of a classic like A. E. Housman. I don't know why he should: the classics remained always alive in his mind, not dead as with many 'pure' scholars.

With the family funds running down, the boy was partly dependent on scholarships, and he wanted to try for Winchester – 'Manners Makyth Man', etc. But his headmaster forgot to send in his application in time, and the boy had to be content with a scholarship at Clifton, then a comparatively small foundation. He consoled himself by sending his boy, Bevil, to Winchester – who was less suited to that more intellectual atmosphere than his father would have been.

Q. was not altogether happy with Clifton. He was put off by an unsympathetic housemaster who snubbed him for the over-bright curtains in his study and rated him for the loud waistcoats he wore. He always had an addiction to bright colours: sea-blue shirts with tall stiff collars and bright red bow tie, strong check patterns in suits or knickerbocker tweeds in the country. When he arrived at Cambridge as professor, A. C. Benson (who had wanted the job) remarked in his Diary that Q. dressed like a 'racing tout'.

However, even at Clifton there were figures to remember. The school had a 'character' well known to the literary world in the Manx poet, T. E. Brown, who took the boy for walks and talks. Several of the young scientists were to become Fellows of the Royal Society. There were constant literary talks with the brothers Francis and Henry Newbolt. To the latter Q. accorded two places in his *Oxford Book of English Verse* for his 'He Fell among Thieves' and 'Clifton Chapel'. He would have done better to have included 'Drake's Drum' and even 'Vitai Lampada', which better brings back the place:

> There's a breathless hush in the Close tonight –
> Ten to make and the match to win –
> A bumping pitch and a blinding light,
> An hour to play and the last man in . . .

And with the hearty refrain Betjeman loved,

> 'Play up! Play up! and play the game!'

Q. would not include anything by his Ninetyish fellow-Cornishman, Arthur Symons: 'I could do nothing for him,' he said to me. Symons had reacted from Nonconformity into the cult of decadence, and Q. liked neither.

He had had one emotional friendship at preparatory school, about which he wrote in reply to a query from an Oxford clergyman, the Rev. S. E. Cottam, who was interested in the subject, and had sent him his volume of poems, *Cameos*. Q.'s reply is extraordinarily sympathetic for someone so 'square'.

> *No: I doubt if my school friend 'fell in love with someone else'. It didn't happen to me, anyhow. You see, we were urchins of 14 or under, and maybe our attachment was unconscious premonition of manly love for a woman – which was to come in due course. My adoration of '——' just faded into a sort of sentimental memory, his of me out of his memory altogether – metaphysics had mopped it up like blotting paper. At my Public School I made some friends in the ordinary way, but it was at Oxford that I learned to get and keep (in numbers too, but with two or three 'elected' ones) the friendship which lasts for life, with hooks of steel.*
>
> *So it is that one experience of a very youthful Eros which helps me to respond to the undercurrent of your book: and if you should ever come across one of mine,* The Delectable Duchy, *and turn up a little story, 'School Friends', you will see to what extent I do respond.*

This was written as late as 1935, and is the only reference I have come across in all his writings to a subject that occupies so much space in those of today. He sounds just not interested – and Clifton extraordinarily chaste. There he made friends with J. W. Arrowsmith, who became useful to him in later years and, at Bristol, published half-a-dozen books for him. No doubt he would have found it still more useful to have been at Eton or Winchester. One has often observed Wykehamists and Etonians promoting each other in the literary papers – like the cult of George Orwell promoted by fellow-Etonian Connolly, and now venerated for having gone slumming among the working class. (As if he knew them from the inside, as D. H. Lawrence and I do!)

III

Oxford

Q. adored Oxford, and was to do so all his life – though he spent far more years at Cambridge. Oxford was first love. He grew acclimatised to Cambridge, but was apt to say 'Wc', referring to Oxford, and 'You' to Cambridge folk.

He fancied going to Exeter college, not only for its West Country associations, but because it was then Head of the River, which meant a lot to the rowing man. But Trinity awarded him a scholarship, and there he was intensely happy for some five years. Then a small college of only seventy undergraduates, it formed a body where friendship was at its height, Q. felt that the increase of numbers 'dissipated something of the old domestic life'. This was close and amicable, with all the little ritual observances he appreciated – the proper dress for the right occasions, top hats and morning calls with gloves and visiting cards.

His energy and activities were prodigious. He got his First in Mods (classical Moderations) easily enough, but he was a rowing man, passionately addicted to the river – and this eats up time. There were theatricals, both College and University; above all there was writing. He was very precocious, with a great facility for writing light verse. At Clifton in 1881 he had written a prize poem, defeating Henry Newbolt, which his proud parents had privately printed. He now competed for the Newdigate, and was awarded *proxime accessit* – probably to a poem less good than his own. I don't think Q. liked that much – any more than I did, when the same thing happened to me, and the prize was won by a Rhodes scholar, years older, who has never been heard of since. Q. observed, 'We need waste no time on these exercises, which are of interest only to people interested in such things.'

He was proud to have inherited Newman's rooms in the Garden Quad – with its outlook on the border of snapdragons described in a

[15]

famous passage of the *Apologia*. Q. refers to his sitting-room there as his 'keeping-room', thus betraying all the years at Cambridge, for it is not an Oxford term, but a Cambridge one, like the verb 'to keep' in that sense. It was like Q.'s loyalty to stick up for Newman in the controversy with Charles Kingsley, for all the latter's West Country associations and breezy nautical tastes.

There were famous men about in that smaller, more elect world; Sir Charles Oman told me that we could hardly imagine the way the Victorians put their great men on pedestals. Dr Jowett would come in from Balliol to trot round the garden at Trinity for his early-morning walk. Glimpses were to be had of Mark Pattison in his invalid's chair in the Turl; or of Matthew Arnold 'slipping through the Balliol gateway, trim side-whiskers and lavender kid gloves':

> *Somewhat of worldling mingled still*
> *With bard and sage.*

Walter Pater would come over from Brasenose to a literary club Q. belonged to. There he would sit, 'on the hearth-rug, back to the fire, cross-legged, with the light flickering over his baldish cranium, his moustaches pendulous in the shadow: a somewhat Oriental figure [Pater had an un-English mixture of blood, Dutch and American], oracular when his lips opened and he spoke, which was seldom.' Q. did not align himself with the aesthetes, or the Pre-Raphaelites.

He was in time to hear Dean Church deliver the funeral oration on Dr Pusey, the last direct contact with the Oxford movement of half-a-century before. There were glimpses of Lewis Carroll – that quintessence of the Victorian age – 'clerical, white-choked, flitting, flitting, like a shy bird into some recess of Christ Church'. Rhoda Broughton was rather a notorious figure in Victorian Oxford, for she not only wrote novels but smoked. Q. would catch a glimpse even, 'unavoidable by politeness, for her window bulged on the pavement, caught on the way back from an early training grind by Holywell, of the authoress's breakfast table laid for her, its silver ware gleaming against a bright fire and by the hearth a couple of pug dogs stretched, awaiting their mistress's descent.' Today the lady would be making her own breakfast in the kitchen, and wouldn't dare to have any silver out in Oxford, a burglar area.

Sometimes Robert Bridges would lope in as a guest at high table, and the rumour ran round the scholars' table that 'this distinguished-looking man was a poet, but few of us had met with any of his verse', as yet privately printed. Q.'s associates, with whom he 'dared to team himself up', were a heartier breed: Anthony Hope and A. E. W. Mason, to become novelists as successful as himself; Henry Newbolt, consciously training himself for literature, and C. E. Montague, to become a pillar of the *Manchester Guardian* as essayist in its best days. Montague and Q. were 'far more intimate as friends and rivals in Balliol and Trinity oarsmanship'.

Q. became better known than any of them as an undergraduate writer. He was one of the group that started the *Oxford Magazine*. In its early sparkling days it was mainly written by undergraduates to become well known: Anthony Hope and Michael Sadler, an inspired educationist; D. S. MacColl, a leading art critic; and Cosmo Lang, of all people, to become the Archbishop of the Abdication.

Young Q. was brought in by his senior at Trinity, Charles Cannan, who became his closest friend. He was an inspiring director of the Clarendon Press, who proposed to Q. the idea of *The Oxford Book of English Verse*, which brought him fame as an anthologist and provided a constant, dependable income. I one day said to him, in the familiar study overlooking his garden: 'Little did you think you would strike a gold-mine in your own back-garden, did you?' Q. grinned: 'Well, no, I didn't, did I?'

A rare volume of reprints from those early years of the *Oxford Magazine* shows Q. as contributing practically a third of the volume. A parody of Whitman portrays the young Q. at Trinity:

> *Behold I am not one that goes to Lectures*
> *or the pow-wow of Professors*
> *The elementary laws never apologise:*
> *Neither do I apologise.*
> *I find letters from the Dean dropt on my table –*
> *And every one is signed by the Dean's name –*
> *And I leave them where they are; for I know*
> *That as long as I stay up*

> *Others will punctually come for ever and ever.*
> *I am one who goes to the river . . .*

(And indeed he went down to the river too much for the good of his Schools.)

'Willaloo,' parodies Poe:

> *See the freshers as they row*
>   *To and fro*
> *Up and down the Lower River for an afternoon*
>   *or so –*
> *(For the deft manipulation*
>   *Of the never-resting oar,*
> *Though it lead to approbation,*
> *Will induce excoriation) –*
>   *Keeping time, time, time*
>   *In a sort of Runic rhyme*
> *Up and down the way to Iffley in an afternoon*
>   *or so . . .*

The refrain has Poe's 'Nevermore'. Already one sees Q.'s skill at verse forms and verbal tricks.

'Fire!' records a visit of the United Fire Brigades to Oxford, May 1887:

> *St Giles's street is fair and wide,*
>   *St Giles's street is long;*
> *But long or wide, may nought abide*
>   *Therein of guile or wrong;*
> *For through St Giles's, to and fro,*
> *The mild ecclesiastics go*
>   *From prime to evensong . . .*

'A Letter' to Miss Kitty Tremayne reads:

> *Dear Kitty, At length the term's ending;*
> *I'm in for my Schools in a week;*
> *And the time that at present I'm spending*
> *On you should be spent upon Greek . . .*

No doubt – but O the fun they had in those unclouded days, the blissful security of the Victorian age – until the cloud of the Boer War rose upon the horizon, foreboding the horrors of our time!

One sees how useful these earlier contacts were to him, and being a good fellow they paid off. Mr Brittain, who became a Boswell to Q. at Cambridge, remarks that he was cautious in making friends. On reflection I think he was right: even in my own early years I suspected that Q. was socially selective.

The Victorian gusto for light verse is more understandable in the absence of canned pleasures, wireless and television; they made their own fun, the printed word was everything. Q.'s high spirits found vent here as on the river. Grave seniors would exchange sallies with this undergraduate in the pages of the *Mag.*, no less a person than Sir William Anson, Warden of All Souls, a prime figure in the University, or Professor A. D. Godley with his half-English, half-Latin Goliardic rhymes.

Later on there would be such exercises in linguistic virtuosity as 'A New Ballad of Sir Patrick Spens' in braid Scots:

> *The King sits in Dunfermline town*
> *Drinking the blude-red wine:*
> *'O wha will rear me an equilateral triangle*
> *Upon a given straight line?'*

> *Our King has written a braid letter*
> *To Cambrigge or thereby,*
> *And there it found Sir Patrick Spens*
> *Evaluating* π.

Then follows a long exposition of the proposition, parodying the Cambridge mathematician, Todhunter, who ruled the roost in Q's undergraduate days:

> *The tane circle was BCD,*
> *And ACE the tither:*
> *'I rede ye well,' Sir Patrick said,*
> *'They interseck ilk ither.'*

[19]

And so on to the concluding proof.

Q. carried these frolics down to Fowey. I have always enjoyed the sheer virtuosity of his verses illustrating the vagaries of English spelling:

> *O, the Harbour of Fowey*
>   *Is a beautiful spot,*
> *And it's there I enjowey*
>   *To sail in a yot;*
> *Or to race in a yacht*
>   *Round a mark or a buoy –*
> *Such a beautiful spacht*
>   *Is the Harbour of Fuoy . . .*
>
> *And my leisure's addressed*
>   *To composing of verse*
> *Which, if hardly the bessed*
>   *Might be easily werse.*
> *And the spelling I use*
>   *Should the critics condemn,*
> *Why, I have my own vuse*
>   *And I don't think of themn.*

Half-a-dozen stanzas of it! could any of his dull critics rival it?

There seems to have been no time for serious poetry – that demands a quieter pace and inner experience. A couple of such experiences, which are the inspiration of poetry, he describes in two passages of prose. As a schoolboy standing on a bridge over a stream in Bradley Woods, a favourite spot near Newton Abbot,

> *I happened to glance up on my right and was met by a Vision. 'Twas of nothing more than sunlight slanting down a broad glade between two woodlands that drowsed in the summer heat. But it held me at gaze while the mere beauty of it flooded into my veins, and the mysterious bliss of it shook my young body. Also, when I came to recall the scene, a deep silence held it: the water slid without noise under the footboards, no note of bird broke the afternoon hush.*

He apologises for perhaps making too much of 'a trivial experience'. But these 'moments of vision', as Hardy calls them, give birth to poetry. Another happened when the boy, on vacation from Clifton, was by a creek of the river Fowey at Lerryn.

> *The time of year was late summer, the water smooth as glass; over it the woods hung, their lower branches leaning, here and there dipping a frond to make a ripple. For a second time that drenching sense of beauty which had poured over me on the bridge under Bradley Woods, mastered and took possession of me.*

These quasi-mystical experiences, when time stands still and one is offered some unaccountable inner revelation, are a signal to the poet and a sign of his vocation. Wordsworth based his whole career as a poet upon them. I wonder if Q. was not too engrossed with the outer life to listen to the inner voice, and was thereby the less good poet?

Meanwhile, life at Oxford hurried too fully, too enjoyably, on – and this was not good for scholarship either. Everybody expected him to get his First in Greats. This test falls into two parts, ancient history, Greek and Roman, and ancient philosophy, mainly Plato and Aristotle. He had decided to plump for the philosophy, and was advised that he could neglect the history. This was bad advice – one needs to do at least moderately well to back up one's first choice. He did very well, got αs on his philosophy papers, badly on the history. Samuel Alexander, to become eminent as a philosopher, struggled hard to get him his First on his philosophy papers alone; the historians wouldn't have it, and Q. was awarded a Second.

It has always surprised me that he should have taken against history; for, later in his novels, he showed a good historical sense. When I dedicated to him my first work of historical research, *Sir Richard Grenville of the 'Revenge'*, he wrote me a charming letter saying comically that he had been sitting up late at night with a wet towel round his head reading it. Well, my *Sir Richard Grenville* is not all that hard to read – it has gone into several editions; but it is a work of historical research, and Q. was not geared to that. He was obviously interested in the English past, but his interest was literary and eclectic – he chose what he wanted for his own stories.

Q's Second was a blow at the time – though nothing like the celebrated catastrophe to A. E. Housman, who completely failed the examination.[1] There had been a heavier blow before this, when Q's father died, a comparatively young man, leaving his son 'the head of our house, with my mother, two sisters and two young brothers of school age, and no income – a grim prospect, though mercifully not so grim at the moment as it afterwards proved to be'. At this juncture his mother's father, who had a fair estate, enabled Q. to continue at Oxford – all with the hope of a First in the Schools and the financial security of a Fellowship.

The young Q. manfully picked up the pieces, sold his father's collection of Cornish relics and most of his library, and with the proceeds settled the family in a house in Oxford. 'Thence my brothers attended the Oxford High School as day-boys before going their ways in life.' This sounds pretty dismissive – one has never heard of them since. There, too, his mother spent the rest of her life, while her son worked hard for years to pay off their debts. So much for her extravagance – he has little to say for her.

Thereupon befell another blow. Grandfather Ford announced that he had lost all his money 'in a vain attempt to rescue an elder brother's fortunes from shipwreck'. It sounds like throwing good money after bad. 'That same evening I asked the lady of my affection to be my wife. It was mad no doubt.' What confidence in life it shows! Fifty years afterwards he counted that moment the most fortunate of his life. Well, taking a risk sometimes brings rewards, but it needs good luck none the less.

Trinity now came to the rescue by giving him a lectureship, so that he was able to remain up a fifth year. He lectured mainly on Plato and Aristophanes – they represent two sides of his nature, the idealism and the Comic Muse. The class must have been cheered by the very human young don who could announce, 'As the University is playing Lancashire this morning there will be no lecture on Herodotus.'

At Trinity he had a good friend in Raper, pillar of the Senior Common Room, one of those benevolent dons who 'take an interest' in their young men and help them over stiles in the way. Q. did not take missing a Fellowship too badly, for he never intended a don's

---

[1] The various recent books on Housman make different attempts to explain it.

life: he intended a writer's. Raper encouraged this, and backed his writing the novel he had in mind – *Dead Man's Rock*. Meanwhile, to raise funds, he took a vacation tutorship at glorious Petworth, and there began it.

Years later, when it became my turn to reach Oxford from remote Cornwall – with much greater difficulty, for my people had *no* money, and there was only one university scholarship for the whole county – he called me over from my local grammar school to his study. My headmaster was sending me up for the English Literature scholarship at Christ Church. Q. said that he had coached a boy for it, and 'though he wrote like an angel' ('and talked like poor Poll', I put in brightly), he didn't get it. I remember registering obstinately to myself, 'Well, we'll see.' When I was lucky enough to win it, dear Q. told the press that he had nearly made a fool of himself. However, fortunately I had not registered discouragement.

Q. was inspired by Robert Louis Stevenson, as so many of that generation were, and looked up to him as the Master. R. L. S. is absurdly disconsidered now, though he was admired by better judges, notably by Henry James himself. Q.'s description of how he came to write his first book is of interest to all beginners. The notion of it came to him on 'a warm summer's night, a small garden overhanging a cove, of Cadgwith in Cornwall; the French window open; a fan of light cast out on the turf; and within a number of moths self-immolated and fallen upon an open volume of Plato that I had deserted to wrestle with the first conception of this tale'.

Then invention stalled, as happens with beginners, and he could not think how the plot was to develop. Enlightenment came on 'a zig-zagging uphill road near the little village of Nanstallon [a Roman signal-camp not far from Bodmin], at a bend of which some months later – beside running water – my fluid ideas came of a sudden to a crude consistency, and I felt I could write a story. The next time I passed that way was on a late evening, and the high banks shone with glow-worms. I took the omen.' The next scene was 'an inn parlour in Petworth, Sussex, where I spread out some sheets of foolscap on a red-covered table and began to write' – Q. wrote everything long-hand, and with that same pen, often mended, with which he had got his Second in Schools. Last scene: 'the moment of tearing open the brown paper parcel and holding one's first book, solid, in its binding'. Every writer knows that thrill.

Q. was lucky to win success from the first. The R. L. S. vogue of romantic adventure, really boys' books, was at its height; Q. was not much more than a boy (and always retained a boy's heart). The book took off, and made him some money. He admits that, though the first half went well enough, the second half fell to pieces. Never mind: its success opened the way to literary life for him.

One recognises the Cornishry of the book, the dialect words – 'airey mouse' for a bat; or the young Q.'s expert nauticality and sea-terms – a 'jib-boom', for example (what is a jib-boom?). I can respond here and there to the evocations of atmosphere. 'The slow clock sounded the hours . . . The mice crept out of their accustomed holes. The fire died low and the candles died out; the wind moaned outside, the tamarisk branches swished against the pane; the hush of night, with its intervals of mysterious sounds, held the house', etc. It is Cadgwith Cove, near the Lizard. Q. has transposed thither the name of Readymoney Cove from Fowey harbour, and got his title from the Dodman, the tall headland near Gorran, which people take to mean 'dead man'. Q., who did not know the old Cornish language, knew that 'man' or 'men' means rock; he did not know that 'dod' means turf. That exactly describes the Dodman, well known to sailors – it rears its head over 400 ft high: the mass of rock is covered with turf.

Q.'s years at Oxford were from 1882 to 1887, Queen Victoria's Jubilee Year; they were formative, bubbling over with activity and development, and they remained alive in his mind all his life. He kept in contact too – not without some *contretemps*. A subsequent President, Blakiston, was not Q.'s man. This crusty old bachelor at some point must have offended Q., for in later years he tended to put up at the nearby Randolph, rather than at his old college. On the other hand Blakiston saved his son Bevil from being sent down. This boy, named for the heroic Sir Bevil Grenville of the Civil War, had 'more spirits than he knew what to do with'. He belonged to that pre-1914 generation – of which the irrepressible Horace Cole of Trinity, Cambridge, was the exemplar – which took delight in practical jokes. One day Bevil was returning from some races and, going through the turnstile on Oxford station, found himself held up by an old lady followed by her black Aberdeen terrier. 'I happened to have a bag of flour with me, and you should have seen the expression on that old lady's face when she turned round and saw that her little doggie had gone quite white.'

Later on, Raper suggested to Q. that he should stand for the Professorship of Poetry, and Herbert Warren, President of Magdalen, promised his support if he would stand. This was in 1910, before Q. returned to academic life but was famous as novelist, critic, and editor of the Oxford Books of Verse. When he consented and arranged to do so, Warren snapped up the post for himself. On this occasion Q. was really angry. It might have been excusable if Warren had been the better man – but who would value the views of a Herbert Warren on poetry, as against Q.'s?

When he became professor eventually at Cambridge, academic business brought him back to Oxford more often. He came over to consult with Sir Walter Raleigh about the shape the Tripos was to take, or he was called over to take part in elections. When Raleigh died Q. came to elect his successor. 'I stayed with Bridges [on Boar's Hill]. He asserts that the view from his garden overlooking Oxford beats the view from Fiesole. Well, I don't know about that: but it is assuredly mighty fine' – ruined today, of course, by the immense suburban growth strangling the city since. 'We bumped into Oxford next morning and elected Gordon to be successor to Raleigh . . . and then I toddled aside into my old college and its beloved but rather battered lime-walk.'

Q. told me that he and Bridges had agreed on Nichol Smith, much the better scholar; but Bridges switched his vote to G. S. Gordon, the lighter weight but more popular man – a lesser Raleigh. Q. kept on good terms with the magnificent, but grumpy, old Poet Laureate – not an easy task – and gave him the best representation of any modern poet in the *Oxford Book* (less good on Housman, who in turn properly admired Bridges). On another visit, 'Yes, Bridges has a noble view, and a noble wife, forbye. Whether or no the old ruffian deserves his luck I don't say. He's a spoilt child; but I like him, and he permits my mirth when he gets too oracular.' This is just: Robert Bridges was used to having his own way in every respect, but I doubt if he had much sense of humour, certainly not about himself. However, Q., who had plenty of humour, knew how to handle the immensely distinguished old poet.

We must return to those years before the turn of the century, before Imperialism and the Boer War darkened them for a time: those happy years which Q. recalled in the best of his poems:

> *Know you her secret none can utter?*
> *Hers of the Book, the tripled Crown?*[1]
> *Still on the spire the pigeons flutter,*
> *Still by the gateway flits the gown;*
> *Still on the street, from corbel and gutter,*
> *Faces of stone look down . . .*
>
> *Once, my dear – but the world was young then –*
> *Magdalen elms and Trinity limes –*
> *Lissom the blades and the backs that swung then,*
> *Eight good men in the good old times –*
> *Careless we, and the chorus flung then*
> *Under St Mary's chimes . . .*
>
> *Come, old limmer,*[2] *the times grow colder;*
> *Leaves of the creeper redden and fall.*
> *Was it a hand that clapped my shoulder? –*
> *Only the wind by the chapel wall . . .*
>
> *Ah, but her secret? You, young lover,*
> *Drumming her old ones forth from town,*
> *Know you the secret none discover?*
> *Tell it – when you go down.*

John Betjeman, a good Laureate, regarded this Oxford poem as 'still unsurpassed'.

[1] The arms of the University.
[2] This rare word means a pal.

Family Struggles and Courtship

Perhaps we may pause here, to take into account the *cache* of Q.'s personal letters that have come unexpectedly to light. They enable us to counterpoint our external portrayal of the man with his own inner experience, thus giving us a further dimension, a deeper perspective. Above all, it gives us evidence of the hard struggle he had to achieve what he did from his Oxford years on, the family troubles that beset him. As to this, no one outside the family knew; he was a reticent man, and we all assumed that his course was plain sailing all along, until he came into harbour at Fowey. Far from it: the truth was otherwise.

The trouble was mainly due to the thoughtless extravagance of Q.'s mother, which nearly ruined the family, and brought down a sad blight upon the end of their Bodmin days. In consequence he had an ambivalent attitude towards his native town – no one knew that: happy memories of innocent childhood days, a narrow escape from social disgrace when the true facts of their situation fell upon them. For years they had lived beyond their means; there was a sense of style in the family – and they had social pretensions. We must remember the inspissated snobbery of late Victorians, incomprehensible to us, and the extreme disgrace which bankruptcy, in those days, would have brought. By Q.'s manful effort this was just avoided, but the consequences fell hard upon him and especially upon his talented sisters, Lilian and Mabel, who also had a gift for writing.

On top of this there came the financial failure of his mother's father, from whom the family had expectations. Then Q. added his own extravagance as an undergraduate at Oxford. For, oddly, in spite of the almighty lesson all this amounted to, he had very little financial sense himself. When he eventually married, he handed over his money affairs, paying over his cheques, to his wife – not the least of the blessings he derived from that exceptionally happy marriage. But the

[27]

money worries, and the strain it imposed, postponed that blissful consummation by several years, and meant a long and at times threatened engagement – by the girl's mother, who evidently was unfavourably impressed by what had happened to the Couches.

While waiting for the girl of his choice, he wrote, 'how pitiable and at the same time how absurd this poverty is!' He admitted that, 'had I been saving when first I came up to Oxford, had I not been an extravagant young fool, I should not be where I am now'. But, he excused himself, 'had I lived below my income I should never have been able to keep in the running with the best men, or to have had any influence to speak of in the College. As it is, I got this place [his lectureship] simply because I was understood to have a lot of influence with the men and to know the best of them.' There we have the Victorian picture, difficult for us to appreciate (a democratic society has *some* advantages, as against its horrors).

It was years before Q., so sensitive a man, could come clean about what they all endured – in a letter to his favourite sister, Lilian.

> *Yes, yes, my dear – I have always known about the bitterness of that past – the root of it in the Bodmin days, but the fruit of it later. . . . It was a long stiff job paying off the load of debt I took over in '88 and eventually cleared. Louie [his wife] had no easy time in lodgings for a year or two: but I did work. . . . Now I suppose a lot of people think I've had the luck of it all along. But I never sought, never applied for, a single thing that has come my way. . . . I reckon that the strange upbringing we had taught us both in different ways (yours the harder) the same lesson – never to rely on anything but one's own courage.*

Never a word of these troubles to the outside world. There were also the two young brothers to be educated, though, without talent, they came to nothing and one of them went to the bad. We hear no more of them, never mentioned in a family so bent on keeping up appearances or (to put it more kindly) standards.

In October 1886 the young man went down to Bodmin to take the family crisis in hand – 'with a headache from talking business all day: if there is one thing I detest it is the man who talks of money'. The decision was taken to sell things up and move the family to Oxford; he had at least the security of his lectureship (not much) and what else he could earn from tutoring and by his pen. At Bodmin he packed up what could be saved. Louie had taken on a 'risky bargain', but she was an inspiration to his work to deserve her: 'you have been on the edge of a stammering declaration for years past'. Actually the girl's mother maintained a sullen opposition to her marrying him for some years. The widow of a sea-captain (with a good cellar at her house in North Street, Fowey), she had her own social pretensions – and no confidence in the Couches. The young man was reduced to pleading that his characteristics were more those of his reliable grandfather, old Jonathan, than of more recent members of the family.

Back at Oxford he was house-hunting for them, but could not afford the house he fancied, at £65 a year. 'I feel such a hankering after money upon me that I must go to bed at once and sleep off the disgusting feeling.' Recovered, 'I like the fine high-sounding braggadocio of these old poets: if a man be fit for much, he must have some inkling of it:

> *But if thou wilt prove faithful, then,*
> *And constant of thy word,*
> *I'll make thee glorious by my pen,*
> *And famous by my sword.*

His love letters are very literary, full of quotations from the poets, but one detects the accents of some uncertainty owing to the opposition of circumstances and 'Mrs H.', as she appears – for the daughter had a better-endowed swain after her. Still, 'I make no doubt that one day we shall laugh at these struggles and I shall snap my fingers at poverty. I used to think of sauntering through the world on a modest competency and playing the onlooker at life: but you have introduced me to the love of money-bags.'

He managed to settle his family into a house, 26 St Margaret's Road. His mother was rather taken with Oxford, though I fancy it took her down a peg or two to have to take in undergraduate lodgers to help square the accounts – which still continued unsatisfactory and bills continued to run up.

Meanwhile his lectureship gave him a refuge in college.

[29]

Oxford is lovely just at present with the red autumn creepers covering its walls: already the younger and 'hungry generations' are about buying their baths [tin ones for a bath before the open fire, in those days], their pictures, their books (few), and their cigars (many). It is an odd feeling coming back as a don and I regret my old scholar's gown. The B.A. ditto stamps one as old in a city which counts the generations in four years – the oldest and youngest city in the world. . . . I have not yet dared to wear my new gown. Who, without a struggle, admits to being 'passé'? I have a very strong feeling, however, that London is the place for me.

There was a significant pointer to the future.

Money was scarce, and in the long vacation the young don took a tutorship at Petworth, the splendid Sussex palace of the Leconfields (illegitimate branch of the Wyndham Earls of Egremont). He was there to tutor a young Wyndham for 'Smalls', i.e. Responsions at Oxford, but more of his time was taken up with batheing, dances, balls, country walks thinking of Fowey, where his heart was with Louie. Comic episodes delighted him – Rectory picnics and music there – he was fond of music, and had exceptionally keen hearing. He evidently fitted in well with grand country-house life, entertaining on the large scale Victorians could afford, and much appreciated intelligent Lady Leconfield, sister of Lord Rosebery. Wandering around the vast house he came to the 'Beauty Room', which he did not fancy, sombre panels painted with dead-and-gone Court beauties:

> *Golden lads and girls all must*
> *Like chimney sweepers, come to dust.*

He was writing to Louie – two letters or three a week to keep him in mind; now the harvest moon was pouring in at his study window while he wrote. 'Life took a different channel for me during that week at Fowey' – when they had plighted their troth on a slab of slate in Readymoney[1] Cove, and in the evening they had walked along Hall Walk (where now is his Memorial looking out to sea). Louie had promised to wait for him, until the family debts and his own were

---

[1] Folk etymology has vamped up a story to account for the name; but in fact it means the stream (rid) by the rock (man or maen).

cleared and they were able to marry. Until then the engagement was
to be kept secret – he found waiting 'cruelly hard'. Mrs H. maintained
her opposition: she had 'nothing to say to him'.

Back at Oxford for term he was in his old rooms, but 'as a stranger',
with another man's furniture, bare and dismal. He always liked
comforts, things of taste around him, always flowers in his rooms. 'I
do not think anyone but an Oxford man knows how one gets to love
the old place. My heart begins to jump when I see the old towers
again from the railway and pass the river I have toiled up and down so
often.' He confessed to 'love of old associations and indifference to
change. So expect domestic bliss, for where my heart is there it
remains.'

> *It did seem blessed and peaceful to dine with the old faces again in the
> quiet panelled room; and I caught myself thinking these dons lead a very
> happy life – out of the bustle and racket of this 'go-ahead' century. But I
> reflected on the prospect – as Goldwin Smith put it – of having one's eyes
> closed at last by a scout, and concluded that I had chosen by far the better
> part.*

> *For thy sweet love remembered, such wealth brings
> That then I scorn to change my state with kings . . .*

> *My sweetheart, I am finding already what a tough battle I have before
> me, before I can win. I do not think you can quite realise how poor my
> people are and how heavily handicapped I am at the start. . . . I expect
> there are few indeed who would care to shoulder my load.*

The Wyndham boy was now up, struggling with Smalls. 'I have
been accused before now of rating the intellect of my fellow men
rather low – another way of saying that I am intolerably conceited.'
[Not at all: a perfectly natural recognition of facts, for an intelligent
man.] Here now were the young men 'expensively dressed', some with
tall hats and tall collars.

> *To think that I, whose sympathies always inclined to those who cut
> lectures and who have myself achieved notoriety in that line, should have
> to lecture to the 'hungry generations' that 'tread me down' is Nemesis*

indeed. Hitherto my life has given me a great deal of happiness and gives me the prospect of a greater joy than all.

Mrs H., however, maintained an 'obdurate silence': she discounted 'my callow youth', and this gave him anguish.

Settling the Couch family in Oxford he found 'a tremendous business', but he had been 'careful about furnishing'. Chloe (his mother) has 'a longing to see me in cap and gown – a pleasure which will be, for the present, denied her'. The house he had found for them was in 'a very jolly neighbourhood'. There was good news of Lily, who had received 'astounding praise' from an editor for her first literary effort. 'I am beginning to think you have gone and got yourself engaged to the fool of the family. . . . I hope you are disposed to make the best of a bad bargain.' Lily must have turned in a bit of money with her writing, and eventually came into harbour by marrying an Eng. Lit. don at London University, J. H. Lobban, and settled in Hampstead, where Mabel, who never found a husband, joined her. The two girls made good by co-operating in one or two books, including one on the holy wells of Cornwall.

The ardent lover exchanged his Oxford news for that of Fowey. 'I suppose as the Couch family proposes living in Oxford I shall have to call this my home. But I do not think I can do it. I shall always be harking back to Cornwall and Fowey. . . . It is a weary time waiting here and ploughing through the old work. . . . So be of good heart – the time is not so long now.' It took longer, and was harder work, than he expected, paying off all the debts and providing for the family – a millstone round his neck for several years. He was buoyed up by being 'within sight of the City of Love'. The idea of marriage was a 'most tremendous one': when he thought of it his head was 'full of quotations' – Shakespeare, Browning, Meredith, old ballads – 'stealing out unawares'. It was a very literary courtship.

This did not impress Mrs H., who 'thinks us mere children'. He thought that the best way of breaking the news of their engagement to her was 'to insinuate that I have all my grandfather's good qualities with a few more thrown in. . . . But how about my smoking? If I knock off three pipes a day?' All his life Q. was a confirmed smoker – his only vice (it caught up with him in the end). He found facing his class of spirited youth made him nothing like so nervous as his ungrammatical declaration in Readymoney Cove had done – and, 'I wonder if Mrs Sackville would let me dig up that slab of slate and take it to Oxford with me.'[1]

There he was rowing energetically every day and coaching the Trinity crew.

> *Of course it is a bleak stream as compared with Fowey and misses the accessories that made the river there a thing to love and pray to. But there is something wonderfully calming to the nerves in a long steady swing down the river, the body swinging in rhythm and all the muscles playing in time. . . . If ever you find your husband restive beneath his harness of roses, send him out for a good long pull up the river and he will return to you.*

We should add here that he was physically a strong man, well-nigh tireless. He seems to have taken only an occasional break, on a College holiday, when he strolled about Trinity garden, and in the afternoon went up to the Parks, with good college spirit, to see Trinity beat Brasenose at football.

Or he would be parading the gardens by moonlight, thinking of Fowey and all the times they had gone up-river, punting under the trees at Lerryn, to Pont by the light of the moon, or various times to Golant – where, from the church on the hill one has the deep view of the river below and up across the valley the tower of Lansallos church on the horizon. He was thirsting for Fowey news: 'the very sound of Fowey is to me "like the shadow of a high rock in a thirsty land"'. The best-selling Miss Braddon was there, intending a novel. 'I intend to write something myself about the place some day – so ambitious have I become – in fact have the plot in my head.' We see that when he came to write his *Troy Town* it was no *jeu d'esprit*, no question of some 'foreigner' (as we say) looking for a subject, but a deep affection that was to hold him all his life. 'The autumn of our life, I trust, will always have the glow of the summer that has been.'

Meanwhile there was money to be earned, and he took another

---

[1] Mrs Sackville, a Rashleigh, owned the land. For her story v. my 'Invocation for a Cornish House', in my *A Life: Collected Poems*, 114–15.

tutorship during the vacation, with a rich new family of Harrisons. Some of his letters are dated from Shiplake Court – Matthew Arnold country – near Henley-on-Thames. He seems to have made himself as welcome there, so agreeable a man, as with the grandees at Petworth.

The books that were to win him fame for his beloved, if not fortune, were shaping in his head. *Dead Man's Rock* had been begun at Petworth, where he had actually shaved himself, 'thus saving 3d each time. Vive l'économie!' Apparently a Victorian gent. didn't even shave himself. In his letters he quotes French verses quite a lot, and Louie said, when they went to France later, that he spoke it fairly fluently. He was always pro-French, like Kipling, and – like any civilised man who knows the record – anti-German. Down at little Fowey there was now a good deal of gossip about the young couple: 'we may be foolish but at any rate we are obstinate'. At Oxford he was coaching the Trinity crew, but wants to labour a bit on a second book; he has an idea that will do, but it needs hammering into shape. This would be *Troy Town*.

In March 1887 he wants to get his book finished by the end of the week – Nagel, one of his colleagues, has gone off to the Bodleian to look up points for him. 'For the past twenty-two hours snow has been falling: the apple-trees in front of my window have still a heavy load.' His people were moaning at freezing, and thinking there was something to be said for Cornwall after all; but they were making the house in St Margaret's Road very nice and planting by the gate. His friend Cannan wants him to go up to the Lakes with him for 'glissades' in the snow. 'My bow window has an excellent seat in the full blaze of sun' upon a white Oxford. Since last summer he feels that he has 'a world to conquer . . . you have put so many schemes in my head'.

In May, good news: Cassell's accept his book and want him to sign up for another. They favour him using the simple initial 'Q.' – already well known from the *Oxford Magazine*. To the family he was always Arthur, and never liked his second name Thomas. About the book he had the usual apprentice doubts: he was 'very much afraid of the miserable venture', and absurdly condemned the 'badness of the work'. Oddly enough, he never liked this book which gave him such a vested interest in Fowey as 'Troy'. To Cassell's he wrote, 'As I am striving to free my people from money difficulties I should be glad to anticipate even at a loss and sell the book out of hand.' This was *Dead Man's Rock*. 'The new story aims at being humorous. . . . Really, it's the kind of book that would be enormously helped by small and clever illustrations amid the text – like the new editions of Daudet's *Tartarin*.'

A later letter from St Margaret's Road continues: 'In consequence of an entanglement in my people's affairs, I am in a position in which I urgently need ready-money [Readymoney Cove!] . . . As I have the plot of Troy Town in my head, I could get on with it at a fast rate, supposing you wanted it.' Happily they did – he was lucky in that, from this time onward, he never had any difficulty in getting his work accepted, indeed work piled in on him. In August he was able to take a brief holiday at Homburg, rendered fashionable by the Prince of Wales, the future Edward VII, and his exotic entourage. Q. wrote from the Hotel du Parc that he had forgotten to sign his agreement (no negligence of that sort once he was safely married). After that his address would be 'The Club House, Fowey' – to become so familiar – then Wargrave for Shiplake Court where his tutoring chore continued.

From 1888 we have letters to Louie's sister Jane, 'Jinny', who had already got a husband in Joe Blamey: they lived at Caragloose,[1] down the coast in the parish of Veryan, where Q. and his beloved could get on with their courting, away from the disapproval of Mrs H. One gets a delightful impression of Jinny, a more attractive one to me than her sister who was – not to mince matters – a snob. Even Jinny, who was not, kept a parlourmaid. She had had a good laugh at *Troy Town*, but Q.: 'I'm not hard on Fowey, only on some of the ways of it.' He had now made his intended move to London, and wrote from Cromwell Road that he had caught cold and rheumatism by going to hear Patti sing: 'She made me fall on the neck of an aged chaperon, who sat next to me, and sob.' Next time, 'I will bring walnuts in my hat-box and build you a salad that will make you sit up' – here was the connoisseur of good food, as of wine. From these good friends hampers of good things come to and fro – a pheasant, cheeses, honey: family affection ran more in that direction, in spite of Mrs H.

From May 1889 there is a touching letter to Jinny on the loss of her

[1] The name means the rock in the wood.

'little maid' of three, whom Q. loved. He could not have trusted himself to speak what he felt, sensitive as he was, only write.

> *It's a perfect day here – the Park full of carriages and the carriages full of people who look as if they had no trouble in life. And yet I don't suppose there's one in a hundred but has lost somebody, and many those that are dearest to them in the world. And how about those who drove along the same road seventy years ago? What's become of their hopes, loves, ambitions, and all the rest? Why, all gone to find out the true values of those hopes and loves – work over, lovers found again, and if they were good, a better world left behind them.*

He was aching to tell Jinny and Joe how much he has learned from them. 'The fashion is to shut up one's heart, and if I were *speaking* to you I should never dare to tell you. . . . When I come to Fowey or to Caragloose I have always found help. . . . I am only struggling after a good that I shall never attain . . . you do see the sweetness of life and the happiness of home and beauty of love.' The 'little maid', in her short life, had brought something of this into his, as well as into theirs. 'A young man of "this so-called 19th century" must thank you with all his heart for it.'

Here, for once, he exposed his heart, as so rarely – except in his letters to Louie. Now from North Street he wrote that he was 'waiting for a definite statement from Cassell's before fixing the date of the "w-dd-g" (can't write it out loud, 'cos I'm so shy)'. They had been up to St Winnow, lunching on the river; today above the Sawmills. He would send on the Dumas when he got back – Jinny seems to have been more of a reader than her sister. However, Louie was the only girl for him. From Shiplake Court he wrote that it had been

> *cruelly hard waiting so long – and now, if I seem light-hearted next week, please Jinny, don't think your grief has touched me lightly; or that, because I've reached my dear desire, I have forgotten the little heart I lost on the way. . . .*
>
> *Heaps of employment have been put in my way as a set-off against leaving the Harrisons. They would have another Trinity man to take my place. If this day three years, I have been told of the joy and pride I have in her today it would have seemed a wild exaggeration, as it would have been outside my comprehending.*

They were married – at last – in Fowey church on 22 August 1889. From their honeymoon we have a letter from Lustleigh, evidently retracing the scenes of his youth.

Mr Bennets, at the Post Office here, is a mild but worthy man, and wears his spectacles on his bump of intelligence instead of on his nose – for effect. He is shaped thus [Q. draws a fat figure] and is my heart's delight. An old lady (visitor) came in yesterday while we were buying sardines and tapes, and wanted to know the way to Lower Eastleigh. So Mr Bennets said, 'First you goes up there' (pointing to the chimney), 'and then takes a turn to the left' (with his eye on the bacon-rack), 'an' then you pops round the corner like as it may be round that' (with a finger extended to the tall clock), 'an' then 'tis slap in your face same as I be t'ards you, mem.' I thought the old girl would have fainted, but she thanked him hurriedly and rushed out into the fresh air: and he observed airily to me, 'Fact is, I be that driven wi' visitors, I dunno where they be or where they bain't.'

Here was the budding novelist, with the professional observer's eye and ear for talk. 'We found a bath here, a High Church service, and some ripping sweets called toffee-humbugs – so we're quite happy, and the inhabitants look after us and say, "How young they be, to be sure!"'

V

London:
Literary Life in the Nineties

Q. had moved to London in 1887, on the threshold of the Nineties, which were such a wonderful time of promise for all beginners in the trade of writing, journalists, novelists, even poets. For there were innumerable papers and periodicals to write for, many of good standards, for a variegated public. Writing was everything; where today it has to lag behind television and radio, their ephemera geared to the masses with their mania for Bingo. Opportunities were such that an active-minded, ambitious youth like John Buchan kept himself as an undergraduate at Oxford by his writing and as a reader for publishers, who were welcoming and on the look-out for likely young men.

Once more there was a good friend to take care of Q. in London. John Williams, a Trinity man, was chief editor at Cassell's. They were a distinguished firm, who continued to publish Churchill, from their premises off Ludgate Hill, La Belle Sauvage, destroyed by the barbarians in the Second War they unloosed on Europe. That imprint went back to a tavern, patronised by Pocahontas in her time in London. She was taken as patroness by taverns, some of which called themselves 'the Indian Queen' – hence the name of the village, Indian Queens, in Cornwall.

In his late Memoir of *A. J. Butler*, Q. tells us that Williams played elder brother to him, 'imparting his knowledge of all the haunts and out-of-the-way corners around Fleet Street, Ludgate Hill, and "the Row" – a knowledge that ranged from quiet City churches [so many since destroyed] and the Halls of guilds with their libraries [ditto], to the special dishes of uncanny restaurants and wines of recondite cellars' – these all too well appreciated. He describes La Belle Sauvage, known to its familiars as 'The Yard', as it was: 'approached by an archway, the first turning to the left as you go up Ludgate Hill. By the passage, perennially blocked by a carrier's van, or vans [it was

still the London of Dickens] you came to the Yard, and at the end of
it to a door, a stone staircase and a lift with authors upon it, ascending
and descending.'

In the depths of the premises were the steam-presses which
'laboured in travail with the firm's productions – *The Quiver, Cassell's
Saturday Journal, Cassell's Popular Educator, Cassell's Magazine, Chums,
Little Folks*, and what not'. The publishing world sported many more –
plenty of elbow room for authors ascending and descending. Presiding
over the establishment was Wemyss Reid, another firm backer of Q.
Known as a good fellow, he soon acquired a host of friends – too
many, I should have thought, for concentration. A close friend was
the firm's illustrator, Alfred Parsons, with whom Q. kept up correspondence over many years. Through him he came to know a number
of artists, Edwin Abbey, Francis Millet, and Sargent. He was called in
to chat away while Sargent painted his celebrated portrait of Ellen
Terry as Lady Macbeth. Among theatre people were the beautiful
Ellen herself, and George Alexander who was producing Wilde's plays
with much *éclat*. On the edge of this circle hovered Henry James, with
his hopeless desire to be a successful dramatist. Barrie was a closer
friend, a colleague in writing for the papers, on the way to making a
fortune by his plays.

When Cassell's founded the weekly *Speaker*, with Q. as its regular
contributor, this greatly extended his literary acquaintance. For a
galaxy of talent appeared in it: Barrie and George Moore, the poet
Richard Le Gallienne, of the improbable name, and H. W. Mas-
singham. Among the poets were Yeats, William Watson, and the
excellent but unfortunate John Davidson, who wrote a fine poem,
'Thirty Bob a Week', which Q. unfortunately did not include in his
Oxford Book – too stark, I suppose. (Q. did not like sadness in poetry.
Davidson drowned himself at Penzance.)

The Speaker was printed in La Belle Sauvage, 'where I used often to
meet and lunch with Oscar Wilde, then in a magnificent coat of
astrakhan, editing *The Woman's World*, and sometimes with George
Moore. The both of these were good enough to treat me always as an
intelligent listener – a game at which I can claim some ability to play.'
He never talked for mere effect, as these Irishmen did; and he had his
own brand of whimsical humour, unlike theirs. One does not find Q.'s

name in *The Yellow Book*, along with fellow-Cornishman Arthur Symons; nor was the unhealthy Aubrey Beardsley among his artist friends – Q. was, above all, *healthy*, in every respect, perhaps to a fault.

The Speaker was a Liberal paper – in those days the Liberals had all the talents – and the politicians writing for it are too numerous to mention. Some of them combined politics with writing, such as John Morley and James Bryce, most successful as ambassador to Washington. Q. did not like Augustine Birrell: 'That man takes himself much too seriously, and nothing else seriously enough.' His intuition was justified. Birrell was later made Chief Secretary for Ireland: it was owing to his inefficiency that the Government was not alerted to the Easter Rising of 1916 in Dublin, with its appalling consequences.

I appreciate more among all these luminaries J. A. Spender – if only for his dictium at the fading out of the Liberal *Nova*: 'The longer I live the more I see that things really are as silly as they seem.' Q. wouldn't have approved of that – to the end he remained hopeful, as if whistling to keep his courage up. (He died just before D-Day 1944.) *The Speaker* was eventually absorbed into a new Liberal weekly, *The Nation*, and that in turn was engulfed in the *New Statesman*. Q. couldn't bear the inflexion of this paper under the ineffable Kingsley Martin as editor (Muggeridge couldn't stand his physical proximity, any more than I could his intellectual smell). Q. would from time to time growl, in his endearing way, that he wouldn't take the paper any longer; but, such was his loyalty, he was still taking it when he died.

For Cassell's he did any amount of miscellaneous work, some of it hack-work. Like so many of the best writers he never minded turning his pen to a good proposition, or to useful purpose – like Dickens or Thackeray, Dr Johnson or Goldsmith. Of course, one recognises those elect spirits, and the critics who over-value them for every book they do *not* write. But the greatest artists are usually those who can turn their hand to anything, good journeymen as well as good craftsmen. Even an elect writer like Gautier, as much of an aesthete as Baudelaire, if asked to insert into a newspaper article enough matter to fill a vacant eleven-and-a-half lines, could always oblige. So, it is clear from his work, would William Shakespeare.

Q. was always a good craftsman, even in his journeyman's work, though I suspect that he is under-estimated partly on account of the latter, the sheer bulk of his writing. For Cassell's he edited a three-volume collection of tales for boys, *The World of Adventure*, and another such collection, *The World of Romance*. Later still he was ready to do any number of miscellaneous jobs, like editing a series of select *English Classics*; or, even as professor, presenting the Bible in more readable shape for children, or a whole series of miniature *King's Treasuries of Literature*. Ernest Rhys, the inspirer of the famous Everyman Library, was always a good friend (I was present in the study at the 'Haven' when Rhys came down to visit and discuss the *King's Treasuries*).

I fancy that all these jobs must have militated against concentration on bigger creative work. Here we may remember that, again amid such miscellaneous journalism, Arnold Bennett achieved *The Old Wives' Tale*; while Somerset Maugham, amid much inferior stuff, wrote another classic, *Of Human Bondage*.

Perhaps Q. did spread himself too widely, but in these early years he was writing for dear life, all day and into the night. In March 1890 he was writing from lodgings in Ledbury Road that he had passed Mrs Harrison in Regent Street, out already in her victoria. No time to speak, he was in such a rush: 'up to my wrists in grime and printer's ink, writing notes and articles to the sound of slamming doors in La Belle Sauvage. . . . A melancholy steak for lunch in the City. But Wemyss Reid and I worked like mad.' He got back in time for dinner, 'instead of 11 p.m. as last week'. But such was 'the penury that follows on imprudent marriages'.

Next month, to Joe Blamey:

> *Upon my word I never have time in these days to turn round . . . so much work to be done just now that I shall take months getting it out of a tangle. I only took this* Speaker *work on with the idea of either altering the paper a great deal or giving it up if I can't get my way. And as I seem to be getting my way against a pack of dolts, and as my blood is also getting up, I mean to sit tight and fight 'em.*

Dead Man's Rock had been dedicated to the memory of his father, *Troy Town* no less appropriately to Charles Cannan, practically a second father. 'Few have the good fortune of a critic so friendly and inexorable'; then, with one of those happy turns of phrase which came so readily to him, 'if the critic has been unsparing, he has been used unsparingly'. Someone described the book as having something of a *Cranford* atmosphere. With Q.'s first two books we have the two sides of his creative work already foreshadowed: adventure story or historical romance on one side, social comedy on the other.

The Splendid Spur had been published in 1889; fifty years later, it was translated into Arabic by one of his pupils. It tells the tale of Jack Marvel's adventures from Oxford during the Civil War, all the way down along the Great West Road, to the battles of Bradock Down and Stamford Heath. The dedication tells us that 'under the coat of Jack Marvel beats the heart of your friend Q.' – spirited and gallant, especially towards ladies in distress; also innocent, I should say.

I fell in love with this book at my elementary school at Carclaze at the age of nine; and somehow I learned that the writer lived over there to the east beyond the Gribben headland. The book made such an impression that I am not surprised to find how much has remained in my head over seventy years. Not the ins and outs of the plot, but, more clearly, gestures, words, scenes. There was the gesture of Jack 'tossing his gown to the porter' at the gate of his college; the pickpocket baking a hedgehog in clay under a hedge; the Puritan villain of the piece trailing his foot and his unforgettable name, Mr Hannibal Tingcombe. He was white-haired: did that suggest the albino vicar, villain of *Jamaica Inn*, to the young Daphne du Maurier, devoted follower of Q. along with me in our early days?

In October 1890 the first child was born, a boy given the name of Bevil, after Q.'s Civil War hero, Sir Bevil Grenville. 'He won't be good-looking, going to be absurdly like me.' Writing from the Clubhouse at Fowey, 'I have to go up again this week, then I may have a week off. Atkinson, Rogers and I dined at the Solferino, Thursday, and went to a music-hall afterwards: a very good wind-up to a day which began in a drive from Paddington to the hotel at 4.30 a.m. And included seven desperate hours of scribbling in Fleet Street.' Atky, his closest friend at Fowey, a bachelor character who lived up the river at Rosebank, was back and 'we rowed along the coast for a bit this morning'.

For *The Speaker* he was engaged to write literary causeries and reviews, and a short story each week. To Wemyss Reid:

> *Your readers must be pretty well tired of finding a short story by Q. every week; so perhaps I had better do something else this time. Why has Barrie ceased work on this line? . . . I'm utterly dissatisfied with myself just now. Almost every day brings a request from some quarter or other for a short story. I feel I shall never write a big book, and it worries me.*

Here was the fix he had got into, through debts and early marriage – though he was twenty-five at the time. George Gissing contemporaneously refused to give himself to any kind of literary journalism; though opportunities offered, he hated editors, he said, and preferred poverty. Q. would not have accepted that, and in fact did not lower his standards; Gissing wrote something of a classic on the dilemma, *The New Grub Street*.

From Fowey he was writing to Jinny, 'their tongues are going like windmills. I have the half of a paper to write tonight for *The Speaker*: perfectly useless to try and work in the middle of all this.' Here was how one got about the country in those days: 'I meant to train to Falmouth, lunch at the Hotel, cross in the ferry to St Mawes and walk up the coast . . . to be at Caragloose a long time before dark, and would walk on next day to Mevagissey and St Austell and catch the train back. . . . The Hockens are standing on their head with excitement.' At Par Station he had met Jinny's mother, talking all the time 'a lot of Veryan scandal. No doubt your vicinity is not quite such a Babylon as it is painted.'

Many of Q.'s early short stories were written in the train between London and Cornwall; or were conceived 'under the stars over Plymouth Hoe in night-pacings through an interval thoughtfully provided for me by the Great Western, breaking trains on the way home'. They appeared in a number of periodicals, in both Britain and USA; most were subsequently collected in various volumes, *Noughts and Crosses, I Saw Three Ships and Other Winter's Tales*. (He had a good ear for titles.) Next year he was writing from St James's Street:

> *My own heart, I'm pretty well used up and must easy off for just a little while before starting on the finish of the Pavilions [*The Blue Pavilions*]*,

*which will have to be written tonight. I did a causerie last night, which
took me till 12.30, and then I felt much too exhausted to begin a story.
So I sat and thought one out for an hour, and early this morning I
trotted off to Reid to explain that I was going up to the office in Fleet
Street, with paper, pens and tobacco, and wasn't to be disturbed by a soul
till I brought him the story written: which happened just before 3. Then I
went out and drank a half-bottle of Graves with my lunch and felt as if I
wanted six. . . . Just got back home and am going to rest for a couple of
hours, and then I shall be fit to tackle the 'Pavilions'.*

We see the way things were with him, the strain of his writer's life.
Cassell's had had 'an offer to run dear old *Dead Man's Rock* through
some newspaper for a small sum: 'you claim these amounts, don't
you?' Reid wanted him to dine at the Reform Club to meet George
Moore. One way and another he was meeting everybody in literary life
in those years, his social life an added strain. Down at Fowey Mrs
H.'s home was being sold up: 'It is hateful to have an old home broken
up in that way.'

The Blue Pavilions of that year was another adventure story, but with
a twist: the aim 'to infuse a sprinkling of the Shandean into an
unhistorical-historical story which ran straight from a beginning,
through a middle, to an end. Such a story had to deal with eccentrics,
who are as natural in an English story as plums in a pudding.'

That autumn he had a complete nervous breakdown – and what
wonder? He once described to me what happened: on the railway
journey he was making to London he could neither sit nor stand, but
had to lie out full length on the compartment seat. In London,
insomnia and 'a nervous fear of crowds amounting even to shrinking
from crossing the street'. A specialist gave him the advice he was only
too happy to take: to leave the city and live by the sea. 'Fleet Street
was not really my life. I made a great many wonderful friendships
there. It was worth it for that alone, but I don't think I got anything
else out of it.'

I rather doubt that. It meant a sacrifice for him: it rather put him
out of the running in literary life. Writers like Barrie, George Moore,
Shaw and a host of others kept their footing there; Henry James spent
his winters in town, even Hardy regularly came up for the season,

Kipling lived not far away. London remained a literary and cultural metropolis right up to the Second German War, and until the penal taxation of the modern state dispersed writers and drove many into exile abroad. Q. came to be regarded as a provincial.

> *All happiness must be purchased with a price, and part of the price is that, living thus . . . to breathe clean air, to exercise limbs as well as brain, to tread good turf and wake up every morning to the sound and smell of the sea and that wide prospect which to my eyes is the dearest on earth . . . a man can never amass a fortune.*

His London friends made fortunes in those days, when the going was good – 'but as it is extremely unlikely that I could have done this in any pursuit, I may claim to have the better of the bargain'.

That 'wide prospect' he found at The Haven, on the riverside above Polruan Ferry, looking across the estuary, to the river's mouth and out to sea. For years now he had been footloose and restless, for ever changing residence from one place to another, eventually homeless, living in hotels and lodgings. With The Haven, he and his little family found a home which he never left until he died.

From a rowing trip down the Warwickshire Avon he made a pleasant book, illustrated by Alfred Parsons. Here Q. was perhaps a precursor, in a field which Edward Thomas was to make his own, book-making too, and get more credit for. Both men were good craftsmen in prose, and Q. has virtually a prose-poem about Shakespeare's resting place, with 'the whisper of Avon running perpetually'. We might regard this as a first announcement of what was to become a constant concern with Shakespeare, as critic and later editor. At the time, we see the inspiration for his most-anthologised poem, 'Ode upon Eckington Bridge, River Avon'.

> *O pastoral heart of England! like a psalm*
> *   Of green days telling with a quiet beat –*
> *O wave into the sunset flowing calm!*
> *   O tirèd lark descending on the wheat!*
> *Lies it all peace beyond that western fold*
> *   Where now the lingering shepherd sees his star*
> *Rise upon Malvern? . . .*

I don't know whether this represents some foreshadowing of the Boer War, the clouds that were gathering in South Africa. The Ode itself is a celebration of peace, against the battles of long ago that had been fought out along the river, Q. himself always moved by the sound of running water. Of his short stories I am inclined to think them the best of his creative work, himself one of the finest of our short-story writers.

VI

Life at Fowey

Life at Fowey was immensely enjoyable; but it took Q. a long time to recover from his breakdown, some eighteen months or so. This experience was more important than we realised. G. K. Chesterton, after his comparable breakdown – from overwork and over-drinking – was never quite the same man again, some *élan* went out of his work. Q. recovered himself, and went on to write his best books and to a fuller, more rounded career, a public life.

For many months he could not face a train journey; he wanted to see Wemyss Reid about *Speaker* affairs, but could not go up to London. The paper made an agreement by which he could write as and when he could: this provided a stand-by for the time. Meanwhile he kept his name before the public by collecting his short stories into books. A friend suggested his making an anthology of Elizabethan lyrics by way of recreation. Hence came into being *The Golden Pomp*, which started him off on yet another line, as anthologist, and led to bigger things.

Good for his health were his physical activities. He had a little seven-ton cutter, the *Vida*, 'a thing of beauty', in which he sailed in the estuary and along the coast; there was also the bright red rowing boat – Q.'s old love of colour – a familiar sight on the water. In this, to the end of his days, he would row across to the steep garden patch by Bodinnick, which he called 'the Farm' – vegetable, flower garden, orchard, apples and plums – where he worked. He took long walks in those days, when he thought out his stories, and he enjoyed horse-riding. He told me of the days when he would ride over the mile-long, hard sands of Crinnis beach on *our* St Austell bay – ochre-coloured coppery cliffs, the island rock from which it takes its name, not a soul in all that empty space of sand, sea, sky. Now popularised under the name of Carlyon Bay, vulgarised into a Lido with swimming pools, vast Entertainments centre to which people troop from far and wide.

The entertainments of Victorian Fowey were of a simpler, home-made character. Q. joined in the frolics; it used to amuse him to watch the effect of the doings of the little place upon his London guests. They might be greeted at the tiny railway station (now closed) in the valley up by Penventinue – pronounced Pennytinny – by circus people, clown and all, girls be-ribboned and in fancy costume, or by the inevitable brass-band frequent at our feasts.

Barrie came down several times in these years, brought his wife to stay in rooms, and would spend hours playing with Bevil: 'he is my favourite boy in the wide, wide world' – though, when he grew up, he was succeeded by other Peter Pans. Barrie wrote to the Dutch novelist, Maartens, whom he and Q. admired: 'It is but a toy town to look at, on a bay so small [it is an estuary!], hemmed in so picturesquely by cliffs and ruins that, of a moonlight night, it might pass for a scene in a theatre.'

A. J. Butler would come down from Cassell's to fall for the delights of sailing, second to his Victorian crush on mountaineering in Switzerland. 'La Vida es Sueño', this good linguist declared, who in the intervals would help Q. with his anthology. Butler had been met at the station by a troupe of Pierrots and Pierrettes, and next by a Scot in bright yellow Tartan. In return he would chaff Q. for his ignorance of geology, and Cornwall the most interesting and variegated county geologically in the whole country! One day, a ship's ballast of volcanic tufa from Naples having been piled up by the roadside for road-metal, Q. led him to it, all unsuspecting, to impress him still further with what we could do in the way of geology.

All these literary folk had little idea of the *historic* interest of Fowey – how important it had been in the Middle Ages in the cross-Channel fighting with France: hence the 'ruins' Barrie saw. They were blockhouses of the time of Edward IV, when an iron chain ran across the harbour to block the entrance. There was the rambling castelled house, Place of the Treffrys, dominating the huddled roofs of the town below – with the tradition of the spirited lady of the house, in the absence of her husband, repelling French invaders by pouring molten lead upon them from the bulwarks. The grand parish church below, with tall four-stage tower uplifting its head, itself bespeaks that period, fourteenth to fifteenth century, the Hundred Years' War with

France. The Ship Inn, across the churchyard, was the house of the Elizabethan Rashleigh, who sailed his ship, the *Francis of Foy*, to serve under Drake against the Spanish Armada. There they all are, the townsfolk of those days, Treffrys and Rashleighs, gathered in their bulky tombs, under their stones and brasses, in the church which Q.'s family attended.

The house he chose for himself, The Haven, was just the right home for him. Mid-Victorian, it had been built by some naval person, hence the rooms were all named for ships of yore. Not too big, it was yet in a prominent position on the long street, with a narrow strip of garden bordered by diminutive Cornish elms. One never saw Q. out in the garden, he would have been far too conspicuous a target for visitors, with the Fowey Hotel looking straight down upon his roof. With Place itself grandly withdrawn within its walls, The Haven was the *point d'appui* of the town – a Mecca for me as a schoolboy.

The house was certainly exposed, and to all the winds that blow. It had a special feature, a little balcony giving on to the street: I used to imagine Q. appearing on it to address his fellow citizens – as I expect he did on festive occasions when they came to honour him. A good thing the house turned its back on the street and looked across the harbour to Polruan,[1] (Penpol in his books) for he was often intruded upon.

> *Why so many people mistake it with its modest dimensions for a hotel, I cannot tell you. I found one in the pantry the other day searching for a brandy-and-soda; another rang the dining-room bell and dumbfoundered the maid by asking what we had for lunch; and a third, a lady, cried when I broke to her that I had no sitting-room to let. We make it a rule to send out a chair whenever some unknown invader walks into the garden and prepares to make a water-colour sketch of the view.*

In January 1891 a letter to Jinny had announced that Q. wanted to run over to Paris for a week in May, when the Salon opens: 'I want to see the pictures.' He had just been correcting proofs of his book of stories, hoping to publish simultaneously in the USA. Cassell's gave him 100 guineas outright for *I Saw Three Ships*, and £85 for his

---

[1] The name means the pool of (St) Ruan.

translation of René Bazin's *Une Tache d'Encre*; while he also edited a volume of legends, *The World of Romance* for them. All this would help him through the bleak year of 1892; meanwhile a retainer from them gave him some security. Jinny was evidently good fun, with a regular Cornish sense of humour: she would shove one leg of Joe's trousers into the other, 'only by way of proving that a man is what a woman makes him'. Meanwhile Q.'s own boy should have been 'tucked' – taken out of baby-clothes – a month ago.

In April Q. was at Christchurch, Hampshire, presumably sailing. His journey on Easter Saturday took him to Bournemouth, then via the Somerset and Dorset line to Templecombe, thence by South-Western to Exeter, where he caught 'The Cornishman'. The trains were quite empty, though he came by 'modest second class' (why not?). He himself was 'seedy', but had been out for a day's fishing with a brother of Professor Tylor of Oxford. They had sailed until the Gull Rock was in sight, in a horribly loppy sea, and fished with fair success, and not seasick. 'I continue to improve. For three months I haven't had a night's rest, to speak of, and that *does* take it out of one. In fact, it's been melancholia, or something very like it.'

In this interval *I Saw Three Ships* came out, dedicated loyally to Wemyss Reid, his friendly editor at Cassell's. This draws on the old West Country rhyme we used to sing at Christmas:

> As I sat on a sunny bank
>   – a sunny bank, a sunny bank –
> I saw three ships come sailing by
>   On Christmas day in the morning.

'In those West Country parishes but a few years back the feast of Christmas Eve was usually prolonged with cake and cider, "crowding" and "geese dancing" till the ancient carols ushered in the day. . . . Christmas fell that year on a Sunday, and dancing should, by rights, have ceased at midnight.' The congregation struggled up to church, high on its headland, their heads slanted against the south-wester that blew up-Channel.

One recognises the scene: it is Talland church, the bell-tower detached from it, grouted into the living rock. All round in the churchyard are Q.'s forbears:

Life at Fowey

By Talland church as I did go
I passed my kindred all in a row;

Straight and silent all by the spade
Each in his narrow chamber laid . . .

I planted my heel by their headstones,
And wrestled an hour with my kinsmen's bones.

I shook their dust thrice in a sieve,
And gathered all that they had to give.

He was a great one for the consoling rituals of life, and always kept high Christmas, himself decorating the house the day before and keeping it up to Twelfth Night. Bidden over to Christmas tea in the dining-room, table laden with good cheer, one would never forget the scene as day darkened and all the lights of Polruan came out, winking across the water.

Sometimes he would celebrate it with a poem: 'Christmas Eve' –

Friend, old friend in the Manse by the fireside sitting,
  Hour by hour while the grey ash drips by the log,
You with a book on your knee, your wife with her knitting,
  Silent both, and between you, silent, the dog . . .

Silent here in the South sit I; and, leaning
  One sits watching the fire with chin upon hand . . .

Veterans are my books, with tarnished gilding:
  Yet there is one gives back to the winter grate
Gold of a sunset flooding a college building,
  Gold of an hour I waited – as now I wait –

For a light step on the stair, a girl's low laughter,
  Rustle of silk, shy knuckles tapping the oak,
Dinner and mirth upsetting my rooms and, after,
  Music, waltz upon waltz, till the June day broke:

Far old friend in the Manse, by the grey ash peeling
  Flake by flake from the heat in the Yule log's core,
Look past the woman you love. On wall and ceiling
  Climbs not a trellis of roses – and ghosts – of yore?

By New Year 1893 he had recovered, and was finding Fowey a bit lonely, with Atky away, a man much after his own heart. Fowey gossip for Jinny was that

> *Annie Carnall fêtes it in Hindoostan – at a Rajah's Court, where a new carriage and milk-white steeds and a train of black attendants attend her to and from the bath – the* bath, *mind you! She takes 'em! Mrs Davis's report: 'I suppose she will come back as she went' – alluding to Miss Carnall's matrimonial prospects. For if . . . you believe she's already a member of the Rajah's harem, you do her an injustice. The Carnalls, though plain, are chaste – at least the women are. . . . Mrs Charles Treffry [of Place] has written to her friends that she is delaying her departure to the Continent. . . . The Continent turns out to be Guernsey.*

Here was the material from which the Troy Town books came.

This year he brought together one of the best collections of his short stories, *The Delectable Duchy*. Once again luck was with him: the title caught on. He thought of it that Eastertide while walking over the sands at St Ives. Ever since, people have been referring to the county of Cornwall as the 'Duchy'. A quite different entity from the county, it refers to the collection of estates both within and outside Cornwall that go to the upkeep of the Duke, eldest son of the reigning monarch. This goes no further back than 1337, when the Duchy was constituted as an appanage for the Black Prince. Cornwall itself is immemorial.

The Prologue describes Q.'s introduction of a visiting journalist, expecting to cover Cornwall and know all about it in a week, to the amenities of Fowey – rowing him up the river and sailing out to sea. 'The water was choppy, as it is under the slightest breeze from the south-east, and the Journalist was sea-sick.' Then came the town, exploring church, town hall, dilapidated block-houses, 'the old Stannary prison' – I think Q. has got that wrong, for that was at Lostwithiel, up-river, Stannary town and Duchy centre.

I have always been charmed by this volume from early days. 'Cuckoo Valley Railway' pokes fun at the opening of the little line from Bodmin Road (now Parkway) to Wadebridge. The valley is that of the Camel, 'where I have seen the boom of a trading schooner brush the grasses on the river-bank as she came before a westerly wind, and the haymakers stop and almost crick their necks staring up at her topsails'. The little engine was named *The Wonder of the Age* and would stop anywhere along the line at the locals' convenience, to pick up a christening party, for instance. 'The town of Tregarrick stood three miles back from the lip of this happy valley, whither on summer evenings its burghers rambled to eat cream and junket at the Dairy Farm by the river-bank, and afterwards sit to watch the fish rise, whilst the youngsters and maidens played at hide-and-seek in the woods.' (Today they would be indoors playing Bingo.) Tregarrick 'possessed a jail, a workhouse, a lunatic asylum, and called itself the centre of the Duchy', sc. county. So this is Bodmin.

The touching story, 'The Drawn Blind', starts off with the visit of the Judge of Assize, sheriff and all, to the Court on Mount Folly. 'Silver trumpets sounded a flourish, and the javelin-men came pacing down Tregarrick Fore Street, with the Sheriff's coach swinging behind them, its panels splendid with fresh blue paint and blazonry.' We go back to the Age of the Saints with 'Legends of St Piran', patron saint of miners, one of the most important saints of the lot.

Most of the Cornish saints came over from the more saintly South Wales, sailing on mill-stones. A leading Roman historian at All Souls, Ian Richmond, had a fancy that they came across the Bristol Channel in their coracles, with a mill-stone to give it ballast; you fixed your pole in the hole, attached your flap of a sail, and there you were on your way.

In bidding farewell to his journalist, as he looked out over Fowey that night – in this case the patron saint, St Finbar of Cork, Irish, not Welsh – this petition escaped him: 'O my country, if I keep your secrets, keep for me your heart!'

That same year Q. put together a volume of his early light verse, mainly parodies, from the *Oxford Magazine*, to which he continued loyally to contribute. This little volume, *Green Bays*, he did not bother to reprint, and rightly – though he could always turn out light verse at request, to amuse himself or others. Now it was:

> *I can't afford a mile of sward,*
> *Parterres and peacocks gay;*
> *For velvet lawns and marble fauns*
> *Mere authors cannot pay . . .*

The harbour is not mine at all:
I make it so – what odds?
And gulls unwitting on my wall
Serve me for garden gods.

There are always gulls around The Haven; and, beyond, ships riding at anchor, or gliding by, in or out:

These, madam, are my daffodils,
My pinks, my hollyhocks,
My herds upon a hundred hills,
My phloxes and my flocks.

By 1894 Q. enjoyed full health again and was getting through much miscellaneous work for publishers, editing two volumes, *The Story of the Sea*, to come out later, writing critical articles for various periodicals, and reading for his anthology. Next year came the short-story collection, *The Wandering Heath*, with its verse as epigraph:

They call my plant the Wandering Heath:
It wanders only in the West:
So flower the purple thoughts beneath
The sailor's, miner's, mother's breast.
O hearts of exile! still at home,
And ever turning while ye roam!

The title is but the translation of the Latin name, *erica vagans*, of our purple heather so common in Cornwall, all over downs, heaths, moors, that it is sometimes called Cornish heath. It consoles exiles who come across it overseas, as I used to find in California, where a border of it flourished along the terrace of the Huntington Library.

The Prologue is a characteristic exchange between the Poet and his wife about people not reading his poetry – and neither does she. So he presents her with a poem to mark New Year's Eve.

Now winds of winter glue
Their tears upon the thorn,
And earth has voices few,
And those forlorn.

[54]

And 'tis our solemn night
When maidens sand the porch,
And play at Jack's Alight
With burning torch,

Or cards, or Kiss-in-the-Ring,
While ashen faggots blaze,
And late wassailers sing
In miry ways . . .

Then welcome to New Year:

For though the snows he'll shake
Of winter from his head,
To settle flake by flake
On ours instead;

Yet we be wreathèd green
Beyond his blight or chill,
Who kissed at seventeen
And worship still . . .

He had completely recovered, with the circumspect care of his wife, happy family life around him; plenty of work in request; outside, river and moor and sea.

His sea-stories are often among the best; later, a whole volume of them was selected. One of them appears here, 'The Roll-Call of the Reef', which turns on a piece of folk-lore I had never heard of. 'Here was one of those word-padlocks, only to be opened by getting the rings to spell a certain word. . . . But you'll never guess the word. Parson Kendall, he made the word, and locked down a couple of ghosts in their graves with it; and when his time came, he went to his own grave and took the word with him.'

A 'Letter from Troy' gives an endearingly funny account of a first meeting of the citizens under the Parish Councils Act. Since they never had less than sixty-five members on the Regatta Committee, everybody expected to be on the Parish Council. The Chairman held that the Parish Councils Act was the logical result of Magna Carta, and 'would have the effect of making us all citizens of our own parish'.

[55]

All the local characters – and characteristics – appear in fine flower, well differentiated.

> *Simple, egregious, delectable town! As I leaned out last night, watching the young moon and smoking the last pipe before bed-time, a dozen gay balloons rose from the waterside and drifted on the faint north wind, seaward, past my window. Another dozen followed, and another, until from one point and another of the dark shore a hundred balloons soared over the water, challenging the stars.*

Troy was celebrating its emancipation or enfranchisement.

The Golden Pomp: a Procession of English Lyrics from Surrey to Shirley came out early in this year, 1895. Q. had put a deal of work into it in the previous three years. It is dedicated to A. J. Butler, who had helped him with it. That Ninetyish figure, Richard le Gallienne, thought *The Golden Pomp* (it comes from Ovid) a wonderful title for a book; I have never liked it – Q. was never pompous. The volume initiated his career as anthologist – famously followed up.

An anthologist needs to have, first, knowledge; secondly, perception and sympathy; finally, judgment. The volume in itself shows Q. to have these qualities, and more. It serves to introduce us to two new sides of his many talents – as scholar and as critic. Everywhere the classics, Latin and Greek, are present in his mind, offering standards of comparison and often whence the inspiration for a particular poem came. Sometimes it was from French, in which he was fairly well read. A more surprising feature was his acquaintance with madrigal and musical sources.

He defines his area at the outset, and makes clear his preference for the early period, the Elizabethan, more simple and romantic, over the Caroline metaphysical poets. Few of them make any appearance; though he respects Donne, we are given much more of Herrick. 'It is a book of Lyrics. . . . I take the Lyric to be a short poem – essentially melodious in rhythm and structure – treating summarily of a single thought, feeling, or situation. This circumspection includes the Sonnet, and excludes the Ballad and the Ode, in which the treatment is sustained and progressive rather than summary.' Excellent: what clearer definition could one want? Then – 'the lyrics in this volume are flowers of the first and incomparably brighter of these two creative days'. Since his time taste has moved on to a better appreciation of the second.

The book is equipped with a wad of Notes at the end; here an unexpected degree of scholarship is evident, eclectic and personal, coming from a love of literature not mere academicism. And he had kept up his Classics. These earlier poets all received the Latin education of their time; he is no less able to tell us when the poems are imitated from Catullus or Horace, or are inspired by a line from Virgil or Ovid, in one case by a 'famous epigram' of Posidippus. Even a Herrick poem, we learn, comes out of Ausonius; or a phrase, 'the god unshorn', translates *imberbis Apollo*. Then comes an illuminating comment on Ben Jonson, who appears 'most spontaneous when most imitative': 'Drink to me only with thine eyes' is 'meticulously pieced together from the Love Letters of Philostratus'.

Q.'s sharp eye detects that Shakespeare's 'the lark at Heaven's gate sings' echoes Lyly's 'the lark . . . now at Heaven's gate she claps her wings'. Or he notes how effectively Keats turned William Browne's phrase – of whom Keats was an admirer – 'Let no bird sing' in 'La Belle Dame sans Merci'. He knew the importance of the plague year 1593 to Nashe, though naturally not to Shakespeare's Sonnets, for their dating had not yet been definitely settled.

He ranged all over the song books of the madrigalists – Morley, Robert Jones, Campion and Rossiter, Wilby, and rarer ones like John Mundy or Henry Youll. He has a fascinating tradition from Devon that goes right back to Herrick's time at Dean Prior – not far from his schoolboy days at Newton Abbot. Here was the scholarly side to Q. but illumined by his *love* of poetry. Not much evidence of that in today's practitioners, or pretenders to practice. For the uncooked verse that dominates in the media displays no love of their medium as an art.

By now Q.'s name was something to conjure with among his own folk, and in December 1895 he was the guest of honour at a large dinner of the Manchester Cornish Association. In those days our tribal consciousness was such that there were prosperous Associations of the kind, not only in London, Manchester, Birmingham, but in the United States, South Africa and Australia. His speech was reported *verbatim*, and very amusing it was: he was a good-humoured man, full of jokes, though he could be testy and grumpy too.

The couple's second child had been born that year, a girl, named Foy Felicia. Barrie stood godfather, but used always to call her 'Fay' – typical of him. His wife had a hard time of it, even a dangerous one, over this birth, so there were to be no more children. At New Year he could at last afford to take her on her first trip abroad – though he was 'put out' by Scribner's delay in paying the £200 they owed him. Their tour took them to Cannes, Monte Carlo, Genoa, Turin, then back to Paris, and home for another Cornish Association dinner at Birmingham. Louie's letters are naively ecstatic: she found Hyères 'the most lovely place I have ever seen in my life', but was almost equally impressed by the fact that the Tremaynes (of old Cornish gentry) were at their hotel. She was going 'to risk my little all at Monte Carlo' – and duly lost it: the Q.'s never had any luck with money. Once, Q. told me, he actually backed a Derby winner; when he went round to look for his bookie, he had vanished, 'welshed' on him.

In July they were off again on a short cruise. At Galignani's in Paris he had noticed several of his books published abroad by Tauchnitz, for which no payment had been made. While in August Regatta Week fell at Fowey, when 'ready-money becomes a matter of importance. Will the state of the chest [at Cassell's] allow an advance of £40?' I expect his wife saw to that.

Christmas 1896 required a further advance. 'I want to start on my fortnight's holiday with a light heart if possible.' An advance of £50 would lighten it. Then,

> *a fine old-fashioned Christmas here with a Christmas tree, and on the terrace a military band (self-invited)! Perfect weather, too, on Christmas day, and today again; and the boy heaped up to his neck with toys, and not yet able to decide which to play with first. . . . We are just starting for an excursion and lunch up the river. Sunday, Dec. 27th.*

In *Adventures in Criticism*, 1896, he brought together the best of his critical essays to date. In 'Poets on their own Art' he shows that it is the poets themselves who, over the centuries, have best known the rules of the game. 'Most of them claim *inspiration* for the great practitioners of their art; but wonderful is the unanimity with which they dissociate this from *improvisation*. They are sticklers for the rules of the game.' From a survey of what the poets have said on the matter it appears that the first lesson is 'that Poetry is an *art*, and therefore has rules'.

These are made by their peers, not by the man in the street, by popular, uninstructed taste. For all Q.'s life-long liberalism, he knew that taste, judgment in the arts, is an aristocratic matter.

> *'Her poetry has been one of England's divinest treasures: but of her population a very few understand it' – only 'the elect who happen to possess, in varying degrees, certain qualities of mind and ear. . . . The worship of it as one of the glories of our birth and state is imposed upon the masses by a small aristocracy of intelligence and taste.'*

He brings home a point that should be obvious – a first rule of criticism is to rise above one's own personal bias. 'It is a truth too seldom recognised that in literary criticism, as in politics, one may detest a man's work while admitting his genius.' Here he exemplifies this: he could not like Charles Kingsley, while he regarded his brother's *Ravenshoe* as 'almost wholly delightful'. He found parts of *Westward Ho!* detestable, yet he recognised that Charles was much the greater of the two. Similarly he detested Disraeli's politics, but could admire the novelist. He disliked Kipling's politics, but 'worshipped his genius' – as I, when a young Leftist, spoke up for right-wing Roy Campbell's poetry, to his surprise.

A notable example of this salutary discounting of personal preferences is Q.'s treatment of Stevenson. His admiration for the Master did not preclude him from criticism of the work. '*Kidnapped* is a capital tale, though imperfect.' *Catriona* similarly, 'with an awkward fissure midway in it'. Put the two together, and you have a more all-round book as 'Memoirs of David Balfour', not challenging artistic integration. And yet, when R. L. S. died, it was 'Put away books and paper and pen, Stevenson is dead. . . . For five years the needle of literary endeavour in Great Britain has quivered towards a little island in the South Pacific, as to its magnetic pole.' I have remembered that image since reading it first as a schoolboy.

Q. criticised with the authority of a creative writer himself: he knew what was to be done and how to do it. Further, it throws light on his own fiction: he was not a mere spinner of yarns, but a conscious artist in telling his tales and writing his novels. He was not taken in by mere 'length and thickness'. Though he became a friend of Hardy's he diagnoses just how *Tess of the D'Urbervilles* is less true to life and art than George Moore's *Esther Waters*.

> *The story of Tess, in which attention is so urgently directed to the hand of Destiny, is not felt to be inevitable. . . . To reconcile us to the black flag above Wintoncester prison as the appointed end of Tess's career, a curse at least as deep as that of Pelops should have been laid on the D'Urberville family. Tess's curse does not lie by nature on all women; nor on all Dorset women; nor on all Dorset women who have illegitimate children; for a very few even of these are hanged.*

Q. recognised that Hardy was extrapolating from his own unhappiness, and so his last two novels got things out of proportion.

There was an interesting exchange of letters with Hardy, who was very sensitive at criticism and detested most critics. Q. had described Hardy's Boer War poems as 'dreary'. The older man took him up and answered that there was

> *a curious correspondence between the expression and the thing expressed. The romance of contemporary wars has withered for ever, it seems to me: we see too far into them – too many details. Down to Waterloo war was romantic [was it?], was believed in: since then even the Jingos have in their secret hearts an uneasy suspicion that drums and trumpets are not its true insignia – a point I tried to make in some verses called The Sick God.*[1]

---

[1] Hardy's Boer War poem, 'The Sick Battle-God', begins:

> In days when men found joy in war,
> A God of battles sped each mortal jar . . .

and ends:

> Let men rejoice, let men deplore,
> The lurid Deity of heretofore
> Succumbs to one of saner nod:
> The Battle-God is god no more.

Wasn't Hardy being over-optimistic? There will always be plenty of humans who like war and fighting; but perhaps there has been a decline in the cult of war as romantic.

Later, 'I found your views to be so entirely my own that I incontinently forgave you the "drearily".'

In fact he did not, for years later Hardy remembered that early criticism. 'I thought wrong – something you wrote in your salad days when you were more dogmatic than you probably are now. It was when I was interested in novels, which I have not been for the last 20 years or more. It did not much hurt my feelings. I simply said to myself, "He be d——d: I know better." ' Here is the real (if buried) Hardy. He went on to say,

> *As to any other kind of writing interesting me (than novels) I sometimes wonder if it is not beneath the dignity of literature to attempt to please longer a world which is capable of such atrocities as these days have brought, and think that it ought to hold its peace for ever. But they bring out heroism, though at what an expense!*

The answer to that is plain: not to attempt to please, but to cultivate solipsism.

An earlier letter of Hardy's reveals the persuasion from which sprang *The Dynasts*, to which Q. had given a welcome.

> *I have long thought that some new, modified, or revived means of expressing how life strikes us must develop as novels grow inadequate. In my own case it was inclination, or rather reversion to a primary instinct, towards verse that led me away from prose fiction, which I never thought of at all in my early scribbling days.*

Q.'s own principle was to see life steadily as a whole, keeping good and ill in proportion. He was a well-balanced, happy man: are we to say that he too was only extrapolating from his different circumstances? He was quite ready, if not to throw overboard, at least to discount, one of his chief recommendations in the eyes of the public. 'I hold it best that a novelist should be intimately acquainted with the country in which he lays his scene. But, none the less, local colour is not of the first importance.' He regards it as secondary, and even places it under the heading of 'Externals'. That is going too far, in my view, for locality, region, spirit of place, enter into the internal as well as the external character of the work, even into its essence: into Flaubert's Normandy or Daudet's Provence, as much as Hardy's Wessex.

As against 'externals', he gives us a rare insight into the inner process when he writes: 'his unspoken ambitions; the stories he tells himself silently, at midnight, in his bed; the pain he masks with a dull face and the ridiculous fancies he hugs in secret – these are the essentials, and you cannot get them by observation, let alone mere documentation. If you can discover these, you are a Novelist born.' In other words, it is the inner life of the imagination that counts. About this inner life Q. was silent, as Buchan was. But a later letter, when he was occupied with academic work at Cambridge, lets us know that his mind was still teeming with stories, plots, incidents there was then no time to write up.

Q.'s principle is that the novel rests upon 'the abiding elements of human life, the constant temptations, the constant ambitions, and the constant nobility and weakness of the human heart. These are the essentials, and no amount of documents or local colour can fill their room.' Thus he would set no store by the 'documentation', the mere accumulation of material, that stuffs out the 900-page abortions – the bigger, the worse – that fill the book-stores of Fifth Avenue. He might well have pleaded for himself, though he did not, that some of the world's finest fictions are very short: *La Princesse de Clèves* or *Manon Lescaut, Adolphe, Candide* or *Le Neveu de Rameau*.

Of course Q. was a moralist. In a generous treatment of John Davidson,

> *I cannot accept his picture of the poet's as 'a soulless life, wherein the foulest things may loll at ease beside the loveliest'. It seems to me at least as obligatory on a poet as on other men to keep his garden weeded and his conscience active. Indeed, I believe some asceticism of soul to be a condition of all really great poetry.*

We do not have to agree with him: this is Q. He derived some fun, too, from what he did not like. 'I must protest that the vilely sensual faces in Mr Beardsley's frontispiece to [Davidson's] *Plays* are hopelessly out of keeping with the sunny paganism of *Scaramouch in Naxos*. There is nothing Greek about Mr Beardsley's figures: their only relationship with the Olympians is derived through the goddess Aselgeia.' I do not know who this lady was: she does not appear in the classical dictionaries. Has Q. invented her? – a joke of his: I suppose the goddess of wantonness.

He could be downright in these earlier criticisms; as professor, a later avatar, he was more indirect and given to qualifications – though already too much addicted to the subjunctive. He inveighs against 'the assumption of many critics that only within the metropolitan cab radius can a comprehensive system of philosophy be constructed, and that only through the plate-glass windows of two or three clubs is it possible to see life steadily and see it whole'. There is a fine period flavour in that.

Moreover, he was effective in argument – he should have got his First in Greats on that alone. He has a devastating piece on literary censorship, an issue still alive today; but much worse in his day when it was comprehensively exercised by book clubs in control of the market, and by railway bookstalls such as W. H. Smith in England and a Mr Eason in Ireland. Mr Eason had defended his censorship of a book by the *avant-garde* Grant Allen. Q. noted the triviality of Mr Eason's 'assumption that his opinion is wanted on the literary merits of the ware he vends . . . struggling to do his best in circumstances he imperfectly understands'. Mr Eason, as director of a business concern, was responsible to his shareholders; 'as supreme arbiter of letters, he stands directly responsible to the public conscience. These functions should never be combined in one man. I range myself on the side of those who would have literature free. But even our opponents, who desire control, must desire a form of control such as reason approves.'

Q. was a man of principle; but cautious – hard to pin down.

He was now not merely embedded in local life but had become its leader. 1897 was Queen Victoria's Diamond Jubilee, and for weeks ahead he threw himself into the preparations for the great day, 22 June. In a letter to Sidney Colvin, who was editing Stevenson's Letters, he describes how Troy Town went off its head, the local band under his windows early, while he didn't get to bed till three next morning.

I worked the people up and we lined the streets with trees from end to end, put up arches and criss-crossed all between with lanterns and bunting till I had a mile of green bazaar. And we fed 1850 handsomely by the waterside – let alone 350 sailors, British and foreign, Swedes, Russians, Italians, infidels and hereticks; and marched and counter-marched by hundreds in fancy dress under the lanterns, and then danced till the gunpowder ran out of the heels of our boots. . . . And we hadn't a man drunk: a few merry, but not-what-you-may-call-drunk. The town has been shaking hands on it ever since.

Here is a specimen of how Q. involved himself in the jollities of local life. He was a member of the Yacht Club, to become its Commodore, in proper sailing outfit; took the leading part in organising the annual Regatta, himself starting the races. For the local Grammar School he took a hand in training the boys for boat racing. Then came the Cottage Hospital, for which he put out a little ivory-bound booklet of light verse, a rarity now: only 300 copies, signed fully in that beautiful hand.

> *Though Shakespeare needs no Pyramid,*
> *Milton nor Urn nor Pall,*
> *I've yet to learn what good they did*
> *For our Cottage Hospital.*
>
> *Though Pope could perfect Art command,*
> *And Shelley Lyric skill,*
> *On our Subscription List they stand*
> *For absolutely nil . . .*
>
> *The Shilling you in me invest*
> *Will help maintain a Cot:*
> *The money spent on all the rest*
> *Admittedly will not.*

It might even bring an unsuspected reward:

> *For should his fame hereafter swell*
> *And grow by leaps and bounds,*
> *This volume you may some day sell*
> *For* Several Hundred Pounds!

[64]

One cot in the Hospital was already occupied by a Scot, one
MacGregor, of whom there is an amusing ballad. He had tumbled off
the jetty:

> *'Twould not have been so hard if*
> *He'd struck the water flop*
> *But the Betsy Jones of Cardiff*
> *Was what he pitched a-top.*
>
> *From deck to hold he bounded,*
> *And there in anguish lay,*
> *Unpleasantly surrounded*
> *By tons of china-clay.*

Picked up, he was wheeled through the streets in a porter's barrow to
the BUILDING –

> *– An unpretentious Building*
> *In the severest taste,*
> *With no superfluous gilding*
> *Or statuary graced . . .*
>
> *And, summoned all with urgency,*
> *The Doctors did display*
> *Their sense of the emergency*
> *Each in his different way.*
>
> *But one and all conceded*
> *With graceful etiquette*
> *That what the fracture needed*
> *Was – chiefly – to be set.*

Here was a case for the Cottage Hospital – so purse out your shilling.
Christmas was observed with regular ritual. One year the tree
ordered from Place – the Treffrys' estate – had 'Gardener Gale
written on every twig of it, the whole thing three-quarters dead and
the rest faded'. So it was 'heaved to cliff', in the regular phrase at
Fowey. However, Barrie had sent the Boy a parcel packed with gun,
pistol, sword, trumpet and other implements. Another year Q. ordered
a handsome hand-organ from Harrod's, such as used to play at
Shiplake, and the Boy borrowed his sea-boots for a stocking.

[65]

He extended his public service to the county at large with his editorship of the *Cornish Magazine*. This brave venture has to be seen against the background of the disaster that had overtaken Cornwall in the last decades of the nineteenth century. The end of copper-mining and the calamitous decline of tin-mining meant that Cornwall – which had been a world leader in these respects – lost one-fourth of its population to emigration. Most of these poor folk emigrated to the United States, others to South Africa and to Australia – to contribute their skills to building up the wealth of these countries overseas. They left whole villages practically empty and derelict. What was to take their place?

The little land made a marvellous effort to recover. Fishing continued from the small ports and harbours; dairy farming improved, market gardening and the growing of early flowers and vegetables for up-country markets. Here the Great Western Railway was the prime factor, as also in boosting the Cornish Riviera as a health resort. An hotel industry grew up. In spite of impoverishment this was the time when the proud venture of building the first cathedral in the country since the Reformation was undertaken.

All this is reflected in the pages of the *Cornish Magazine*. It has more than a nostalgic interest, though that is reflected in the illustrations from the Newlyn School, led by Stanhope Forbes, today coming to be appreciated again. Morton Nance's drawings appear, who was later to become the leader in the revival of the old Celtic language. We have photographs of the fishing fleets coming into harbour with their catch – as one used to see the myriad lights of the Mevagissey fishing boats in our bay at night, before the war of 1914–18.

There are photographs of Truro cathedral being built – it had got as far as choir and transepts. We have the great house of Mount Edgcumbe, as it was before it was gutted by the Germans in their Second War, when it lost most of its treasures, the accumulations of centuries, pictures, china, the archives, family documents and papers. One sees the vanished interiors, for the house was much diminished in rebuilding; the terraces and gardens, the English, French, and Italian gardens all in perfect trim – of which only the last remains, to be enjoyed by the good citizens of Plymouth.

One article has memories of Helston Grammar School under

Coleridge's son, Derwent, when Charles Kingsley was a pupil. The under-master was C. A. Johns, the naturalist whose *Flowers of the Field*, a classic, still retains its place. Emily Hobhouse – her mother a Trelawny – was to become famous as the 'Florence Nightingale' of the approaching Boer War: she wrote about Cornish miners in the Far West of the United States.

On the literary side Q. got a poem out of Yeats, to whom he described the aim of his 'tribal magazine'. He was trying to make out of it something more than an ordinary local journal. He hoped that there was an audience 'that will read sound stuff about its own county. . . . And I am trying to combine this stuff with good writing, and especially with good poetry. I believe you have Cornish blood and can sympathise with an effort to do some good for this corner of the world.' True, Yeats claimed some Cornish affiliation through the West Country Pollexfens; it did not amount to much, nor did his poem. Q. should have recruited Arthur Symons, Yeats's 'dear friend'. Something came from the manly W. E. Henley, and verses from the less manly A. C. Benson, son of the first bishop who set everything going in the new diocese. Contributions came from Eden Phillpotts; Baring-Gould; Charles Lee, a master of dialect, whose *Cornish Tales* are still worth reading; and H. D. Lowry, a short-story writer of promise who died young.

Contemporary celebrities receive praise: Alderman Treloar, Lord Mayor of London; Sir Richard Tangye of Birmingham; Fanny Moody, of the glorious voice, the 'Cornish nightingale', with the tiara the miners of Johannesburg presented to her – the touching story of the hush that descended upon the vast crowd of rough miners waiting for her to appear on her balcony and sing to them into the night, the exiles from home, reduced to tears.

The *Magazine* continued for less than a year, from July 1898 to May 1899, then folded up for lack of support, quality too high. Q. must have been relieved to be quit of it, for think of the work it entailed, all longhand, with no secretary! His daughter told me that she and her mother were constantly called in to help, answering letters, etc, while Q. regularly wrote after dinner to midnight and beyond.

He was now free to write what is perhaps his best novel, *The Ship of Stars* (1899) – paradoxically, because it is largely autobiographical, when he found it difficult to write about himself in straight autobiography. His boyhood at Bodmin is in it, and then Oxford – the boy Taffy, who is himself, gets there, though his father dies, as Q.'s did, and narrowly missed having to go down. It is a love story, but turns upon a wreck on the terrifying North Coast of Cornwall, which piled up a ghastly record of wrecks in the last days of sailing ships – with no harbour between Padstow (with dangerous shifting Doom Bar at entrance) and Bideford:

> *From Padstow Point to Lundy Light*
> *Is a watery grave by day or night.*

Hence he had a public purpose in mind: he was urging the building of a harbour of refuge along this coast, and he dedicated it to a leading M.P., Leonard Courtney.

> *We held many meetings all over the Duchy to advance this project . . .*
> *but when I pleaded for it before an audience largely composed of South*
> *Wales ship-owners, I was discouraged on the ground that such a harbour,*
> *without an area of commercial profit behind it, would only tempt ships'*
> *captains to be careful of life at the expense of commercial delay.*

Q. was angry at this. Years after, he wrote, 'I have never since that evening, or at any time during a twenty-odd years' service as Chairman of a Harbour Commission [at Fowey] felt any considerable sympathy for the whines of ship-owners, or been warmed-up by their after-dinner hiccoughs over the glorious record of our Mercantile Marine in the late War.'

The end of the story was tragic; for then 'I was young and conceived myself bound to obey an almost puritanically severe artistic conscience.' After the wreck in his own life, 'in these later years when so much of one's instincts insensibly tend towards *reconciliation*, I dare say the last chapter had been happier'. It is right as it is: he saw the tragic side of life as well as the comedy, and was capable of writing about it. He knew the 'facts of life', too, well enough, but was content to give them only a glance. 'There's wantonness, for one thing – six love-children born in the parish this year, and more coming. They do say that Vashti Clemow destroyed her child. And Old Man Johns –

him they found dead on the rocks under the Island – he didn't go
there by accident.'

The Ship of Stars is full of the fun of early life in the county town,
headquarters of the DCLI,[1] Mecca of the county militia's visits, the
boy listening to their bugles in bed at night. Over his head hung, as
over so many other children's:

> *Matthew, Mark, Luke, and John,*
> *Bless the bed that I lie on:*
> *Four corners to my bed,*
> *Four angels round my head;*
> *One to watch and one to pray,*
> *Two to bear my soul away.*

His window 'looked upon the Town Square, and across it to the
Mayoralty [sc. Judge's Lodgings]. The Square had once been the
Franciscans' burial-ground, and was really no square at all, but a
semi-circle.' Here was the centre of the town's livelier events, the
movement and noise mingling with the stories the boy told himself in
bed. Here is the born novelist. His girl friend was always asking for
stories, 'but never seemed to admire him at all for his gift' – he would
never have said that in his own person. 'It's not memory with him: it's
something else.'

There are the scenes we recognise from his *Memories*.

> *Often he had sought out the trout pools on the moors behind the towans,*
> *and lying at full length had watched the fish moving between the stones*
> *and water plants; and watching through a summer's afternoon had*
> *longed to change places with them and glide through their grottoes or*
> *anchor among the reed stalks and let the ripple run over him.*

The grown man, tethered to that desk between the windows in his
study, was really an out-of-doors man, unlike so many writers.

Then it is Oxford.

> *Taffy sprang out of bed and ran to the open window. The gardens lay*
> *below him – smooth turf flanked with a border of gay flowers, and beyond*

---

[1] Duke of Cornwall's Light Infantry: then, I think, merged with the
Somersets.

the yews with an avenue of limes. A straight gravelled walk divided the turf. At the end of it two yews of magnificent spread guarded a great iron gate. Beyond these the chimneys and battlements of Wadham College stood grey against the pale eastern sky.

It is the view from the garden of Trinity.

Now it is May morning on Magdalen tower. 'The clock below struck five and ceased. There was a sudden baring of heads; a hush; and gently, borne aloft on boys' voices, clear and strong, rose the first notes of the hymn:

Te Deum Patrem colimus,
Te laudibus prosequimur,
Qui corpus cibo reficis,
Coelesti mentem gratia.'

All Q.'s nostalgia for Oxford is in it; but, unknown to him, it was to be Cambridge for him.

We are given a scene of wrecking the parish church. Talk of nature imitating art – this is what happened some quarter-of-a-century later when Low Church Philistines wrecked the church at St Hilary. We have a Nonconformist Revivalist preacher – as it might be Billy Bray, so celebrated in his day, with his dancing and skipping for joy, like David before the Lord.

Folklore, folklife, rare words – the book is crammed with such knowledge, all taken in Q.'s stride, quite naturally. He knew that the arms of the Moyles (now a grand family in Salt Lake City) is a mule, a rebus on the name. Over the gateway to the old manor house of the Moyles, Trevissick, across the fields from Trenarren, their mule is carved. I dare say Q. knew it; for he has a story of smugglers coming up our valley from the cove (and Trenarren has cobbled cellars large enough to stow away a cargo of brandy). We find terms of art, and words I don't know – like the bal (mine) maidens 'spalling' the tin ore. Nor do I go back to Honiton lace-making; or the sinister sound of the crake foretelling a man drowning. 'It's Langona crake calling the drowned!' – North Coast folklore, I don't think we had it on the South Coast.

Q. ceased to write regularly for *The Speaker* in 1899; to help the family exchequer he undertook to do, what Charles and Mary Lamb had done for the comedies and tragedies, *Historical Tales from Shakespeare*. It brought a typical postscript from Swinburne, to whom it was dedicated: 'You may like to know that the author of *Aylwin* is a great admirer of *The Silver* [sic] *Spur*.' This was Watts-Dunton, who had Swinburne in his charge; the poet in return always spoke up his friend's one work – so did Watts-Dunton.

Old Fires and Profitable Ghosts was one of Q.'s finest volumes of short stories; if one selects the best out of his work, one can place him with Flannery O'Connor or Willa Cather. He did not have the vulgarity of a Maugham or the brutalism of a Hemingway. Like Willa Cather, he was addicted to the short novel, or *novella*. *Ia* (1896) was one such, and had no success with the public. Mr Brittain thinks that, for all its rightness of length, it was too short to buy. To my mind the explanation is simpler: the title is too short – for all that the patron saint of St Ives was the Irish Ia. (The 'v' crept in by infection from the Huntingdonshire St Ives: historically, our place was always St Ie's, as Fowey was, more sensibly, Foy.)

He tells us that *Ia* was a re-writing of 'Once Aboard the Lugger', a short story in the new volume, in which a determined sailing lass gets her reluctant man into her lugger, takes him out to sea and captures him. In *Ia* Q. gives the tale a more acceptable *dénouement*: the strong-minded female renounces the man not in love with her – of course, in Q.'s view he is unworthy of her. Better than the love interest is the character of the doctor, a good man, based on Q.'s father. He had not been the usual general practitioner of the time, handing out coloured waters to the locals, but 'a sceptic on many points of traditional medicine', opposed to nostrums and an advocate of proper hospitals and effective nursing. His brother, another doctor, died young from septicaemia contracted in an operation.

'The stories in this book are of *revenants*: persons who either in spirit or in body revisit old scenes, return upon old selves or old emotions, or relate a message from a world beyond perception.' Did Q. believe in ghosts? 'The Room of Mirrors' is a London tale, of hatred, two enemies, one in pursuit of the other, who finds an identity in the man he hates and cannot live without him whom he kills. Q. took up this theme again in the last novel he was to complete, *Foe-*

Farrell, dedicated 'To anyone who supposes that he has a worse enemy than himself'. It is odd that this theme should have haunted him, for no man had less experience of enmity.

Several stories in the book have a historical basis or had their original suggestions in fact. 'A Pair of Hands', an early favourite of mine, is pure fantasy, like 'Old Aeson', arising out of the happy domesticity of The Haven. 'The Mystery of Joseph Laquedem' was based on a mystery in Fowey folklore. Anthropologists will know that in primitive societies there are regular insults which, given expression to, will arouse the populace. In Fowey the prime way to produce an explosion was to ask, 'Who killed the Jew?' It seems that a Jew had been murdered for his money, in some previous century, on a quay by the waterside, in circumstances never cleared up. A good subject for Q.'s combination of curiosity and imagination to work on.

He was never wanting for companionship at Fowey. I am only surprised that he should have put up Robertson Nicoll, a Nonconformist hack in literary journalism – but he was a fellow Liberal, knighted by Lloyd George, whose taste in literature was not high. Barrie was a regular visitor, who envied Q.'s domestic happiness.

Kenneth Grahame came down to Fowey at this time, fell in love with the place and became one of Q.'s closest friends, addicts of the river and pottering about in boats. Grahame brought his fiancée down, and was married from The Haven. Anthony Hope was best man, and hired a hurdy-gurdy man to grind his organ outside and wake the household on the day. Kenneth Grahame was a natural bachelor, who should never have married, least of all the dreadful woman who drove their only son to suicide. For this boy Grahame wrote his classic *The Wind in the Willows*, and the river is mostly the Fowey.

In 1899 we find Q. selling up the household at St Margaret's Road in Oxford, presumably on his mother's death, though he says nothing about her, merely that it was 'dreary work wading through bills, letters, etc. The girls have a few things of their own to claim; poor dears, they broke down yesterday very badly, but are plucky again today. . . . I have no responsibility for a single debt; but it is all terribly wearing, a hundred times worse for the girls than for me.' However, work wouldn't wait: there were the last few pages of the *Tales from Shakespeare* to be done.

In February a blow struck the beloved Jinny and the family at Veryan.

> *Just as I am beginning to scribble again in no very high spirits after the 'flu, comes a wire that my sister-in-law's house down the coast has been burnt down, and here's a pretty mess to be looked after! I suppose we shall be receiving the refugees in a few hours. . . . And these are the circumstances in which a man sits down to begin a* causerie *for the* Speaker.

The Ship of Stars was half-written: 'the idea of the thing had rather taken hold of me, and I hope to finish it out of hand'. Meanwhile there was the furnishing of The Haven to be seen to: if Cassell's would let him have £100 advance on the book 'it would be a great favour and convenience'. By New Year 1900 he was writing that he had enough stories for two books, so prolific was he after his recovery – and Fowey had helped to accomplish it.

The most interesting literary correspondence of Q's to survive is that with Robert Bridges, and we are fortunate that it has survived in entirety on both sides. Happily too it gives a more genial impression of Bridges than the usually accepted one. One knew him only as old and Olympian; the Poet Laureate never made any concession to popular tastes. He speaks of his 'literary detachment', and he was a very superior person, a pure aesthete, dedicated to poetry and music, of an absolute integrity, aloof and hard to know. People found him rather formidable. Today, naturally enough in such a low-grade society, he is not appreciated, his poetry under-estimated – as it was not by those better capable of judging, Housman and Q.

Surprisingly it was Bridges who took the initiative and very much wanted to know Q., admired the work and evidently liked the man. In the letters he is constantly pressing Q. to come and see him – Q. much more engaged on every side, who appears as the more amusing and better letter-writer. (It brings home again what a pity it was that his letters were not collected while there was yet time.)

Twenty years Q.'s senior, Bridges, in his direct way, wants to make his acquaintance, having known him so long by his writings. Would he come to lunch or dine at the Savile Club? – it was then, along with the Garrick, the chief *rendezvous* of writers and artists. This was early in 1893; Q. replies that he has not yet recovered from illness which made 1892 a blank year for him. Bridges had been a doctor; he had just bought a book of Q.'s of the 9th thousand, so he had no need to work at such high pressure. Bridges had been reading a book of Q.'s verse, disappointed that he was not married to the Muse, still flirting.

Next month, after reading two more of Q.'s books – would he come and see him at Yattendon, just off the direct line to Newbury? Q. replies that he would never be able to say anything in verse; he agreed that *Noughts and Crosses* was, if anything, the best of his books, 'the others are child's play'. He is now working at a sea-book – standing and dictating he finds good for his nerves – so that boys may know some sea-history, and the difference between a brig and a brigantine, a davit and a stanchion.

Bridges insists that one couldn't beat the first page of *Troy Town* for form. Nor could one the old sailing ships properly rigged, and so beautiful. 'We live in excellent, unassailable dullness, in an old comfortable Manor House, in a small out of the way village in pretty country, and we would take great care of you.' That spring was so fine for sailing that Q. had 'accumulated two months' arrears of work, alienated the affections of my publishers, and saw starvation in the middle distance'. He had been reading Bridges' 'Humours of the Court' and goes into it in detail. His mother's old servant calls his book of stories 'The Detestable Duchy'.

Bridges particularly admired 'A Corrected Contempt'; the doctor tells Q. off for writing so small, it involves more muscular effort. The critic Gosse had declared Bridges' new book of poems as tottering 'on the edge of inanity' or triviality. (Gosse could be an ass, like most critics.) Q. admires the beauty of John Davidson's diction, but is shocked by his 'Ballad of a Nun', where he exhibits the Virgin Mary as encouraging harlotry. At Christmas 1894 he was at his window watching vessels exchanging messages, with his Code Book in hand.

Bridges was generous about Davidson's 'high imaginative poetic faculty of diction', but he must have 'a hole in his vast hull somewhere – has got among a shabby lot in London'. Q.: 'It's a dirty little lot that

runs about Fleet Street just now; and Davidson is much too good a
fellow to have any truck with them – or should be. I wish you could
speak to him like a father.' (This accords with Q.'s lasting disapproval
of his fellow Cornishman, Arthur Symons, too.) Now Davidson has
produced a novel, *Earl Lavender*, which deals with 'unmentionable
indecency'. Q. has heard 'some rather ghastly reports of that set he's
so thick with. If the man won't be helped, why, he won't.' Both
Bridges and Q. were high-minded Victorian prigs. Davidson was a
good poet; what was chiefly wrong was his poverty: he could not make
a living by his pen. Eventually he came to settle at Penzance, but in a
fit of depression drowned himself there.

Bridges recommends illustrations for Q.'s sea-book: 'nothing in
that line will ever come up to a full-rigged frigate with her fore-sail
backed'. Here is the enthusiasm that created his fine poem:

> *Whither, O splendid ship, with white sails crowding,*
> *Leaning against the bosom of the urgent west?*

There is a mandarin element in the discussion between these two, in
those days of *élite* literary standards. Did Bridges know the 'jolly
choriambic measure' in Ben Jonson? He replied with detailed suggestions for re-casting the dialogue in a story of Q.'s. Meanwhile Barrie
is in 'a windy lodging house on the hill here, writing Scotch pathos
with one hand and holding the house together with the other'. Q. is
bent on earning enough money to buy a small 10-tonner and go
fishing: 'surely such an end justifies my means'.

Q. never found time to call or stay at Yattendon, though invited in
almost every letter, so Bridges at length, in May 1895, came to Fowey,
'one of the most poetic-looking places in England'. Thence to
Falmouth and St Ives, where 'Leslie Stephen wants to sell his house
for £1000' – this is the house of his daughter's *To the Lighthouse*. He
went on to Plymouth, fascinated by the different kinds of ships and by
being conducted inside a conning-tower. At Oxford he retired from
being a candidate for the Professorship of Poetry – he did not fancy
himself as a professor; in fact the more academic Courthope was
preferred. Bridges considered Daudet a 'second-rate fellow'; here he
was wrong. 'They told me he was a beast.' (He was partly paralysed

from syphilis.) Bridges had attended the Greek play at Bradfield, badly acted – the *Alcestis*, 'a thoroughly bad play'. Here was the superior, not to say supercilious, side to him.

In December '95 Q. was fully engaged writing 'bad verse', the disease had attacked him when his head was full of good prose stories. When he has done with the Muse, Bridges writes, 'send her on here to me. She has not been seen in Berkshire for ever so long.' He was having to contribute a booklet to young Binyon's Shilling series of poets: he suggested the title 'Lyra sesquidenaria, or the Shilling Liar', but they wouldn't have it. Q. meanwhile was distressed by 'this Johannesburg business', the Jameson Raid, and by the country not distinguising between Right and Wrong. In Cornwall distress was so dire that the miners were begging for turnips, while 'we eat the tops'. He was now fitting out the *Vida* with 'a new suit of Lapthorn's sails' – Bridges should come down and sail in her. Q. jokes about the drains at The Haven being choked while reading Suetonius. An autograph hunter had addressed his request to 'The Harem, Fowey'.

Bridges considered Suetonius 'filthy', always looking for scandal. He disagreed with Q. about 'Endymion': through all its immaturity one could see Keats's 'splendid poetic imagination'. Q. (quite rightly): 'I can write as good verses as Alfred Austin', the poor Poet Laureate at the time. Bridges: 'you have a pretty gift for verse – but not yet done it justice'. He has been making Yeats's acquaintance, whom he likes and has 'the highest opinion of his poetic faculty; but he is squandering himself on Rosicrucianism and Hibernian politics'. Bridges wisely maintained political as well as literary detachment, and kept to his ivory tower.

He paid a price for this: his poetry was largely unknown, except to the discriminating few. It was the duty of the literary papers and critics to make it known. This they failed to do. Bridges did not mind criticism – he took little notice of it; but when a man brought fish to market, it was the proper job of 'these self-constituted authorities to notify the public'. Neither the *Athenaeum* nor the *Spectator* had even mentioned his new book of poems. 'How dishonest these reviewers are! . . . I know how this is done, and why; and who does it.'

This simple answer is that third-rate people are apt to behave in a third-rate way: a Bridges would have even more reason to complain today, when poetry is overlooked by the media in favour of stuff that is printed as verse but might as well be printed as the prose it is. The result was that, when Bridges was made Poet Laureate, he was almost unknown to the general public. It should have been Kipling, of course, but a Liberal government would never subscribe to so justly accusing a voice.

In 1900 Bridges gave a warm welcome to Q.'s *Oxford Book of English Verse*, and made a point that few notice – how much work Q. had put into it and the new ground he ploughed. Most people take that famous anthology for granted, they have no idea of the difficulties Q. surmounted. The textual scholar Grosart had sent him a seventeenth-century poem as 'unpublished', when Q. from his wide reading recognised it as one of Ben Jonson's known poems. What would people have said if he had accepted Grosart's word: 'isn't he dire?'

Bridges did not always agree with Q.'s choices, who was 'more catholic and tolerant'. But here, for the only time, we have Q.'s own view of the book. He could not appreciate Gray's Odes. 'Awake, Aeolian lyre', etc apparently awoke only the risible faculty in him, and Dryden is 'but *libretto* to me'. 'Too much Tennyson – nowadays he seems a voice quite hollow of thought.' This is revealing of the reaction after Tennyson's long ascendancy, and it is not fair to him. Q. defends the large amount of Landor and Meredith. At the last moment he had had to hack about the last 100 pages – the weakest part of the book, we may agree.

We are rewarded too by Bridges' own view of his work on Hopkins' poems, for which *he* has been unfairly criticised. 'They are so very queer I am afraid they would get more abuse than praise. And they are terribly difficult to edit' – three or four versions of some poems, usually two. He had tried to get Hornsby to devote one of his finely printed books to an *editio princeps*, but had failed. We see that Bridges was wise to wait for a change in the air, after the war of 1914–18, before launching Hopkins upon the public.

He had lately met Henry James, and 'snuffed up a vast quantity of incense' – wonderful what 'age and a white beard will do for one's reputation'. In 1908 he moved from Yattendon to Boar's Hill at Oxford, where he built a house, 'Chilswell', and longed for a visit from Q., who never came – too much drawn into politics, Bridges supposed. However, when Bevil came up to Oxford, the old boy would leave a card on him and invite him up. He had shown himself ready to help Q. with the music for his Coronation celebrations at Fowey, and equally to alter a word or two in his own Odes for Q.'s criticism.

When war came the Poet Laureate embarked on his remarkable anthology, *The Spirit of Man*. He thought that professional consolation was usually ineffective, and that true consolation was a raising of the spirit. He would value help from Q.'s 'wide anthological labours'. A good deal in Q.'s *Pilgrim's Way* he would not pass (Q. was always more *popular*, in the best sense): 'I respect my own originality as much as I do yours. . . . My book will be very queer – but all the better for that.' What a Mandarin Bridges was! Q. was not, and allowed years to pass without responding to the older man's reproachful invitations. Evidently Bridges, a choosy man, liked Q. very much – and of course he was more companionable than the handsome, alarming old poet, with his direct attack and headstrong ways, caring for nobody much or for what anybody thought.

When Q.'s son died, Bridges wrote, 'for a long while your sorrow was very constantly present with me', but he was afraid of an intrusion. 'You never would come to stay with me, and since my house was burned I have been unable to ask anyone.' He was taking refuge in Postmasters' Hall in Merton Street – if Q. was over in Oxford would he come to see him? In 1925 Q. was coming up specially to vote for Asquith as chancellor of the university – 'a forlorn hope. The abjects are gathering against him.' Bridges cared for none of those things – and a good thing too; Asquith should have been elected, a far more distinguished figure than the second-rate Cave whom the Tories pushed in. Asquith said peaceably that some people wouldn't vote for him because he was a Bachelor (he had never taken his M.A.), others because he wasn't a bachelor (i.e. on account of Margot's notoriety).

Bridges was engaged in his esoteric experiments in prosody, and from 1920 in founding the Society for Pure English, to which he recruited Q. He wanted nothing in the nature of an academy – whose conception of the language would be static: he would have nothing to do with such a body. His idea was the clarification and direction of living usage. We see how very much his own man Bridges was, an utterly original personality. No wonder people fail to understand him: for most of them he was too academic, an accomplished scholar in several languages, while himself rejecting academicism. In 1924, at eighty, he undertook a visit to USA – which Q. would never do; he wanted to meet Mencken, the authority on American linguistic usage as forthright as himself.

In 1929, at eighty-five, he produced his long poem, *The Testament of Beauty*, which had an immense success – at last! 'The incredible laudations of it have swamped whatever modest confidence I may have had in its worth.... Still, I enjoyed writing the poem.' (One is conventionally supposed to make that sort of disclaimer: there is no need to do so.) He was hoping to come over to Cambridge to see Q. 'one day soon'; but, having corrected a second edition of his great poem, he died at eighty-six. By all counts it was an extraordinary achievement. All his long, dedicated life he had lived for beauty, and that was his religion – as much as for Ruskin or Proust. He spoke to me of Joyce – 'Joyce's aesthetics are *m-my* aesthetics'; and told me that he had sent the poem to Joyce, Gorki, and the King, George V – an extraordinary trinity, *sui generis* like everything about him.

VII

Public Man

The Boer War, which broke out in October 1899, made Q. a public figure in the West Country, and cost him his popularity for some time. Without being simply pro-Boer, he was opposed to the war, along with one half of Liberal, and all Radical, opinion. He was not ashamed to call himself a Radical. The Boer War was made partly by the uncompromising stance of their leader, Paul Kruger, still more by the British High Commissioner, Milner, with his German heritage and education. More flexible minds were against it: the cleverest brain among the Boers, young Smuts, wanted to maintain peace, nor was Lord Salisbury's Cabinet at home bellicose: it had made no preparations for war, and was in fact caught napping.

The war made Britain unpopular throughout the world, except for her own colonies, which came to her help; she presented the spectacle of a big power bullying a little one. Actually, the initial advantages were with the Boers. A good patriot, John Buchan, thought that Britain was only marginally in the right; I venture to think marginally in the wrong. It was a historic disaster that the war ever took place.

Today we can see it in a longer perspective. The Boers lost the war and won the peace. If Britain had kept the upper hand in South Africa there would have been no Apartheid: difference of attitude towards the blacks was an underlying issue. We can see that there was something to be said on both sides. However, the mob in England, particularly in London with the popular press, was not merely blatant, but vulgarly jingoistic. (We must remember how uneducated the people were then.) This attitude of mind was anathema to a sensitive and just man like Q.; he was courageous enough to come out and risk his popularity – when his living depended upon it – in an unpopular cause.

An out-and-out pro-Boer was the Cornish M.P., Leonard Courtney, a doctrinaire figure, consistently pacifist. Q. was hardly a popular platform performer, but Courtney got him to take the chair for Lloyd

George at a public meeting, when this was a risky thing to do. For this impassioned pro-Boer had been hounded off platforms, his life threatened. While Q. was speaking a note was passed to him that a man in the audience was out for Lloyd George with a revolver. The platform was stormed and the meeting broken up, though Lloyd George got away without harm. Such was Q.'s initiation into political life.

Britain was unpopular most of all in Holland, and Q.'s friend, Maarten Maartens, was caught between two fires. Q. did his best to console him. 'The war has made me unhappy too. On many points we should not agree: for Kruger and his party seem to me to have behaved in a way that made it very hard for England to use patience.' This was just; but the back-veldt Boers had no comprehension of the situation in Britain any more than they have today. 'I have always believed that by patience the war might have been averted, and still believe that force is no final remedy for South Africa.' How right he was!

He went on, 'I see no hope against this accursed militarism through which we are all moving towards slavery until those who, in all nations, believe in spiritual things organise themselves to make this belief felt.' This was written at the outset of the twentieth century. Some hopes! He ended, 'but I don't think this hopelessness lessens the obligation to shout in the wilderness – scattered and inefficient as we seem'.

Sailing always provided relief from worries, public and private. In August 1901 Atkinson took Q. and Bevil for a splendid sail up the coast, in his yacht *Airy Mouse*. 'We carried a stiffish breeze all the way.' Atky had been preparing dinner ever since they passed the Start; he had brought Q. tea at 10 minutes to 6, and was now washing up, Q. writing in pencil in his bunk while his boy was dressing. 'We may go up to Totnes for a tramp on the Moor, then sail round to Torquay.' Next day, Q. was routed out of bed at 4.30;

Day was just breaking and a steam yacht offered us a tow out. . . .
Dartmouth harbour mouth 5.15, Torquay 7.30 – a tearing fine breeze
and as we rounded Berry Head, lo and behind the British Fleet a-riding
at anchor – the Fleet back from manoeuvres. We sailed in close around
the Hecla, Prince George, Repulse, Mars *and* Majestic *– a lovely*
morning and really it was worth while for such a sail and such a sight.

[81]

*Torquay is looking lovely. They won't let me have any time ashore to
see the town: but (though you won't believe it) my temper is sweet. At 12
noon we all went off for a bathe below the Imperial Hotel – one of the
best bathes I've had. This afternoon we are to drive to Teignmouth, catch
a steamer to Exmouth and Budleigh Salterton, and home by about 8.
Yesterday we went up the Dart – ate lunch in a meadow by Totnes,
caught a Bosey car to Paignton and sent the Boy to Kingswear by train,
while Atky and I walked through Brixham and around to Kingswear by
coast, batheing at Babbacombe and reaching home at 7.30. . . . I wish
you were here – we'd conspire to have a few hours' quiet in Torquay –
though the place is packed with bluejackets and the steam launches are
buzzing past us every minute.*

Those were the days!

The reaction from the Boer War produced a Liberal revival throughout the country, and Q. was caught up in it, speaking on political
platforms for Liberal candidates at election time throughout the
county. In return he had his fair share of political abuse from Tories.
He told me that he was once in a compartment in a train – first class,
of course – with a couple of prominent Tories who were discussing
their election tactics, until they looked up and saw the opponent
present. They then said that they hoped that he would not betray their
confidence. Q., a better gentleman than they, retorted: 'What do you
take me for?'

If it were worth it, we could look up the local papers of those years
before 1914 and trace his speechifying and the political line he took,
when party divisions were acute and party feeling ran high. But
nothing is staler than stale politics. He was more usefully employed at
Fowey as Chairman of Commissioners of the Harbour, of the Sub-
commissioners of Pilotage for that area, President of the Mercantile
Association, as well as J.P. All these local jobs, especially the last, gave
him material for his stories.

The Tory government at the turn of the century, however inefficient
in running the war, made the greatest step, perhaps of the century, in
social progress with the Education Act of 1902. This represented the
achievement at last of Matthew Arnold's years of campaigning for a

national system of secondary, i.e. grammar school, education in which England was backward, held up by sectarian strife.[1] The campaign was carried through to success by a major civil servant, Sir Robert Morant. He converted the Prime Minister, Balfour, to it – who duly paid for his good work by a heavy defeat at the next election.

The Act released a flood of idealism on behalf of educational progress throughout the country. It gave County Councils wide powers in regard to both elementary and secondary schools, the authority to levy rates to build and support them. They were to appoint a supervisory Education Committee of councillors and to recruit to it other persons of experience in education. Q. was co-opted to this: who more suitable? The secondary schools were largely based on the public schools – re-made and reformed under the inspiration of Dr Arnold's Rugby. Clifton itself had been founded on that model. Cornwall was a poor county and there was hardly any provision for secondary education – none at all, for example, in the populous china-clay district of St Austell.

A large programme of school building and equipment was to be undertaken, and some opposition overcome. Q. threw himself into the work, and laboured hard at it during the early constructive years, as Vice-Chairman, then Chairman, altogether for some thirty years. A dedicated team of three pushed the programme through: R. G. Rows, a Methodist local preacher and natural philosopher, supplied enthusiasm and rhetoric; Q. gave authority and distinction; F. R. Pascoe, of an independent, buccaneering spirit, provided organising drive.

As the result of their efforts the county was girdled, in as many years, with a dozen grammar schools, as well as pushing forward on the front of elementary education. Q. took a good share in both, visiting schools from one end of the elongated county to the other, and functioning when he could as governor of several schools in his vicinity – usually on speech days and at prize-givings. It was on one such occasion that I first set eyes on the man who was an inspiration to the schoolboy receiving a prize at his hands – naively surprised by his appearance: more like a weather-beaten sailor than my fancy of what a famous writer would look like.

News from The Haven was mingled good and ill. Andrew Lang

[1]   cf. my *Matthew Arnold: Poet and Prophet*, ch. 6.

asked Q. to call on his cousin visiting Fowey, wife of McCunn at Liverpool University, professor of what he couldn't remember. (He was not a bad professor of political theory, for what that was worth.)

The Boy is learning Latin with me, is quite clever at it, and I am growing quite keen. I should like to make a 'pretty' scholar of him: but he'll go to school and then Lord knows what will happen. It is a lovely language, if some blundering idiot of a master doesn't spoil it for him. And I'll always believe that a boy who really gets hold of Latin, has something to keep his brain clear for life.

Alas for his hopes: Bevil turned out a fine young fellow, but no scholar at all.

Nor had he any luck with his family again on the financial side. An uncle at Penzance, who was quite well off, died leaving all his money to 'the less amiable members of the family'. During his last illness these had kept him from any communication with the others, especially Q.'s sisters Mabel and Lily, who could have done with some help.

But it's no use fussing over spilt milk and one really can't compete against people who are able to behave like that. The day at Penzance was made too horrible – the most squalid business I ever went through. But it's over, and I don't find it hard to put out of thought – wasn't born to be helped much by relatives, it seems: so must sit up and fend for myself.

He had better luck fishing: after finishing off a story, he then pulled the long line, and 'achieved a fine sole, several plaice, four or five gurnards and sundries, and almost caught an octopus. . . . We spend our evenings on the river and come in to a late supper.' Then, 'why on earth do women always think it is a pity to have more than two in a family? I can never understand it.' (I can.)

Next, 'the critics are all saying nice things about my Oxford Book of Verse. So the work and the journey to Oxford haven't been wasted. It *was* work too. But it's a beautiful book – though I say it as shouldn't.'

I received *The Oxford Book of English Verse* from him. 'I have tried to range over the whole field of English Verse from the beginning, or from the thirteenth century to this closing year of the nineteenth, and to choose the best. . . . The numbers chosen are either lyrical or epigrammatic.' He sensibly modernised spelling for the sake of the reader, except for Spenser, whose deliberate archaism is part of his artistic intention, and Milton, who might reasonably be modernised. Q. did not wish 'to discourage many readers for the sake of diverting others by a scent of antiquity': a good rule to apply – to Shakespeare also.

The anthology was received rather coolly at first, but soon took its place as 'the finest anthology of English verse that had ever been published'. We must remember that today, when it has been re-edited, disconsidered and elbowed out. It had sixteen editions before Q. himself revised it.

For his revised edition I persuaded him to cut down Meredith's too lengthy 'Love in the Valley'. It is curious how much addicted his generation was to that poem: many of them had a memory for verse that has been eroded – G. M. Trevelyan could recite whole stanzas of it. Anyway Q.'s taste was his own. Any fool can criticise any anthology, and many have criticised his *Oxford Book of English Verse*; its later replacement was not altogether an improvement.

He makes a crucial point, much overlooked today, when he says, 'the Muses' house has many mansions'. When traditional, representational painting held the field, it was more tolerant of the non-representational and abstract than the latter was when it went ahead. Similarly with architecture. An historian knows that fashions change. The current preference of the media for uncooked verse is no less intolerant of what is regular or traditional. Q. regarded our traditional poetry as 'indigenous, proper to our native spirit, and it will endure'. He was more optimistic than I am.

The new year 1901 brought *The Laird's Luck and other Fireside Tales*. His short stories were much in request, in USA too, where McClure of *McClure's Weekly* was an admirer. As Q. said, 'work tumbles in', lucky fellow. His later Preface gives us further insight into his writing. 'I remember Grant Allen's – that good man – upbraiding me once that I was squandering into short stories a number of ideas and plots that, economised and treated one by one more spaciously, might have lasted me for life as a commercial outfit.' We might say that, if he had taken time off from the chores of public life, it might have gone into the big book his generation expected of him.

However, he liked to tell a plain tale his own way; as for 'plots, notions, ideas, I had so many in head or in notebook that no man – let alone the indolent writer I have always been [!] – could live out the stock'. Then comes something surprising. 'Worst of all is that I was born – or conceive myself to have been born – a better writer of lyrics than of novels: and on many nights for years have gone to bed haunted by lyrics of my own composing – to wake and find that the words, even the lilt that fitted them, have vanished beyond recapture.' We may suspect here that his busy way of life, without the necessary solitariness (contrast Hardy), prevented him from giving himself to poetry; and from boyhood his mind had been given to inventing stories. That was his true *métier*.

Certain ideas had followed him in and out of dreams so that they re-appear in various forms – he had an active dream-life, and was a light sleeper. These recurring ideas could be given different backgrounds and locations. We note him turning more to history for these – to the Napoleonic war in the Netherlands and in Spain in this and successive books. I discern, from a hint, that he read Napier's big history for the Peninsular War. 'Margery of Lawhibbet' is a tale of 1644, when Charles I's army followed Essex's into Cornwall and cooped it up in the narrow peninsula around Fowey. We have mementoes of it in the King's eloquent letter of thanks – no doubt written by Clarendon – posted up in so many of our churches. Or again along Hall Walk opposite Fowey where a stray shot narrowly missed the King.

Plenty of sea-terms as usual. 'There came into sight around the Dodman Point a ship-of-war, running before the strong easterly breeze with piled canvas, white stun-sails bellying, and a fine froth of white water running off her bluff bows.' In another tale we meet with a 'Dutch pram' – I don't know what a Dutch pram is. So many of these proper terms will have gone out with sailing ships. We should notice the numerous rare words this conscious artist uses – part of his artistic inheritance from the Nineties.

'Three Men of Badajoz' is an exciting tale, with a climax of horror, and the authentic psychological point – corroborated in the war of

1914–18 – that fear, flinching from danger through cowardice, is apt to drive men mad. 'You enter the village of Gantick between two round-houses set on each side of the high road.' That is Veryan, at the back of Pendower beach. We call them 'witches' houses', set there so that no witches could enter the village, having no corners to them. More folklore appears in the Christmas Eve ceremony of baptising the apple-trees in the orchard with last year's cider, circling around while chanting,

> *Here's to thee, old apple-tree,*
> *Whence to bud and whence to blow,*
> *And whence to bear us apples enow.*

We learn that it is unlucky to watch anyone out of sight – Lot's wife, I suppose: I see the rationale, or suggestion, behind it.

For Q.'s birthday, 21 November, Jinny sent up a hamper as usual from the country: a pheasant, etc. He had made 'a vow to finish a novel before my birthday, and actually kept it by a shave – finishing it off about 10.30' the night before, 'happy though exhausted'. This would be *The Westcotes*. That same week he had 'captained a hockey team against Falmouth and whopped them. They *were* surprised.' Meanwhile a lady novelist had descended upon Fowey; she came to his birthday tea, Beatrice Harraden, 'a little dark queer person: not particularly eccentric though, except for smoking cigarettes in the public streets. She doesn't do it by way of showing off. Why the dickens she should I don't know.' She must have been *very* advanced. He himself was engaged in reviewing Mary Coleridge – a really distinguished writer, not a Harraden.

Next year appeared *The White Wolf*, more fireside tales. In the Prefaces for the collected reprints of his fiction – which he wrote in the late Twenties – we observe a defensive note.

> *I have a knack of forgetting my stories almost as soon as they are written; with an incurable habit of persisting on my own line, careless if my audience dwindle or no. I have still the assurance that I have been able, in various ways, to touch many hearts, and am still able to touch some. . . . A novelist who traffics with sex and suicide, domestic bickerings and disillusions, is playing the very easiest game in the world. Any*

illiterate can make a hit with such a theme, if his mind be of the sort to descend to it. But to people a wide stage with characters at once good (as most are) and brave, in patience or adventure – that is the artist's test.

It is more difficult to make good men, in fiction or biography, as interesting as the bad – the Macbeths and Iagos *are* more interesting than the Romeos and Orlandos. Q. succeeded in filling a wide stage with his brave fellows and good women – but what would he think of the thuggery and buggery, the mugging and drugging, the homosexuality and Lesbianism, that take up so much of modern novels? He was lucky that his vogue lasted long enough to justify a collected 'Duchy Edition' of all his Tales and Romances – and that he had another career to move on to, as professor and critic at Cambridge.

This volume returns to the West Country, with a story 'I heard in a farmhouse upon Dartmoor, and I give it in the words of the local doctor who told it. We were a reading-party of three undergraduates and a Christ Church don. The doctor had slipped on a boulder while fishing the river Meavy, and sprained his ankle.' Hence the doctor. Another tale, 'King o' Prussia', brings in the celebrated smuggler Carter, who was 'king' of Prussia Cove near the Lizard. 'The Burglary Club' makes fun of Cornish juries.

> *'They acquit oftener than other juries,' said the Judge; 'and the general notion is that they incline more towards mercy. Privately, I believe that mercy has very little to do with it.' 'Stupidity,' said the High Sheriff sententiously. His own obtuseness on the Bench was notorious, and had kept adding for thirty years to the Duchy's stock of merriment.*

Cox *versus* Pretyman' is an Assize Court yarn.

> *We are not litigious in Troy, and we obey the laws of England cheerfully if we sometimes interpret them in our own way. I leave others to determine whether the Chief Constable's decision, that one policeman amply suffices for us, be an effect or a cause, but certain it is that we rarely trouble any court, and almost never that of Assize.*

Q. took his duties on the Bench seriously, but had a reputation for inclining to leniency, as one would expect.

The Westcotes is a tale of charm, if one may use the word, and

[88]

tenderness. Mr Brittain calls the theme one that 'very few writers would take the trouble to handle at all, unless it were to poke fun – the love of an unattractive middle-aged spinster for a man much younger than herself.' He seems to have had a *tendresse* for spinsters left high and dry on the beach; sometimes they catch the boat, or their man, and come into harbour.

Appropriately this tale is dedicated to Henry James, a maiden lady himself. Q. confesses that it 'wants all the penetrating subtleties of insight, all the delicacies of interpretation', which James would have brought to the lady. Such was not Q.'s way: he left the tale to speak for itself. Henry James was not a popular author in those days, but Q., more easily appreciated, paid tribute to the Master's genius, 'a mystery in operation', and assured him of 'a sense almost of personal loyalty, the sustained and sustaining pride in good workmanship by which you have set a common example to all who practice, however diversely, the art in which we acknowledge you a master.' Not everybody recognised Henry James as a master in those days: his books did not sell, and he had reason to complain, 'Nobody ever understands *anything*.' Q. did not belong to his school, but he understood.

Henry James was touched, and replied in a characteristically orotund letter in his old lady's, not always decipherable, hand:

> *This is a brave and moving, a really romantic surprise, and an incident, every way, that fills my eye with the tear of appreciation. I am more touched than I can tell you with your friendly voice out of the past, the far past and the great sea-spaces – in blue sea-spaces I think of you, have thought of you, as immutably poised. . . . Behold me then wearing your charming tribute in a conspicuous place and causing my aged vision to shine a flash in the light.*

And so on, interminably.

Some thirty years later Q. said that, for this *novella*, he had 'cut his canvas down to the size that seemed to him best suited to the subject. Publishers nowadays follow one another in a craze to standardise the length of novels. They forget that the length of *Manon Lescaut* differs in the nature of things from the length of *Don Quixote*.' His old schoolfellow, the publisher Arrowsmith of Bristol, and his friend, Wemyss Reid, of Cassell's 'were content to trust the author in this matter of his art'. The tale is placed in Devon during the Napoleonic war, so that the French prisoners much in evidence around Plymouth and on Dartmoor then are to the fore in the book, which has a distinct French flavouring. He had got up his French history, knew about the *dragonnades* of Louis XIV's reign, while the text has not a few Gallicisms, along with the rare words he fancied.

The year 1903 saw no less than three books. The admirable *Hetty Wesley* we have already recorded, with its reception from Methodists at the time. *The Adventures of Harry Revel* begins at the Barbican in Plymouth – which fortunately survived both the Blitz in our late war and the intentions of the Corporation – and ends with the Peninsular War in Spain again. Q. intended to dedicate it to an old Devon friend, who then died and 'now cannot twit me with the pranks I have played among his stories of bygone Plymouth'. Later he tells us that 'its eccentrics were actual food for my own boyhood's enjoyment; and, to be frank, I would not cast off the painter of a frail boat with anyone too proud to ship Miss Plinlimmon and Mr Benjamin Jope for company'.

Two Sides of the Face begins with a tragic story, 'Stephen of Steens', of which the author says 'the reader, if he care enough for me to think the tale worth his studying, will perceive that it might easily have been stretched out into a long novel by help of psychological analysis and long forceful conversations and oaths.' This is just, for the hero of the story was a man with a complex. It is based on the actual story of an eighteenth-century yeoman near Helston, who was somehow legally done out of his rights to his property and was by way of being ejected from the home that had been in the family for generations. Not understanding his case, he fortified the house and held out with his faithful retainers at gun-point. The Sheriff and his posse mounted an assault, but failed at first with loss of life. So Roger Stephen was outlawed, the house eventually stormed. Q. gives the tale a different ending from the historic fact – a flight and pursuit to Dartmoor for its end. Once more we see him sufficiently versed in Cornish history. Legitimately he shuffles names about. He calls the Sheriff Sir John Piers of Nansclowan, 'the little baronet whom Walpole never could bribe'. This is Sir John St Aubyn of Clowance, of whom Sir Robert said, 'Every man has his price except the little Cornish baronet.'

Continuing his defensive note, Q. held, 'after my experience, that the capacity to feel poignantly the tragedy of life and the acquired play of humour upon it are equally of divine communication and equally respectable'. 'Shakespeare's Christmas' was of more than local application, and appeared in various issues. However, in those days the identity of Shakespeare's young friend in the Sonnets – the obvious person, his young patron, Southampton – had not been perfectly realised, and Q. fell, like so many, for the simple mistake of taking 'Mr W.H.' to be Shakespeare's man, when in fact he was the person to whom the *publisher* dedicated the Sonnets years afterwards.

Fort Amity, 1904, was dedicated to Henry Newbolt – in these dedications we have a roll-call of Q.'s friends as they made their way along their various paths of life. 'Two schoolfellows, who had sat together in the Sixth at Clifton, met at Paddington some twenty years later and travelled down to enter their two sons at one school.' (But they chose Winchester.) The elders discussed the project of the story, for it was to be serialised in Newbolt's *Monthly Review* – Q.'s school-friendships paid off. The themes were to be honour and friendship; the story that of a soldier's love crossed by his sense of honour. 'Let these deciduous pages commemorate the day when we two went back to school four strong. May they also contain nothing unworthy to survive us in our two fellow travellers!'

The scenes are those of the Seven Years War as fought in Canada – Ticonderoga and on to Frontenac; Fort Amity is Fort Amitie.

> *Can such a story, if at once true and exemplary, conclude otherwise than in sorrow? The great artisans in poetry and prose fiction seem to consent that it cannot. . . . The theme is a variant on a great commonplace: and, following my habit, I let the incidents and characters have their own way without the author's comment or interference.*

Shining Ferry has an autobiographical Preface.

> *It is now almost a quarter of a century since I took up the duties of chairmanship over the Elementary Schools, some 360 in all, of my native county, which extends almost a hundred miles from Morwenstow to the*

Lizard. These duties involved long journeys over many outlandish roads (in days when the motor-car was scarcely known) and long colloquies with country parsons and country teachers, all unaware that in more populous England an age was passing, and that in that passage some hurt to honest conviction and more to honest old-fashioned learning could only be at best, and with all the good will in the world, alleviated.

That is kindly put, but in fact, the advance of elementary education had been held up for decades in the nineteenth century by the sectarian squabble and the Nonconformist envy of the Church. This nasty spirit surfaced again after the great Act of 1902, and managed to defeat the Liberal government's measure for improvements in elementary education. Nonconformist ministers campaigned bitterly against rate-aided support going to poor Church schools.

In Q.'s earlier days the strife had been bitter; in 1928 he was writing optimistically, 'those painful days are now over; and almost over, I hope, the sectarian squabbles we had to carry at the back of our minds over journeys by rail and every kind of ramshackle hired conveyance. But I happened to be in the midst of it, and an agent sensitive to its tragedy, when I wrote this book.' The tragedy in question is the closing down of a poor old dame's school, which had done duty in our villages (at tuppence a week according to my mother and father, neither of whose parents could afford even that much regularly for their too numerous progeny) before rate-aided schools came into being – and the poor old dames lost their livelihood. All over the country parsons and their wives had done duty teaching in little Church schools. Nonconformists were adamant against giving them any aid. Q. did his best, in the transition to state education, to help Church schools to keep going and help to fill the many gaps. He could do no more as Chairman, often with obstruction to contend with in the County Council itself.

Oddly enough he found that he had almost totally forgotten this particular book, until he read it again for the collected edition. He was the more surprised because 'it dealt seriously with one of my strongest feelings – hatred of tyranny and the deliberate cruelty it engenders and specially under the cloak of religion'. That was the theme of his admirable *Hetty Wesley*. '*Shining Ferry* deals with my own folk too,

their ways, and – at a side-glance here and there – their actual
histories. The story of the old ferryman Nicky Vro, for an instance, is
in effect a truthful annal of the poor, and I am glad to find that in
telling it I had avoided excess of sentiment.'

But why apologise for sentiment? It is an ingredient in life, and as
good an ingredient as any other in a book.

From a Cornish Window, 1906, is of interest for the personal light it
throws on this author so shy of direct autobiography. This discursive
book lets us into Q.'s convictions about politics and his technical
expertise about poetics. Its date was the high-water mark of the
Liberal revival – never again such hopes. In its Dedication he speaks
of the years during which 'the author has striven to maintain a cheerful
mind while a popular philosophy which he believed to be cheap took
possession of men and translated itself into politics which he knew to
be nasty. . . . I have fought against it for close upon seventeen years,
no small slice of a man's life.'

That takes us back to 1890, when imperialism gathered strength,
which Q. detested. The fierceness of his anti-imperialism is surprising; he hated the Jingoism of the Nineties, thought Jingo verse 'rotten',
despised the popular press that featured it, and disliked the expansion
of British rule. Still he had the justice to admit that 'there might be
many worse worlds than a world so ruled'. There might indeed! – as
the experience of the century since has brought home to us.

He quotes a verse of Kipling's as exposing the flaw in his view:

> *The 'eathen in 'is blindness bows down to wood and stone;*
> *'E don't obey no orders unless they is his own . . .*
> *All along o' dirtiness, all along o' mess,*
> *All along o' doin things rather-more-or-less.*

Wasn't Kipling perfectly right, when one looks at the mess made of
Rhodesia under the name of Zimbabwe, or Uganda, or Nigeria, or the
Sudan? Far worse than a 'mess', such black states reduced to a
shambles, terrorism, massacres of each other – when British rule not
only kept law and order and dispensed justice, but was altogether
more civilised and humane.

Against Kipling Q. cites the optimistic Liberalism of Meredith,

[93]

about which he is unconvincingly enthusiastic. 'He will always preserve the strength of manhood in his work because hope, the salt of manhood, is the savour of all his philosophy.' Hope! No wonder that Hardy has lasted better. Actually Hardy was liberal in his inclinations, without entertaining Liberal illusions: he did not confuse the way he would like things to be with things as they are. I agree with Kipling and Hardy, not with Q., and certainly not with Meredith.

Q. would recommend Meredith to us on the ground that 'he has never grown old, because his hopes are set on the young' –

> *Keep the young generation in hail,*
> *And bequeath them no tumbled house.*
>
> *A younger generation reaps, etc.*

Yes – look at it today – everywhere drugging and mugging, their idea of sport reducing even their football matches to a shambles. Sport? – I agree, with Kipling, that what they need is discipline.

Q. goes in detail into Meredith's metrics, 'no single poet was ever more untiring in technical experiment'. One must respect the mandarin world of culture these people belonged to, the passion which Victorians, indeed the whole nineteenth century, had for poetry: they remembered it and could quote reams of it. Not today – but, then, undisciplined, uncooked verse is not memorable.

A letter from Meredith, in his neurotic, self-conscious hand, says: 'your *Ship of Stars* has given me a timely distraction in this roar of War. [January 1900.] Taffy is heavenly of my infancy, and the writing flows through me, as good literature does. You are one of the few whom I can read in these days.' Next year again: 'your work always gives me pleasure, for it is literature and well thought out. We have little of it at present, in spite of much cleverness.'

Being addicted to poetry had its advantages for criticism: there was, for instance, the difference between being a scholar and a judge of poetry. 'Dr Grosart was by no means a safe judge of characteristics in poetry. With all his learning and enthusiasm you could not trust him, having read a poem ... to assign it to its true or even its probable author.' The same holds good of Shakespearean scholars today.

An autobiographical passage brings his background home to us.

[94]

*I was born and bred a bookman. In my father's house the talk might run
on divinity, politics, the theatre; but literature was the great thing. Other
callings might do well enough, but writers were a class apart, and to be a
great writer was the choicest of ambitions. I grew up in this habit of
mind, and have not outgrown it yet.*

One gets a glimpse of where he got his ethical perfectionism from:
first, his home; then the ideal inculcated at Clifton, the next generation
on from Arnold's Rugby; topped by the pervasive influence of T. H.
Green at Oxford. Q. was a Platonic Idealist.

To descend from those heights – there is naturally a great deal
about Cornwall, something about his interest in public affairs, including Liberal politicking, and his activities particularly in boats. Best of
all are the parts about sailing. There is a thrilling account of working
into the lovely estuary of Salcombe, over the bar at the entrance, in
full view of the historian Froude's house, The Moult. And a breathless
tale of the return journey down the coast, in rough weather, to
Plymouth and on into Fowey. 'On the whole, it was not too soon for
us that we opened the harbour and

> *saw on Palatinus
> The white porch of our home,*

though these were three or four times hidden from us by the seas over
which we toppled through the harbour's mouth and into quiet water.'
Good sailor as he was, he concludes, 'while the sails were stowing, I
wondered how I should like this sort of thing if I had to go through it
often, for my living'.

The month of October ends with one of the finest pieces he ever
wrote, 'Laying up the Boat': I chose that to represent him in *A Cornish
Anthology*.

The year 1905 saw an interesting proposal from the Clarendon Press
at Oxford, which recognised the scholarly side to Q., for all his being
a popular author. They wanted a short history of English literature,
with a volume of selections to illustrate it. Sir Walter Raleigh wrote,

*I despair of making the 17th century a child's theme. What am I to do
with Donne? Burton? Dryden? . . . Any help that I can give you on the
spot, in my quality of Gossip [godparent] to the Press, I will gladly
furnish. . . . If you can see your way to it, Stopford Brooke, who has
reigned for twenty years, will topple from his throne.*

Q. was well disposed to the idea, and Raleigh went into it in some
detail, suggesting that the story should be built around individual
names. The Press were 'hungry' for it, and also wanted a volume of
selections for schools. Nothing came of this: Q. was too busy, and
anyway did not fancy himself as an historian. A fascinating letter of
Raleigh's on early Scots poetry shows him a better scholar than he
(and others) gave him credit for. This brilliant, but rather indolent,
man should have written the book himself.

Sir John Constantine, 1906, was Q.'s choice, though not the most
successful, among his novels. Much influenced by Cervantes, a
favourite with him, it deals with the quixotic adventures of a Cornish
knight in Corsica, during its eighteenth-century struggle for freedom.
'A hundred and fifty episodes, two sermons, and a number of moral
digressions, have been omitted.' I could do with omissions of the
subjunctive, a foible with Q., which I find tiresome. An adventure
story, it is yet a very personal book: 'here is interred part of the soul
of the Bachelor Q. . . . we are surely ghosts if we keep nothing of the
blood which sent our fathers like schoolboys to the Crusades.' One
can appreciate the spirit in fiction, without being of it, or even agreeing
with it in history or in life.

> *To them was Life a simple art*
> *Of duties to be done,*
> *A game where each man took his part,*
> *A race where all must run . . .*

(That was the Victorian world, a society worth living in; from today's,
better to withdraw.)

> *They went about their gravest deeds*
> *As noblest boys at play . . .*

The Victorian who wrote those uplifting lines, Monckton Milnes – did Q. know? – was the greatest collector of pornography in the age.

Q. was much taken by that oddity, a liberal-minded German – who had written a book on the English addiction to 'Fair Play' – and lifted a sentence: 'The English have maintained both in art and literature the modest tradition of the play-attitude.' Very unlike Goethe or Thomas Mann, we may say, neither of whom could claim any modesty – let alone madmen like Hölderlin or Kleist or Nietzsche, well in the German tradition. Q. takes for epigraph some lines about knighthood:

> *For knighthood is not in the feats of war . . .*
> *But for a truth, or for a woman's sake.*

Oh well! – knight-errantry, one might call it.

However, the tale is topped by his thorough knowledge of the sea and its ways – such a bonus to a writer. He knew well the south coast of Cornwall from sailing it – the horrible Manacles off the Lizard, for instance. ' "Lost his bearin's! And him sailin' her in from Black Head close round the Manacles, in half a capful o' wind an' the tides lookin' fifty ways for Sunday! That's what he've a-done, for the weather lifted while we was haulin trammel," ' (whatever that might be). Many good ships and hundreds of lives have been lost on those shark-toothed rocks. The loss of the liner *Mohegan* left an impression with us for years in the Cornwall of my youth.

> The Gauntlet *being in ballast, and the tide high, Captain Pomery found plenty of water in the winding channel. . . . He had taken in his mainsail, and carried steerage way with mizzen and jib only; and thus we rode up on the tide, scaring the herons and curlews before us . . . until he let down his remaining canvas and laid the ketch alongside . . . one of the seamen, who had cast a stout fender overside [what is a fender?], stepped ashore.*

It is the entrance to the Helford river. Sea-terms! – I can't tell a binnacle from a pinnacle. And here is a dialect word I still don't know: some shanty kept 'liddening (as we say in Cornwall)' through someone's head.

Rattling adventures – all improved with wide reading in English literature, rare words, and always an apt classical quotation. As for personal reflections – 'Dissent in the first generation is usually admirable [is it?] and almost always respectable. . . . But Dissent in the second and third generation usually rests on bad temper.' He should know, for old Jonathan Couch had belonged to the first generation of Methodists, who make their appearance in the book. What accounted for the extraordinary effect of Wesley's preaching, without any external advantages? Because he spoke 'with authority'.

And the moral of the book? Q. was a stalwart upholder of liberty; yet 'liberty has its drawbacks. . . . In any struggle for freedom the real danger begins with the moment of liberty.' We have in our time reason to reflect on the long struggle for freedom from the tyranny of the Tsars in Russia. That tyranny overthrown, Lenin was asked by a visiting Westerner if there could not be a bit more liberty. 'Liberty?' said he; 'what for?' Russia has reason to regret that.

Q. thought that, if he were to re-write *The Mayor of Troy*, it should be shortened by one-third; I agree – it loses effect from too many complications of plot. The story pokes fun at a self-important mayor, who is captured during the Napoleonic war, has many adventures but, when he eventually comes back home, finds that he has not been missed at all. Jonathan Couch gets a salute in passing: 'the second-lieutenant, young Couch of Polperro, is almost out of his articles and ready to proceed to Guy's'. The book ends up with a Regatta. 'Troy on a Regatta Day differs astonishingly from Troy on any other day in the year, and yet until you have seen us on a Regatta Day you have not seen Troy.' At the time in which the story is placed the then famous Saltash fishwomen gave an exhibition race in their large gig. When Fowey ceased to be a borough in 1834, someone made a bonfire of all the corporation records. 'O Alexandria!' commented Q. Similarly, a Victorian town clerk of Lostwithiel, concluding that – since he couldn't read the medieval archives there, nobody else could – burned their records too. Both towns must have had rich archives.

The book was dedicated to 'Kenneth Grahame and the rest of the crew of the *Richard and Emily*, and with apologies to the Mayor of Lostwithiel, a borough for which I have (with cause) much affection and a very high esteem'. Lostwithiel appears as Lestiddle. The two towns were rivals, of course. 'Rowing quite close up to me the Mayor of Lestiddle asked – for we observe the ordinary courtesies – what bait I was using.' Somehow the exchange on the river gave him a clue, 'and more than the clue. I know now the history of that Mayor of Troy who was so popular that the town made him Ex-Mayor the year following.' Q. apologised for the farcical extravagances of this tale: 'this dearest of small cities lives, breathes and runs its daily self-respecting life in extravaganza, thus confounding the categories of Tragedy and Comedy'. He chaffed at a critic, 'who proved that the Mayor of Troy ought to have been treated as seriously as was the Mayor of Casterbridge: for, argued he, both were disappointed, and one was a Mayor as well as the other'.

The comedy ends upon a sad note. This he defended by referring to his favourite Don Quixote, '*si parva licet*. Where will you find sadder writing than the chapter in which the Don rides home to his native village?' Barrie was much taken with the idea of the story, and had a rather similar notion; perhaps they might collaborate on a play? Nothing came of this: Barrie thought 'the difficulty is that it seems to lead to a grim end and a rather queer view of life. . . . It seems to amount to this: no-one should come back, however much he was loved.' In the end he made this the *dénouement* of his highly successful *Mary Rose*.

Ten years later Q. himself made a play out of *The Mayor of Troy*, but it was war-time (1916) and had no success when put on at the Haymarket. We catch a glimpse of him rehearsing hard from 10.30 to 2.15 and from 6.30 to 11 p.m.: 'Dog's life! the intervals filled up with interviewers who make my soul creep with shame.' He was more disappointed than he cared to admit, for he lost several hundred pounds over it, when he could well have done with a slice of the fortune Barrie was making out of the theatre.

He wrote stoically, 'I have a better sense of proportion than to worry over a little misadventure like that in times like these', and that he intended to try again. He never did – no time for it, though Cambridge put on a performance of his verse-play, *The Regent*. A series of odd happenings 'never gave the little thing a dog's chance'. 1, Henry Ainley, the producer, was too much pre-occupied with the Shakespeare Tercentenary to give his mind to it. 2, A corking bad Press. 3, Zeppelin scares. 4, Sinn Fein (the murderous Easter Rising in

Dublin). 5, Kut (where a British Army was boxed up in Mesopotamia). 6, Cabinet crisis. 7, Rush of holiday weather. The actors went wrong in the Bathroom, and omitted five minutes of dialogue, and the poor scene-shifter dropped dead between Acts II and III. 'Yes: I didn't get so far as Charles Lamb and hiss my own play (though actually that little feat of his crossed my mind at the time).'

I suspect that Q. would dearly love to have had a success in the theatre, like his friend Barrie – and he certainly could have done with the money, as he continued his generous, expensive way of life, economising on nothing. He was keen on amateur theatricals and directing plays at Fowey. We have an account of him at it from the young Compton Mackenzie, whom he directed in *The Merchant of Venice* and *Hamlet* in those idyllic days in Cornwall before the shadows closed in in 1914.

Mackenzie describes his first meeting with Q. 'in that book-lined study of his at The Haven, the windows of which looked out across that enchanting habour. . . . I still see Q.'s library at dusk with the windows blue as sapphires and the fire burning brightly and the half-covered sheet of paper on his desk where he had left off writing.' It was to become a familiar scene to me in the years after the war – but with a difference. Though he was genial and kind as ever, there was a shadow in the background. I was too young to know, though I can sense something of the gaiety and light-heartedness of those distant years. One derives a good picture of the fun they had in Cornwall, the innocent *joie-de-vivre* from the pre-War volumes of Compton Mackenzie's autobiography. The Germans ruined all that.

He gives an account of the discussions they had, particularly over *Hamlet*, Q.'s enthusiasm and readiness to consider the young theatre man's suggestions. He then goes on to discuss Dover Wilson's later editions of the play, which aroused so much discussion, when it appeared in the Cambridge Shakespeare which Q. and he launched together. Among all the points raised over this Mackenzie, oddly enough, never notices the absurdity of Dover Wilson's interpretation of Hamlet's famous line to Ophelia: 'Get thee to a nunnery: why wouldst thou be a breeder of sinners?' Dover Wilson absurdly interprets 'nunnery' as meaning brothel. As usual, the sensible thing is to take Shakespeare as meaning simply what he says.

However, Q.'s own enthusiasm for theatre paid off for him later as professor. In his book on *Shakespeare's Workmanship*, in his Introductions to various plays, and in lectures on them, particularly on *The Tempest*, I have been struck by Q.'s theatre sense and the aptness of his interpretations of what is happening on the boards. No doubt those practical experiences of directing, small as they were, provincial and unprofessional, played their part.

Then there were other platform activities. A general election was approaching in 1910 – in fact, two – and Mackenzie was as ardent a Radical as Q. 'Did you tell me that you had never seen Polperro? If that's so I've a mind to book you for a Saturday meeting there – fishermen have a Saturday night ... and the Sunday we'll devote more or less to the Muses. On Wednesday I go to Liskeard to help in planning out the campaign.'

In January there followed more meetings: another at Polperro on the fishermen's Saturday night off, 'Paignton Monday, Helston Tuesday or Wednesday. Life is *real*, Life is *earnest!*' On the Thursday 'I shall be at Truro all day – Education Committee – returning by the 4.25 from that city', for an evening meeting. In those days it was by no means so easy to get about the country; one wonders how he had time for it all – and to get his writing done. Perhaps this is the place to note, what his family knew – the public hardly at all, he carried it all apparently without effort – that he was a man of quite exceptional energy.

A rather comic situation arose when it fell to him to invite Leif Jones to be the candidate. For, though Jones had been a contemporary at Trinity, he was a Temperance fanatic, President of the United Kingdom Alliance for the Total Suppression of Liquor Traffic. Q. found this a bore – the bore himself used to be known as 'Tea-leaf Jones'. Eventually a local candidate was found in Isaac Foot, father of the Foots, who all regarded the House of Commons – Carlyle's 'Talking Shop' – as the final end and aim of the good life.

Major Vigoureux, 1907, reflects something of Q.'s political interest. This was exceptional, and shows that politics did not appeal to his imagination. The story is set in the Scilly Islands, whence the theme. The proprietor of the Isles, Augustus Smith, was a benevolent autocrat

– said to have exercised *droit de seigneur* too, no doubt to the improvement of the stock there. He had removed the last inhabitants of the little island of Samson from their home – really for their good. 'You maintain the landlord's right to ordain the lives on your estate, and command them to be as you think best. . . . We drew our nurture from the Islands before you ever came to hear of them.' Q. was fond of claiming to be a Radical, on the ground of caring for the roots. 'It is for the roots I plead, against your claim that the surface gives all.'

I read this book, according to habit, in the proper *locale*, the Scillies themselves. Revealingly, I remember nothing of the political theme – only the hilarious beginning when the characters, going home from a whist-party, lose themselves in a Scilly fog and grope round and round – was it? – the parish pump. It made me laugh aloud; and now reminds me that Q.'s novels often begin brilliantly, and tail off towards the end. It is then fair to say that, with this defect, he was not a writer *de longue haleine*.

Later, in a return to the Islands with *Tom Tiddler's Ground*, he made amends to the benevolent Proprietor. However he maintained his stand on principle. 'The late Mr Augustus Smith was a wise Proprietor, far-seeing for his subjects' ultimate profit. But there are two things for which men may excusably be allowed to fight even against the prospects of worldly profit. The one is addiction to their native soil, the other, their jewel of liberty.' I do not agree. The benevolent autocrat removed these peasants for their own good; and he, not they, knew best what that was.

Poison Island, also 1907, Q. described later as but 'a semi-nautical yarn. But I should say that we, lovers of Stevenson, were trying to do what our master had just failed to do in *The Wreckers*', i.e. combine adventure with comedy, RLS with a spice of Dickens. Anyhow he deplored the 'now fashionable Russian trick of endless talk which never arrives at action' – evidently he was no admirer of Chekhov – and preferred 'the curtain to fall on a stage piled with corpses'. (We may note that *Hamlet* achieves both.)

Merry-Garden and Other Stories followed these two – three in one year, and he an 'indolent writer'! I am not engaged in re-telling his fictions, but in sleuthing the man in his work. In a good tale here, 'The Bend of the Road', which he evidently imagined from the train when going over one of those vertiginous viaducts above a valley going down to Looe, we come upon this.

> *Men liked him, in spite of his shyness: his good manners hiding a certain fastidiousness of which he was aware without being at all proud of it. No one had ever treated him with familiarity. One or two at the most called him friend, and these probably enjoyed a deeper friendship than they knew. Everyone felt him to be, behind his reserve, a good fellow.*

This well describes Q., except that more than one or two called him friend – forty years older than I, I did not presume to do so: I came to know him well, and to regard him with affection and (irreverently perhaps) something like veneration. G. M. Trevelyan once came out of his emotional reserve to describe Henry James as 'adorable': that was no less true of Q., really more so (for James was cold at heart).

The things Q. knew about, from his numerous activities and wide contacts with life! In spite of his quixotic attitude towards women he knew that 'above all things women suspect and fear irony: it is not one of their weapons'. Did he know that Americans are almost entirely without this particular tool?

Of the stories 'no one will ever know how this or that one has untwisted itself out of personal joys and griefs, or what root is responsible for this or that leaf or tendril. I wish my books to stand to be judged by themselves, and that no one will ever write a Memoir of me.' Many writers have expressed that wish, but of course it is unacceptable with so distinguished a writer as he was. He speaks of his life as 'broken and patched', but that was after Bevil's death: until then it was a singularly homogeneous one. All that was worth preserving, he says, was in his books – except for 'things private and sacred'. But a *great* writer writes about what is private and sacred – witness Hardy and Kipling, both even more vulnerable men.

From 1908 he was up to his eyes with miscellaneous work, editing a series of *Select English Classics*, no less than thirty-three small volumes, with Introductions: mostly poetry, lyrics, ballads, songs and sonnets, but also essays and smaller pieces of fiction. In 1909 came the delightful *True Tilda*, a favourite with me. Why has this never been made into a film? – it is just the material for one: the jogging of circus-

and fair-folk down the Warwickshire Avon and through Stratford country. All fantasy and fun, with plenty of visual appeal, arising from the original idea he had for a short play: 'Two children – Babes in the Wood – lost and inquiring their way. The various people they meet are kindly or morose: each helps or hinders in a fashion. But the moral to be that, in the end, the children have somehow helped everyone they asked.' Very true to Q., that – each of his mature novels has a moral, a leading theme.

The tale 'just ran with the children's Odyssey as the pen ran; as easy as a dream or as Avon ran once, with bends and turns, through a happy fortnight'. That was when he had made the voyage down the river for *The Warwickshire Avon*. He had an authentic insight into the minds of children through being a family man, but where did he pick up his knowledge of show-folk? – perhaps from their regular visits to the fair-ground at Fowey. The Cockney they speak is rather a literary language, in part derived from his love of Dickens – and none the worse for that.

We are given a hilarious account of a Revivalist meeting in the West Country, and that is true to fact. Tilda's dog, Dolph, is a charming character in the book.

He gave the name *True Tilda* to his sailing-boat: we find him urging his daughter Foy to win her race in it at Polruan, as she did. When she was rowing down the Warwickshire Avon with Bevil's fiancée, May Cannan, her father advised,

> *When you get down to Eckington, land by the bridge and see if the sandstone parapet is still dented with the marks of the tow-ropes which the bargees used to shift there where the towpath changes sides. Your father once wrote a poem there, which got into print. . . .*[1] *Tell May that whoever reported the Avon unnavigable above Warwick must have deceived her. That Stoneleigh can't be navigated is quite inconceivable. But you have seen that lovely Warwick Park, and the building on the live rock: and if you're not all in love with Avon by this time, I renounce you. It's the gentlest stream in England, and the most English.*

Shakespeare's river, providentially.

Lady-Good-for-Nothing, 1910, a book of some power, deals with a

---

[1] 'Ode upon Eckington Bridge, River Avon'.

potentially tragic subject: a wronged woman, like *Hetty Wesley*, physically maltreated by the Puritan humbugs of Massachusetts in the
name of religion. This was a theme that inspired Q. to anger. The
story was based on an historical case in saintly New England. 'Some
years ago an unknown American friend proposed my writing a story
on the loves and adventures of Sir Harry Frankland, Collector of the
Port of Boston in the mid-18th century, and Agnes Surriage, daughter
of a poor Marblehead fisherman.'

Q. confessed ignorance of details of the local scene, never having
been to America, and transferred events and happenings, as legitimately in fiction. The girl is whipped through the streets for Sabbath-
breaking, is protected by the gallant Collector, who becomes her
protector in the more meaningful sense of the word. The epigraph is
from Wordsworth's 'Ruth', 'an innocent life, yet far astray' – and Q.
called his heroine Ruth. She appealed to his imagination more than
any of his women (along with Hetty). 'As I wrote, this wonderful
woman came, like the original Mother of Love, out of the sea to me:
unrecognised as a goddess by the religious, and consequently a
creature to be bruised and beaten.' He remembered 'the mist of
emotion that now and again clouded my writing of her story'. The
theme of hate crops up again: 'Our enemies in this world are dearer
to us than friends. They cling closer.' Did it come out of his experience
of politics, just now coming to an end, and the malice one has to put
up with in that deplorable way of life? He was wise to keep out of the
snake-pit.

His intimate knowledge of the Bible came in handy among those
Puritans. A character says that the proper way to read it is to forget all
about its being divided into verses and take it like any other book.
This is just what he did later on at Cambridge, in editing it readably
'as literature'. One day, while in his morning bath, his bed-maker (at
Cambridge a woman, not as at Oxford a 'scout') shouted in an urgent
telephone message: 'The *Daily Mail* wants to know what you have
done with the Bible.'

'Why are the noblest, birds and beasts, so few and solitary?',
someone asks. The reply comes: 'You may include man. The answer
is the same, and simple: the strong of the earth feed on the weak, and
it takes all the weaklings to make blood for the few.' This is rather

stark, the answer a baronet gives, not necessarily Q.'s view. But, of course, he was an 'élitist' – today used in a derogatory sense: all too understandably by the inferior, to elide their difference from the superior. The word only meant the 'elect'.

Q.'s linguistic gift appears in his rendering of the darkie's lingo – as he could also render broad Scots or Irish brogue. Or, for that matter, construct an acrostic, as here. The story ends with the earthquake of 1755 in Lisbon. He had got up the eighteenth-century background, for this book as for others – he did not trust himself further back than the Civil War. The dedication reads: 'To my Commodore and old friend, Edward Atkinson, Esq., of Rosebank, Mixtow-by-Fowey.' Mixtow, up a creek of the river, was the haunt of piratical medievals, John Mixtow a leader among them in the fifteenth century.

An older friend, Barrie, no longer came down to Fowey as in earlier glad days. The failure of his marriage caused some embarrassment – in those days – and left him a sad man. (Why did he embark on it?) But he still regarded Q. as his best friend: 'you are what I miss mostly in London. It would have made a big difference to me if you had been here all these years.' Earlier it had been, 'in these forty years I have met no man that has meant as much to me'. In 1909 it was still, 'I miss you much and always. On the whole I've cared for you more than any other of our calling.' No family of his own, he cherished an affection for Q.'s. He was Foy's godfather, and went down with Q. to visit Bevil at Winchester. Then, in 1909: 'The Boy! to think he is leaving Winchester instead of putting on his pinafore! Tomorrow he will be leaving Oxford.'

The year 1910 was much broken into by public events: the accession of George V – end of the gay Edwardian age – and two General Elections, with Q. as keen a Party Liberal as ever. Barrie had wanted him to become a Parliamentary candidate. The newspapers reported that he had 'caught Radical politics badly', and Tory Kenneth Grahame described him as 'propagating his pernicious doctrines throughout the West Country'. This did not disturb their friendship. When Grahame received the dedication of *The Mayor of Troy*, 'I feel now really officially connected with the place, through its Mayor, and

some day I shall put in for an almshouse, if you have any.' He reported
to their American friend, Purves – who now regularly joined the
friends for sailing and frolics – that Q. looked

> *not a day older and even more beautifully dressed than formerly. Mouse*
> *[Grahame's boy] was particularly struck with Q.'s clothes. I think he*
> *then realised for the first time that Man, when he chooses to give his*
> *mind to it, is incomparably the finer animal of the two and does the*
> *greater justice to his clothes. . . . The farm – 'Priam's Cellars' –*
> *flourishes exceedingly. One sunny day we all went over there with a large*
> *luncheon basket and lunched in the open, in a riot of daffodils and*
> *primroses, with three big foreign ships – Danes and Norwegians –*
> *moored right below us.*

What fun they had in those halcyon years! – before the shadows
began to fall on all of them.

In 1910 Q. was knighted, much to his surprise, for in those days
such things, like professorships, were much less common than today.
No one was more suitable – one might say, a 'knightly' man in the old
chivalrous sense – when one considers the combination of his
achievement in literature and his political services. The Prime Minister, Asquith, a Balliol man, was a good scholar himself and a man of
taste. The prophet was not without honour in his own country, for on
his return from London the band of the Fowey Territorials – which
he had helped to recruit – serenaded him all evening outside The
Haven with 'A fine old English gentleman' and such ditties. I expect
that the evening proved a drain on Q.'s cellar. That autumn the local
Liberals had their fête in his honour, with a presentation to him and
her ladyship. As a Party man, he had had a full share of abuse; he
pleaded that it was a 'queer fate' that had dragged him into politics,
when his only ambition was as a man of letters.

He took the lead in all the junketings to celebrate the Coronation
in 1911. He wrote the pageant, 'This Royal Throne of Kings', for
which Bevil, now at Oxford, designed some of the stage-properties.
Crowded services in Fowey church, the choir singing Q.'s hymn, 'Of
old our city hath renown': Lady Q. and the vicar's wife planting red
chestnut trees (still there) outside the church. The little town, and all
the ships in harbour, lit up at night, lanterns, festoons, arches of

greenery; a ball in the Armoury, the dance led off by the new knight and his lady, everybody in fancy dress. *O sancta simplicitas*!

It was a good thing that he had several books in the bag that year to keep the wolf from the door – all the entertaining involved must have been expensive. *Corporal Sam* does not appear in the collected edition, its stories were distributed among other volumes, as with the earlier *Shakespeare's Christmas*. A volume of Fairy Tales from the French was illustrated by Edmund Dulac. Then came *The Oxford Book of Ballads*, extending his empire as anthologist, and carrying the Oxford Books a stage further.

To the *Encyclopedia Britannica* he contributed a personal notice of T. E. Brown, whom Q. had known as a master at Clifton. Brown had been a servitor (i.e. half-scholar, half-servant) at Christ Church, but – in spite of his double First – he was refused a studentship! A schoolmaster for thirty years, he won fame in his day with his poems in Manx dialect. Q. loyally gave him a place in the *Oxford Book*, though his verse, popular with Victorians, is hardly to our taste – least of all 'A garden is a lovesome thing, God wot' – wot ye what?

In 1911 appeared *Brother Copas*, a rather unsatisfactory book – unlike Q. The subject is the goings-on, the back-biting and enmities in an out-of-date foundation of almshouses, a medieval hospital. Evidently the idea occurred to him on his visits to Winchester, where one sees the ancient foundation of St Cross Hospital, though Q. pleads that his 'St Hospital has no existence at all outside of my imagining'. Mr Brittain finds that the opinions expressed by Brother Copas are pretty much those of the author: 'the same patriotism, the same recognition of the national failings, the same Liberalism, the same dislike of German critics of English literature'.

Uncharacteristic is the disillusioned tone. Q. partly accounts for it: 'In *Sir John Constantine* I expressed (perhaps extravagantly) my faith in my fellows. In *Brother Copas* I try to express something of the correlative scorn which must come sooner or later to every man who puts his faith into practice. I hold the faith still; but

> *He who would love his fellow man*
> *Must not expect too much of them.'*

The first fine careless rapture of the Liberal hopes of 1906 was over – and Liberalism was on the way out for good over most of the modern world.

In a Preface of 1928 Q. tells the omens. This book was written

when the overtaking event of the Great War was already beginning, for some, to cast its shadow ahead. Over a few of us that shadow had seemed to impend ever since the outbreak of the war in South Africa. . . . We carried about with us a deepened foreboding, as men walking in a doomed city, the inhabitants of which will not listen to be warned.

That was still more true in the Thirties, with even less excuse, for we had already had experience of what the Germans were heading for – but the easy-going British would not be warned. Of the promise of the pre-1914 world Q. says sadly, 'Feeble hope and vain! Through the greater arrogance of an enemy came what was yet bound to come – the hour of paying the gods in the blood of young men and their parents' tears.' 1914–18, and yet again – unforgivably – 1939–45: 'a ruined age', as a poet of the seventeenth century put it.

Next year, 1912, produced a varied crop of work. First, a new novel; since, with Q., cheerfulness would keep breaking in, it was a comedy, *Hocken and Hunken*, in the vein of *Troy Town*. He thought it a better book: 'it comes near to annoying me when people praise *Troy Town*; which to its author – who has practised some criticism in his time – seems unworthy to rank with the little comedy set out in the following pages'. He had never worried about the popularity of his books compared with other writers', but it irritated him when people preferred the less good. But, then, they never *know*.

He followed this with a translation of that somewhat mysterious poem, *Pervigilium Veneris*, of the refrain echoing through the ages:

Cras amet qui nunquam amavit; quique amavit cras amet.

He had already edited the Latin text, with an Introduction that reminds us that poetry shifts its appeal – a salutary reminder when we are confronted with the 'verse' of today. He also made verse translations from the Homeric Hymn and the Winter section from Hesiod's *Works and Days*. It was fortunate for him that he kept his classical scholarship in trim, as also his wide reading in our own literature. Some of it went into his next *Oxford Book*, that of Victorian Verse. And, of course, regularly along the years he had been editing, with Introductions, or producing selections from, such poets as Coleridge, Tennyson, Matthew Arnold.

So that it should not have been such a surprise to everyone, himself included, when there came the call to Cambridge.

Cambridge.
War-time 1914–18

Q.'s first acquaintance with Cambridge came through his friend at Cassell's, A. J. Butler, who had been a Fellow of Trinity. They kept going a joke between them that Butler had never heard of Oxford, nor Q. of Cambridge. Butler took Q. down on a brilliant hot weekend, when the University voted against degrees for women. Neither of them approved of this reactionary step.

On the Saturday they dined with the Ad Eundem Club, a small body of Cambridge and Oxford members in equal numbers, who alternated dining together once a term and, 'forgot that they are grave or were ever rivals'. (It also served the purpose of advancing common causes and each other's interests.) Q., a devoutly clubbable man, became a member. On the Sunday he dined at high table in the hall of Trinity, grandest of English colleges, though declining to admit that it surpassed the hall of Christ Church.

At this point he makes a distinction that 'while a Cambridge man reverts to Cambridge as a *place*, gracious and hallowed by the feel of great men as well as by those of his own transient youth, it does not lay on him just that spell which binds an Oxford man to *personify* Oxford, to enshrine and adore her as veritably and ineffably mother and mistress and queen.' This was an old-fashioned way of expressing his feeling for Oxford, but old-fashioned loyalties were of the essence of his nature. Enjoyment of life was no less strong and he undoubtedly enjoyed his Cambridge years, if with a different inflexion from the Oxford days of his youth. Cambridge gave him a pulpit, and he became a 'character' there – almost as much as Dr Johnson was in eighteenth-century London.

His appointment as King Edward VII Professor of English Literature – in those elect days when such things mattered – made something of a sensation, it was so much out of the ordinary. He was not the first, but his predecessor, one Verrall – a run-of-the-mill

academic – had been fatally ill during the year of his tenure and
unable to construct anything of the School which the foundation of
the Chair was intended to bring into being. Everything was yet to do –
and what a challenge this was to a man whom the public looked upon
as simply a Stevensonian best-seller. However, Q. was not simply that:
they overlooked the scholar.

Some fuddy-duddies in the University did not hold with the
academic study of English Literature, and opposed the new School.
Others had different ideas of how the subject should be treated, and
of what should go into the Tripos. Further opposition came from the
English Association, a national body outside. They continued to
oppose Q.'s ideas for the new School and the programme he worked
out; he took their opposition to heart, and was angry at it.

In general, this imaginative appointment, which easily might not
have worked out so brilliantly as it did – in the event it made literary
history – was warmly welcomed. The *Cambridge Review* regarded it as
'the most popular which could possibly have been made'. A. C.
Benson, Master of Magdalene, put his finger on the need when he
wrote,

> it is really a great opportunity. There are many men here interested in
> literature, but there is no centralisation. What we want is a man who
> will really found and organise a School. Everything is ready for this, and
> what is needed is a strong personality, to do for us just what Raleigh has
> done at Oxford. It is not only stimulating teaching that is wanted, it is a
> social centre for individual energies.

The situation and the prospect could not be better put. Benson's
private reaction was less generous. The archbishop's son thought Q.
'not quite a gentleman because of his cavalier disregard of social
invitations' – this of the most sociable of men![1] Benson thought him
'amiable but somehow common. I don't like his dress nor the scent of
smoke and drink he diffuses. He looks like a racing tout.' Friend and
schoolfellow Newbolt informed Benson as to his 'strange background
– a mixture of fisherman and country doctor, with a wife of a lower
class who is tiresome; very ugly, waxed moustache and very irritable'.

[1]   D. Newsome, *On the Edge of Paradise*, p.288.

[112]

Newbolt informed Benson that Q.'s mother 'had been a lodging-house keeper at Oxford'. Nothing unrespectable in that – after her extravagance had nearly ruined the family. What snobs the Victorians were!

Benson thought better of it on reflection. 'Quiller-Couch is at all events *a figure*: he is an amateur, of course. . . . If they were going to take an amateur, why not me?' Here was the source of the feeling behind the depreciation. We can imagine what mutterings there would be if things went wrong. Q. confessed that he was in a 'hideous funk' – a quarter of a century since he had lectured to undergraduates, and a whole new School to create. Still, it was a grand opportunity, not only for the university but for him. He was now near the end of his vogue as novelist and writer of short stories. He was to win a new public with his Lectures, beautifully produced by the Cambridge University Press, to become a front-runner with it while continuing with the Oxford Books. Meanwhile he had a new generation at Cambridge to play with, and they gave him a welcome from the first.

Sir Walter Raleigh, Q.'s opposite number at Oxford, gave him good support. A Cambridge man by origin, Raleigh spent his life in professoring, at Liverpool, Glasgow and Oxford – and didn't think much of it.

I am glad that Cambridge played up. If it is as decent to you as Oxford was to me, you won't lack. I hope you'll get a handful of people who want to write, not to teach. I spend most of my time trying to avert the schoolmasterisation of English Literature in this University. But the love of mankind for system and rules will defeat me. I suppose orthodoxy and creeds and tests were invented to prevent men of no intelligence seeing to be the asses that they are.

Still more so today, when there is a kind of academic sub-culture (if 'culture' is the word for it) sufficient unto itself – at any rate with its own self-sufficiency.

Raleigh and Q., both highly gifted men, were at one in their humaner ideal of a school of English Literature, and in their aims for it – though both over-optimistic in thinking that it could turn out writers, for writers are born, not made. Still Q. did his best to blow on a spark wherever there was one, and to encourage writing rather than pedagogy.

It was his residence at Jesus College that made all the difference and made him at home – in time it became a second home. At Cambridge, as at Oxford, a professor is elected Fellow of a college, and it makes a good deal of difference which. L. H. Courtney discussed the claims of various colleges, hoping that Q. might go to St John's, to continue the sequence of eminent Cornishmen there, Henry Martin the celebrated missionary to India, Bishop Colenso, John Couch Adams the astronomer, himself. Jesus got in first with its offer of a Fellowship. Q. could not have been happier – or probably as happy, in a big college, overloaded with scientists and such. There were not too many Fellows at Jesus – Q. by far the most eminent; he shortly became king of the Senior Combination Room and was 'spoiled' by the undergraduates, who made a regular 'character' of him, while he took part in their fun.

His rooms at Jesus were charming, but small – up above the First Court as you approach the College along the 'Chimney', the passage between two walls, the Master's garden on the right. He had only one sitting, or 'keeping', room and the tiniest of bedrooms, a cupboard of a bathroom. In time he was allowed to use the guest-room across the way as his dining room – presided over by the fine Nicholson portrait of him. Everything was kept in apple-pie order, almost ritually, his writing materials, pen, paper, paper-knife, etc, always in the same place, the room filled with flowers. How he disposed of all the papers, manuscripts, letters that flowed in on him I cannot think – a litter of papers accumulates around me wherever I work. In short, *pace* Benson and Newbolt, he was a perfectionist – something of an aesthete.

At first Q. brought his wife up to Cambridge and thought of a house there. But she didn't like it – naturally enough, she was out of it; rather put off, too, by her first dinner party, when a Darwin – one of the ruling families there, and notoriously *gauche* in manners – asked her how much money Q. made by his books. It was eventually decided that he would live in college during term time, while their home would remain at Fowey, to which he would return for vacations, half the year. Thus he would continue his public work for Cornwall too. It proved an admirable arrangement. He took to bachelor life in college

once more like a duck to water; Lady Q. kept the home fires burning
and had her bridge-parties at The Haven.

We have an amusing letter to 'my dearest Deare', of January 1913,
describing his installation in college rooms – and also the subsequent
pattern of journeys between Cornwall and Cambridge.

*From Paddington I took a 4-wheeler to Liverpool St. and there got into a
Restaurant car. Dinner at 7 (halibut) lasted on until we reached
Cambridge at 8.5 punctually.* [One couldn't rely on that today.]
*Hansom to the College here, and then the fun (?) began. There was a fire
in the rooms, and the bed was made: so much for the credit side. The
'bedmaker' (no scouts here, only a lot of women) had gone home, leaving
neither a plate, nor a glass, nor a knife, nor a fork, nor even a cake of
soap: not a candle, nor a candlestick. Two thin blankets on the bed, and
no bolster. I sent round the porter to scout for a few things such as a glass
and a lamp: while I plunged off into Cambridge to buy a tin of mixed
biscuits and some candles.*

*The man couldn't raise either biscuits or a candle (the buttery was
shut, and at 8.30! on a day when all the college was coming up!) About 9
o'clock, when I had returned with my stores, came a knock at the door
and in came the Master, profusely apologetic. 'His wife was ill: had been
laid up for a month; Nurse in the house, and Would I come over to his
Lodgings* [sc. Lodge at Cambridge] *and have some supper?' I declined
very politely. Then he promised me a set of Don's rooms, well furnished,
by Tuesday next; and I told him, still smiling, that I would look for
lodgings to fill up the interval. You should have seen me standing in this
bare and ridiculous room, heaped around with my luggage and packing
cases. But I had easy top hand all through the discussion, and my spirits
were rising rapidly, the whole thing being so absurd.*

*When he had gone I mixed myself a good glass of whisky and began to
undress. It was then I discovered the absence of soap: so I washed with
shaving soap! and then something in the pattern of the wash-hand stand
started me laughing, and I sat on the bed and fairly shouted with mirth.
What's more, I slept like a top: having rummaged out a bolster,
uncovered but clean, and helped out the blankets with rug and dressing
gown.*

*This morning the old bedmaker called me, and the same silly game
began – tiny jug of hot water, nothing but a bar of yellow soap, etc. But I
was taking none of it, and fairly made her skip for cans of hot water, etc.,
and by 9.15 was sitting down among the packing cases to a pretty good
breakfast – excellent sole and a boiled egg (no egg-cup, but a serviceable*

tea-spoon). At 1.30 I am lunching with the Master and shall have a
serious talk with him. After luncheon I have a mind to inspect the river
and the Varsity Eight. . . .
   Letter from Smith, Elder this morning, enclosing cheque for £50 for
cheap edition of Corporal Sam.

This was to be paid to his wife's account. When he found lodgings, she and 'the Babe' (Foy) were to come up at the end of the month.

Such was the novelist's description of his introduction to many happy years at Jesus, and as professor at Cambridge.

Much depended on the impression his Inaugural Lecture made. (This had been delivered in January the previous year.) Doubtful dons must have been surprised at his appearing in formal morning dress, tail-coat and all – as he continued always to appear for his regular fortnightly lectures. The lecture theatre was packed and overflowing, unaccustomed curiosity aroused (Benson among the crowd). The lecture could not have been bettered, for, underneath the modesty and expressed diffidence, is the cleverness well disguised, the persuasiveness, the tact. Critics were side-stepped from the first. Instead of invoking Stevenson or reminding them of the novelist, the whole atmosphere was Greek, based on Plato's last dialogue, '*The Laws*', 'left unrevised'; quotations which revealed the width of his reading, but with Cambridge men to the fore; a reminder of the Cambridge man 'you gave to Oxford', Sir Walter Raleigh who had built up the new English School there; a special word for Verrall, a stricken man when appointed, and 'following him, I came to a trench, and stretched my hands to a shade'.

His conclusion was from Sainte-Beuve, with its suggestion of his own case, '*si magna licet componere parvis*, delivering an Inaugural Lecture: 'I have written a good deal in the last thirty years; that is, I have scattered myself about a good deal; so that I need to gather myself together, in order that my words may come before you with all the more freedom and confidence.' The words were, as always – though they gave the impression of ease and spontaneity – carefully pondered, even the pauses considered. In short, a formal lecture by him was a work of *art*, even a speech was carefully prepared – a shy man, he was not a spontaneous speaker. (I have his copious Notes prepared for merely a school prize-giving.) With that Inaugural Lecture, as Mr Brittain tells us, Cambridge was conquered 'at one stroke'.

There was something of an actor in him, people have not noticed; and, nervous as he was at taking on the job, he cast himself in a professional rôle, what he considered it ought to be. Hence the self-conscious tone of the lectures (which irritated the irritable Grigson). Hence too the joke of his regular address, 'Gentlemen', to an audience where the women outnumbered the men. Actually, it was a form of protest at women being excluded from being full members of the university – he was a liberal in the matter, in which Cambridge eventually followed Oxford.

The gist of his message, which he was to enforce throughout his tenure of the Chair, was that 'literature is not an abstract Science, to which exact definitions can be applied. It is an Art rather, the success of which depends on personal persuasiveness, on the author's skill to give as on ours to receive.' This sounds to us simple, it is so concise; but that phrase 'ours to receive' implies a whole programme of teaching, the training and equipment, in short an *education*, in literature. Later on, F. R. Leavis made a vociferous campaign about the Cambridge English School being an education in itself; that it might be so is already implied, more modestly, in Q.'s brief phrase.

With this approach 'our investigations will deal largely with style, that curiously personal thing'. They will be always seeking the author's intention, aiming at the concrete rather than at definitions and theories, 'through the sleeve of which the particular achievement of genius is so apt to slip'. He applied this quite trenchantly in a follow-up:

Remember that you are English and to go always for the thing – *casting out of your vocabulary all such words as 'tendencies', 'influences', 'revivals', 'revolts'. 'Tendencies' did not write* The Canterbury Tales; *Geoffrey Chaucer wrote them. 'Influences' did not make* The Faerie Queene: *Edmund Spenser made it: as a man called Ben Jonson wrote* The Alchemist, *a man called Sheridan wrote* The Rivals, *a man called Meredith wrote* The Egoist.

This states concisely the common sense that should not need emphasising, for the biographical and personal approach to the study of a writer, so absurdly depreciated at both Oxford and Cambridge in the succeeding generation. Though it sounds simple, it is really more subtle, and added difficulty to Q.'s task, for it is easier to adhere to structures to instruct the young out of 'movements' and 'periods', 'schools' of thought etc. – more difficult to plan out one's courses without some such framework. Hence the nature of Q.'s Lectures at Cambridge; easy to read – they made popular reading, went into several editions, and sold well – yet they are not so easy to grasp. There is more in them than appears, or than people think.

With a real writer as professor, not just an academic, though his standards were academic in the best sense, it was natural that he should emphasise the practice of writing. In the study of literature 'I want us to be seeking all the time *how it is done*: to hunt out the principles on which the great artists wrought; to face, to rationalise, the difficulties by which they were confronted, and learn how they overcame the particular obstacle.' Here is a task, one of the proper tasks, of real criticism. In the fullest sense it may be impossible to teach how it is done – both Q. and Raleigh had that sense of the limitations of their job – for genius is inimitable: it is so much the essence of an individual, unrepeatable personality. But there are lessons, if secondary ones, that we can learn, tips of the trade, as in any profession; and for the inaccessible element of genius we can at least learn to appreciate it, in its various manifestations – another province of real criticism.

Q. followed up with some useful tips for the practice of writing.

(1) Almost always prefer the concrete word to the abstract. (2) Almost always prefer the direct word to the circumlocution. (3) Generally use transitive verbs, that strike their object; and use them in the active voice, eschewing the stationary passive. Now by attending to the few plain rules above you may train yourselves to write sound, straightforward, work-a-day English.

Beyond that one needs 'something of an ear. Yet the most of us have ears, of sorts.' Here, too, by assiduous practice, we can 'wonderfully improve our talent'.

[118]

Thus Q. encouraged a number of undergraduates to become writers. We do not know them all, but among them were two who became distinguished, Rosamond Lehmann as novelist, J. B. Priestley both novelist and dramatist; Frank Kendon and Gerald Bullet, poets; G. B. Harrison and Basil Willey, scholars and critics, the second of whom succeeded him as professor; and the unteachable Leavis. W. A. Darlington became well known as a dramatic critic; he found Q. a strict supervisor: 'he read everything I wrote, and mostly made me write it again'. He does not seem to have done this for Leavis; but nothing and no one could have taught him to write good English.

The effect of his lectures was said to be 'magical', and something of the effect comes through in reading them. The first year's course was collected in *On the Art of Writing*. In addition he gave informal classes, usually with Aristotle's *Poetics* or the *Ethics* as a basis for discussion. He himself set the bad example of smoking at these (I agree with Benson about that), and even provided cigarettes, as well as coffee, for his guests. Often a few dons attended these, and members would read papers or offer questions for discussion. Even Benson came round after attending one: '4 December 1913: went to Quiller Couch's symposium – about forty men all round the room, smoking and whispering. Two little papers were read, and I liked the calm humorous way in which Quiller Couch raised points. I shudder to think of doing it, but he did it well.'

All this came naturally to him, but before him was the more difficult job of moulding and re-moulding the Tripos. He had had no experience in this field, but shouldered the chore conscientiously. Mr Brittain, who knew this side of him best, said that he 'gave a great deal of thought to the future of English studies in the University'. He went over to Oxford to consult Raleigh, who had had far more experience.

When Q. arrived at Cambridge English studies formed part of the Medieval and Modern Languages Tripos and were weighed down with philology, Anglo-Saxon and Medieval English. To what point? Largely pedantry, to bear up with the form the study of ancient classics took. Q. was not susceptible to the charms of *Beowulf* in the original, and had not the great scholar W. P. Ker's passion for Old Norse. After his first year's experience of how things worked at

Cambridge, he joined up with H. F. Stewart, who became a valued friend, and H. M. Chadwick in a campaign for reform. They prepared a report, with their proposals for a new English Tripos on its own. There was quite a lengthy campaign, for opposition came not only within the university but once more from the English Association.

A letter which he wrote to an official of that body gives one an idea of what he felt.

> *Dear Madam, I thank you for your kind invitation: but regret to say that the name of the English Association has been used more than once in endeavours to defeat my work at Cambridge. I must assume – since the Association has never, to my knowledge, discontinued these attacks – that I have still a long way to go before qualifying to help it in its aims.*

Could there be a more perfect example of the retort courteous, a complete, though polite, brush-off?

Within the University the reformers won. A separate English Tripos was constituted, in which philology, Anglo-Saxon and Middle English were made optional, and in their place candidates could offer Literary Criticism and Comparative Literature. The study of English Literature was no longer halted at the sacred year 1830. Youth, in the pages of the *Cambridge Review*, noted the Professor's 'quiet note of triumph' in what was almost a Second Inaugural. 'Today, thanks to the English Tripos, the Professor of English Literature stands on a new level and surveys a different prospect. Now, as always, he is in arms against professionalism in literature.' I imagine pedantry was meant, for Q. himself was a professional in the true sense. 'Now, as always, he confesses three articles of belief: (1) that Literature cannot be divorced from life, (2) that Literature cannot be understood apart from the men who have made it, (3) that Literature is a living art, to be practised as well as admired.' The young men had got the message.

From the first Q. – with an exceptional energy and *joie de vivre* – was ready to throw himself into both college and university activities, social and sporting, as well as literary and dramatic. He became a member of various clubs and, as a good college fellow, cheered on Jesus' rowing, Head of the River in these years. He was ready with speeches and verses for undergraduate festivities, and to contribute to their papers as well as to the dons'. In November 1912 we find him answering an inquiry for help.

> *I know something of the difficulty of running a University paper, and had a little to do with the start of the* Oxford Magazine, *which is now respectable and dull and promises – Crabbe's phrase, I think – to 'slumber through immortality'. So I am sympathetic – and a little more: for your paper – if it can hold on – may help to do something which in my present ignorance I seem to see as wanting to be done at Cambridge. Just now, my own chief business must be to listen and learn. But if I can give you any little unofficial help I shall be happy: for I think that in a way we shall be pulling in the same boat.*

In the years to come there would be many contributions, chiefly light verse as in old days at Oxford, to Cambridge periodicals. What a contrast to the withdrawn, if not wholly sombre, life of his fellow-Oxonian there, A. E. Housman, in his gaunt rooms in Whewell's Court at Trinity! I like to think of the creaking chair in the front of Deighton and Bell's bookshop in Trinity Street, which each of them occupied in turn on his calls. Housman and Q. were good friends: both wine-bibbers, with eclectic palates, they would exchange invitations, especially to their respective college feasts (at Oxford 'gaudies'). On one such occasion Housman, already engaged to dine at Christ's, had to decline: 'I wish that colleges would show more concern for gluttons and drunkards in arranging their Feasts.' After Housman's lecture in the Arts Theatre his select audience of half-a-dozen would make way for the horde of Q.'s pouring in. No wonder that Housman had more time for pure scholarship – to make him the first Latin scholar in Europe; Q.'s much the more demanding job.

On his arrival at, Cambridge Q. had received a welcome from Housman in his characteristic style. 'Dear Couch, (for I gather that this is how your friends address you, instead of calling you all the names they could)', and expressing pleasure at proposing Q. for the Philological Society. I do not suppose that Q.'s enthusiasm, if any, for that body lasted – one hears no more of it. The relations between the two Oxonians in exile continued on a social, rather than philological, basis.

Eventually Housman graduated from 'Couch' to 'Q', and it became 'will you come and dine with me at our Purification Feast, and be introduced to our fine new Combination Rooms, next door to the Master's Lodge?' (at Trinity). Then, a typically ambivalent letter:

> *I have put off thanking you for* Harry Revel *till I should have read it; and now I shall earn your contempt by saying that much as I like it I like my memories of* Poison Island *more. But when I add that I have read Mrs Henry Wood's* The Channings *three times and am quite ready to read it a fourth, you will see what sort of critic I am.*

One thing one sees is that time hung heavily on Housman's hands, and, for another, what a good critic he was. For *Poison Island* – for all its being inspired by *Treasure Island* and regarded by Q. as a semi-nautical yarn – is the more memorable tale. In it he carried on from *Harry Revel* Miss Plinlimmon, one of the maiden ladies he was so good at creating and was so gallant about.

Cambridge in term, Cornwall for vacations, more than half the year, gave his life a stimulating duality. He did not cease to take a public part at home, he even continued as President of the Liberal Association in East Cornwall until 1912. Earlier the Liberal government dropped a bomb, with its Bill for the detention of the mentally deficient. The measure was based on eugenic principles: not favouring the proliferation of mental defectives, it proposed the segregation of the sexes, and even implied that sterilisation of the unfit would be a good thing.

All Q.'s liberal and humane instincts were up in arms at this proposed invasion of personal liberty. He had all along sympathised with the horror that poor people had of having to go to the workhouse – he had written a story on the theme. He now wrote three Open Letters to the press against his own Liberal government's measure. Here is another facet to his writing. He was good at reasoned argument, often disguised in his Lectures by digressions and jokes, a method of persuasive indirection. Nothing indirect about these: Q. was shocked and angry, his argument vigorous and scathing: it might almost be Swift writing.

In the event the government withdrew the Bill.

In the same year came out his *Oxford Book of Victorian Verse*, dedicated 'To my future friends and pupils at Cambridge, this propitiatory wreath.' He apologised for having to repeat so many of the poems that he had already chosen for the more famous Book. But how could he have excluded what he thought best from the new anthology? 'I should have condemned myself to anthologising the second-rate, and clearing the ground for an *Oxford Book of the Worst Poetry* – which, by the way, might not be an unentertaining work.' Some idea of what this might be may be gathered from the amusing Introduction to a volume of Parodies at this time. No bad parodist himself, he here defines the *genre* concisely. 'Its method consists in a nice apposition of the incongruous, catching as nearly as possible the authentic speech of the bard and applying it unexpectedly, even absurdly, to things beneath his notice. In its easiest form Parody will take his actual words, and turn them to some new and ridiculous connotation.' In this way it follows further that 'Parody must be a form of criticism, and may be enlightening as it is vivacious'.

Hardy gave Q. leave to include any poems of his he wished – 'I frequently think of you in your snug and romantic corner down there.' To Hardy Cornwall always meant 'romance' – the romance enshrined in *A Pair of Blue Eyes*, and the best poems of *Moments of Vision*. Q. told me that whenever he met the old man, all he would talk about was Boscastle and Tintagel and our North Coast. Once and again he invited Q. to break his journey, 'coming from or going into Cornwall – that county which was the scene of the greatest romance of my life'. (That was after Emma's death.)

The chaplain of his old college at Oxford provided some examples in the theological field. This was the irreverent Reverend Ronnie Knox, who had poked fun at some of his seniors' attempt to lay the *Foundations* of Christian belief with an impertinent work pointing out *Some Loose Stones*. He now came forward with another jape, *Reunion All Round*. Q. found it 'diabolically funny, and the great Jonathan himself might have signed it. But I reckon, knowing 'em, that the dons of Trin. Coll. Oxon. must be having a time with this young man.' They were indeed, and Q. was quite right in his inkling – 'I don't give him long to enjoy poking the Common Room fire with a sword.'

This imp was on his way into the bosom of the Roman Church,

which knew of old how to take care of such. He had been one of the brilliant galaxy of friends at Balliol, every one of whom, except Harold Macmillan, was killed in the 1914–18 War. Thereafter Ronnie Knox lived a kind of widowered life, the gaiety gone out with the morning: a sad man, though he did write one more good squib, *Let Dons Delight*.

Among the undergraduates at Trinity to whom Ronnie temporarily, and with doubts, ministered was Bevil Quiller Couch. No intellectual, he was a thorough good fellow, a first-class oar – now a grown man after Q.'s own heart. Such a united family had good times together. They usually attended Henley Regatta – in this last, blissful year, 1913, before the sky fell, 'to cheer Jesus College for the Grand Challenge Cup, Trinity College, Oxford, for the Ladies' Plate, and Bevil – who had just finished his career at Oxford – for the Silver Goblets'.

With all that rowing and boating and seafaring, tragedy once struck Bevil. He put out from Fowey with old friend Atkinson in a small boat, which foundered in a heavy sea. Bevil was a strong swimmer and managed to bring the older man ashore, but unconscious. Bevil climbed the rocks in the storm to get help, but by the time it arrived Atkinson's body had been washed out by the waves. Q. had been very fond of this salty character, and succeeded him as Commodore of the Yacht Club, the duties of which gave him much pleasure.

The daughter, Foy, was good with a boat too. I remember reading a headline in a French newspaper, when in Paris in the 1930s, 'Trois Marins Sauvés par une Femme' . . . 'Miss Foy Quiller-Cough [sic], la fille de l'auteur célèbre', etc. She too had gone out, in bad weather, to bring them in, and made nothing of it when I told her of the headline. She took that sort of thing in her stride, and from girlhood had sailed with Bevil, to whom she was devoted.

Cambridge, 13 April 1913: 'The "May trees" here in full leaf, but the limes have not started yet in Chapel Court.' Q. was engaged in improving his rooms, and lunching with Benson, who had become a friend – they had something of Cornwall in common, for his father had been the first bishop of Truro. The *Times* had come out with a pleasant notice of Q.'s work at Cambridge. He next reported that J. A. Spender had been down to speak, but not in good form: he could not forget that he was standing for the town when the audience was a university one. 'For the credit of Oxford I had to treat 'em to a quieter key' – that went very well. Henry Jackson invited Spender and a score of others to his rooms in Trinity – Q. back at midnight. The Cambridge Union wanted him to speak, as a 'distinguished stranger (h'm!) against Chesterton, who was coming to denounce the Liberal Party. 'A poet has been lunching with me and reading me his verses' – rather good too, but they had made him sleepy. Such were his days now.

In June he was proud of Bevil's 'laying out those Blues. I *know* he's one of the best four or five oars up at Oxford, and I *think* he's easily the best stroke. Great day: Barrie's baronetcy in the morning (I have written) and the Boy's telegram in the evening. I got it as I was dressing for the Pharisees' dinner.' He adjured his

> *dearest Deare*, Don't *let these silly Tories get on your nerves. I know how, being so near* [this would be Treffrys and Purcells] *they irritate and seem to be of vastly greater importance than they are. But really and truly they are of none at all. . . . I go off to join Archdeacon Cunningham's party and see the 'Mays'. . . . Such a pretty sight. Once more the scenes at Oxford and here are so different that you can't set up any comparison. Bevies of smart frocks and sunshades on the Knoll at Ditton and in the Pitt enclosure at Greenway and the towpath packed.*

With the danger to European peace threatening from Germany – the majority of her people (not the Socialists) looking forward happily to '*der Tag*[1] – Q.'s son now joined the Special Reserve, to be called up at once as an officer on the outbreak of war. 'Please God he will never be called upon' – a very different attitude from that prevailing in Germany. His father felt that he had made the right choice, for, if the time should come, 'from what I know of him he would volunteer just the same. I think it's rather fine of him to go in for the real thing like this, instead of the pretty uniform and society play of the Artillery

[1] For the psychological preparation over decades of the German people for War, cf. P. Fussell, *The Great War and Modern Memory*. The attitude in Britain was far otherwise, liberal and civilised – except for the Imperialists, who in this respect were better prepared for the facts of life in the modern world.

Company.' Having sent off this missive to 'my dearest Deare', Q. now had to finish off a paper to read in the Dean's rooms that night.

News from the Duchy, 1913, for all its unpromising title – for fiction – contains some of Q.'s best stories. It was dedicated to Austin M. Purves, 'of Philadelphia and Troytown', who came over with his family each summer to enjoy Q.'s company and the amenities of Fowey. Quite a fat book when it appeared, *Tom Tiddler's Ground* was transferred to another volume in the collected edition; so too with 'The Election Count' which records some of his electoral experiences and makes fun of those unhumorous proceedings. 'Frenchman's Creek' is hilarious and turns the famous Captain Bligh, who had no sense of humour, into a joke. When he visited Helford to make soundings of the estuary during the Napoleonic war, the suspicious locals took him for a French spy and put him under arrest.

In October 1913 came an interesting exchange between Galsworthy and Q., who had commented unfavourably on Galsworthy's book, *The Dark Flower*. From Wiesbaden the author wrote that he had intended it as 'a study of Passion – that blind force which sweeps upon us out of the dark'. For all his gifts Q. had not perceived Galsworthy's purpose. 'You can never have looked first hand into the eyes of an unhappy marriage ... that but lives on the meanest of all diet, the sense of property and the sense of convention.' Galsworthy had known the two extremes – the happiest, 'and the shrivelling hell of the opposite. My gorge rises when I encounter that false glib view that the vow is everything, that people do better to go on living together when one of them, or both sicken at the other.' Galsworthy's book was *not* on the theme 'No duty where love is not'.

> *I cannot and must not be told that, when – in our land of facts and almost terrible love of propriety, with the innumerable forces of authority, convention, property, and fear – some voice makes itself heard to say: 'All this is little worth if the spirit be gone': I cannot be told that this is sentimental, dangerous, destructive, and so forth.*

Galsworthy was evidently much moved, and I cannot but think that he wins the argument. Q.'s own marriage was one of unmitigated happiness. The weakest side of this admirable man was his unbreachable conventionalism. He should have known better: in modern parlance he was a 'square'. There were no further contacts with Galsworthy: I do not think he was much to Q.'s mind.

'Lieutenant Lapenotière' is based on historic fact, the naval officer bringing to the Admiralty the news of Trafalgar and the death of Nelson, then going on to carry Nelson's last letter to Emma – Q. as usual not flinching from sentiment.

All his qualities are in evidence: the sharp observant eye – the pilot's eye 'set in deep crow's-feet at the corners, as all seamen's eyes are. It comes of facing the wind.' There is the folklore ready to hand: he that marries a fool must expect thorns in his bed; the shy titlarks that used to be friends of the race that inhabited Cornwall long ago, and inhabit their cromlechs still; the reason why choughs go red-legged to this day. We recognise the cove at Cadgwith: 'years ago I had been an undergraduate and had made one of a reading party under the Senior Tutor, who annually in the Long Vacation brought down two or three fourth-year men to bathe and boat and read Plato with him.'

He had the heart of an undergraduate still, and did not think it beneath him to exchange verses with them as in old days at Trinity. Now it was Jesus:

> *Q. is for 'Q', in the late Verrall's boots,*
> *His bedder plays draughts on his cast-away suits.*

Those were the loud checks that prim Benson had deplored. In reply he found time for a long poem of 'Avuncular' advice for the College paper, *Chanticlere*. Jesus had been founded by Bishop Alcock, so the cockerel was its totem; Mr Brittain, pillar of college life, had his rooms full of cocks of every description, china, wood, lead, even silver. The verses offer a long list of Don'ts:

> *Frederic, these Rules forgive*
> *For being mostly negative!*
> *'Tis by self-effacing ways*
> *Studious boys deserve the bays*
> *And at length become B.A.'s.*

On 4 August 1914 came the thunderclap of war – at least it was sudden and unexpected by the great body of simple folk, like us who heard of it that brilliant summer day, on the beach at Crinnis where Q. used to ride in earlier cloudless years. He himself was doubly involved – through Bevil, who had been in the Officers' Training Corps and transferred to the Special Reserve. He was immediately called up to serve in the Royal Artillery. Before the month was out he was in France with the heroic B.E.F. (British Expeditionary Force) – all too small to hold up the advancing hordes of Germans, as long intended under the Schlieffen Plan.

Q. himself, as a good patriot, had taken a leading part in the formation of the Territorials in Cornwall. All that long vacation and into the autumn term he was kept busy recruiting, organising meetings, aiding the national effort, bringing home the sense of danger in remote country places as yet hardly aware of it – both by speech and writing.

As a schoolboy of ten I somehow came by his 'Appeal to Cornish-women', written for the County Recruiting Committee. It could not be bettered as an appeal to the women: 'as it is your image the man will carry away with him; because the England he goes to defend shapes itself in his mind as "home"'. Nor could it be better as a statement of the country's case. Germany's case had been put by her civilian Chancellor, Bethmann-Hollweg, with typical German tact:

> *We find ourselves in a state of necessity, and* necessity knows no law. *Our troops have already occupied Luxembourg. Perhaps already they have entered on Belgian territory. (Applause).* That is in conflict with the rights of nations. The wrong which we are thereby doing *we will endeavour to make good as soon as our military end is achieved.*

Observe that for Teutonic tact! And we see that the road is quite continuous up to our own time with Hitler and the renewal of the German attempt to dominate, and enslave, Europe.

Q. pointed out that this was the logical end of the doctrines taught in every German school and university, proclaimed in their text-books: 'Neutrality is only a paper bulwark.' Bernhardi's militarist teaching was simply reflected in the civilian Chancellor's dismissal of the international guarantee of Belgian neutrality as only 'a scrap of paper'. In the lower standards of our own time Hitler did not even make excuses, but went ahead with the sudden evisceration of Rotterdam, and the holocaust of an ancient people, one of the three prime sources – along with the Greeks and Romans – of European civilisation. Q. quoted from Bismarck – Hitler advanced further in that path: *'You must leave the people through whom you march only their eyes to weep.'* The Germans were their own worst enemies: he did not need to go further than their own statements of intention.

It was a sad Cambridge that Q. returned to that autumn,

> *the streets desolate indeed. The good soldiers who had swarmed in upon town and college in August . . . had all departed for France. Nay, already many of them slept in French earth. . . . In the courts and around the Backs the gardeners were sweeping up the leaves, as ever; but no men passed on their way to lecture 'with the wind in their gowns'. In College one seldom met, never heard, an undergraduate. A few would gather in Hall, the most of them in their O.T.C. uniforms after a strenuous afternoon out by Madingley. The scholar read grace with an unwonted reverence:* Sic Deus in nobis et nos maneamus in illo. *As I looked down the hall, this one undergraduates' table reminded me of a road in the West Country a few days before, with the telegraph running beside it and on the wires the swallows gathering, discussing flight.*

Meanwhile, there was – as Mr Brittain reminds us – 'the daily and even hourly agony of wondering what was happening to his only son'.

After a sad Christmas at home, the vacant seat at the board,

> *we returned in January to a vastly different Cambridge. She had become a garrison town. The curfew no longer tolls the knell of parting day. It is not permitted. But when dusk has fallen, and the Mayor and Corporation leave the world to darkness and to me, I walk in the Fellows' Garden, carefully hiding the ardent tip of my cigarette lest it should attract a Zeppelin.*

Now there were lines of artillery horses beside the roads and Jesus Ditch, the horses fetlock-deep in mud, mud everywhere. Especially on the road to the Rifle Butts, where Q. drilled with dummy rifle along with other senior members of the University. Well known in their day – W. H. D. Rouse, Prévité-Orton, E. S. Prior – who remembers them now, except for Q.?

On 20 February he reported, 'I have put in a two-hours' drill: rifle practice: lying and kneeling on a mackintosh. The weather was charming, so I quite enjoyed it. Not the fun I should *choose*: but all these things go by comparison.' His colleague Duckworth and he were to do a training-walk next day, Benson to dine with him in the evening. A full morning's writing; then evening chapel between the afternoon's walk and dinner at St John's. A couple of days later: a sturdy tramp with Duckworth – below Ditton to Baitsbite Lock, across the river and home by the Newmarket Road. Tea with Mrs Duckworth, an hour's proof-correcting, then dinner at St John's, a pleasant time in the Combination Room; proofs 9.45 to midnight. Friday he was to motor to Audley End – 'Lord Braybrooke wants to show me the place.' Down at Fowey Major Bourne wishes to plant a miniature rifle-range in the Grammar School playground – referred to Major Shadwell.

John Masefield wrote to him in May, having returned from working in a French soldiers' hospital. He was appalled by the sufferings of the wounded from the Argonne – from the long journeys they endured before reaching hospital, many dying on the way. Masefield was raising money for a travelling field hospital, and needed £3,500, for fifty beds; he had been promised a motor ambulance and equipment, and was appealing for funds.

From March to October 1915, Q. was on leave from the University on military duty at home. He was given a temporary commission to raise and train a pioneer battalion of the Duke of Cornwall's Light Infantry. In the midst of all this he had to set examination papers for the Tripos, and was a bit late. 'We are almost desperately busy here ... on top of my share of recruiting the War Office made me a temporary lieutenant to work up one company.' Men were pouring in, 'and I am left alone with the O.C. to wrestle with a thousand details of clothing contracts, army forms, billets, etc., besides taking parades and sitting on minor offences'.

With the acute shortage of officers the Colonel and he had to make do as best they could.

*My days for a week have been 7.30 a.m. – 1 a.m. The Colonel gets to
bed at midnight, and then I consider the History of English Literature
1780–1830. . . . I have been drilling and grilling for two hours in the
eye of the sun: if this letter is apparently blotted with a tear it has nothing
to do with the Recording Angel and moreover it isn't a tear at all but
perspiration. I will post the General History and Shakespeare paper
tonight. It is mostly ready and should be despatched with this: but I have
to take the men on a six-mile route march after getting something to eat.*

This, with his excuses, to his junior colleague as examiner.

*My poor wits were wandering when I concluded my last, and also I was
interrupted by a lady who wanted her child to be exempted from
vaccination. You will like to hear of a recruit who begged off parade on
the ground that he 'wasn't took very well this morning'. Suffering from
meiosis? If the fellows weren't so amazingly tractable I don't know what
we should do. They still look on me as an amiable eccentric when I
examine their 160 chins every morning at 9.30. 'I never* belonged
[Cornish usage], *sir, to get shaved but on Saturday night.'*

Then there were toe-nails to be looked at. After taking his company
for a bathe in the sea, he found that he needed to cut the toe-nails of
a large number – 'and they *were* toe-nails, too!'.

Generous as ever, on one route-march through Fowey he took the
whole company into tea at The Haven, filling the length of lawn in the
garden. This was the kind of occasion Lady Q. could rise to, though
they ate the house bare. By June 'we have raised two companies and
have orders from the War Office to continue and push for a battalion.
My own little lot are today 210 strong, and I took 'em a route march
this afternoon after a hard morning's drill.' Meanwhile, 'my boy
continues to write cheerfully from France, and, in the intervals of
fighting, collects large stores of cherries and gooseberries from
deserted gardens in which the roses are smothering the holes made
by shells'.

At the end of September he wrote to Lilian from his 10th D.C.L.I.
Camp at Hayle that he had been left to make a camp with two
subalterns only to help, and had been under canvas ever since he and
she had parted. Next came news of brother Cyril's death – Q. insisted
on paying the bills. On 21 November, 'I travelled up with the dear

Boy yesterday. We parted at Paddington. . . . I came on to Liverpool Street in a beastly train, where luckily I had to keep a set face in a crowd of passengers. But, my dear, what a lift it will be when this filthy nonsense is over.' What a contrast that was with the Germans, who thought that they would have a walk-over in Europe! However, 'not an inch of slackening until the job is through'.

In December Q. dedicated *On the Art of Writing* (what more appropriate? – he could tell his students how to), to Lilian's husband, J. H. Lobban. 'He seems to me to be (on our common job) a sound man amongst many fools.' Here is what he really thought, but didn't publicly say. Today, in an egalitarian society, it needs to be said out loud. He had Lilian to thank for a great bowl of bath soap – just what he was longing for, for his tent. Louie had sent out to Bevil plum-puddings, cakes, cigarettes 'for the whole of his Brigade!'.

Nicky-Nan, Reservist, which Q. wrote in the intervals of his war-work, has the special interest of being a faithful record of how that war took West Country people – mostly by surprise and wonderment. As Paul Fussell brings home in *The Great War and Modern Memory*, the English were neither militarily or psychologically prepared, except for Navy men. The Germans had had war indoctrinated into them for three generations, and taught to regard it as a good thing; peace was thought demoralising. They had always been best at fighting, for centuries providing mercenaries for Europe.

In a later Preface – before the Germans got going at their trade yet again – Q. tells us that in our agricultural areas 'the idea of war was a new thing, as the idea of any special enmity against Germany was a strange one, while that of a General Levy to meet an unrealised emergency lay far beyond the countryside's horizon. . . . The Army seldom came within their ken, almost never within range of their domestic concern.' The fisher-folk were affected differently, for their men were used to serving in the Naval Reserve, and took service as a matter of course. In both Church and Chapel, however, war was regarded as anti-Christian, and along the countryside the difficulty was 'to awaken the sense of private duty in a national danger and (often) to contend with conscience'. This was Q.'s task, and he was as well equipped for dealing with the latter as with comprehending the full extent of Germany's threat not only to Britain but to European civilisation.

Engaged in doing this duty actively, as his son was in France, Q., like the just man he was, turned to the other side of the matter in his book.

Infinite damage was done by the unhelpful who wrote hasty, scathing letters to the newspapers, accusing villages and districts of cowardice; infamous cruelty by people who sent white feathers anonymously to young men already tortured by mental and moral doubts. . . . I can recognise, looking back, that a great deal of this cruelty had its root in panic. But it did much harm at the time, and in the heat of resenting it I wrote this story.

How like him it was to keep so just a balance, while he was himself engaged in serving, and to see both sides with such humanity. One derives a much less respect-worthy picture of just those days at the D.C.L.I. *depôt* at Bodmin from the Letters of D. H. Lawrence, doubtly tethered to his anti-war stance by his Bloomsbury affiliations and his German wife.

Nicky-Nan was a Naval Reservist who got into trouble for not answering the call, while really incapacitated by a growth in his leg he was trying to conceal. That glorious summer of 1914 was like that of 1940:

When the corn is in the shock,
Then the fish is on the rock.

A very little of the corn had been shocked as yet; but the fields, right down to the cliffs' edge, stood ripe for abundant harvest. I doubt, indeed, if in our time they have ever smiled a fairer promise of reward for husbandry than during this last fortnight of July 1914, when the crews, running back with the southerly breeze for Polpier, would note how the crop stood yellower in today's than in yesterday's sunrise.

Polpier is Polperro, and Nicky lives in his part – 'cantle' is Q.'s word – of Jonathan Couch's house huddled over the river there. The Old Doctor is recalled for us, as a still living legend among his people.

They told what an eye he had, as a naturalist, for anything uncommon in the maunds; how he taught them to be observant, alert for any strange fish, and to bring it home alive, if possible; and how he was never so happy as when seated on a bollard near the Quay-head with a drawing-board on his knee, busy transferring to paper the outline and markings of a specimen and its perishable exquisite colours . . . pausing now and again to pencil a note on the margin of the portrait.

We may transfer something of that portrait to the grandson, who inherited the Old Doctor's looks and skill, transposed to literature. We find the familiarity with our people's old folk-ways, as with the men fishing. 'A crabber sits much on the thwart of a boat and drives with his heels against a stretcher.' However,

feminine gossip in Polpier is not conducted in groups, as the men conduct theirs on the Quay. By tradition, each housewife takes post on her own threshold-slate, and knits while she talks with her neighbours to right and left and across the road. Thus a bit of news zigzags from door to door through the town like a postal delivery.

They knew not at all why their country should be at war. Over the harbour lay the usual Sabbath calm: high on the uplands stood the outposts of the corn, yellowing to harvest. Not a soul present had ever harboured a malevolent thought against a single German. . . . Yet the thing had happened.

We have had reason, twice in a lifetime, to know better since.

For Bevil, fighting in France, we may go to May Cannan's autobiography, *Grey Ghosts and Voices.* Daughter of Charles Cannan, Q.'s closest friend at Oxford, she was the girl Bevil was to have married. Q. could not bear to speak of his son; his mother was braver, and would drop into conversation, quite naturally, something about 'the dear boy'.

He was in the earliest fighting of the heroic B.E.F. which, small as it was, fought the Germans to a standstill 'and itself out of existence', but prevented them from ever gaining the Channel ports in that war. To the Germans it was the 'battle of Calais' – they did not get it. May learned that 'it had been touch and go; that at one moment the crack Bavarian troops had found themselves engaged, and held, by a contingent of cooks, grooms, officers' batmen, and some men from an Ammunition Column' (Bevil was with those). He wrote home when the crisis was over; but 'never have I seen such fighting as on the lst,

2nd and 3rd. People may well be proud of the lst Corps (that was Haig's), which held on for three days against more than treble its numbers of Germans.' He was immediately sent up with his Ammunition Column 'to the 41st Brigade who were heavily engaged', and there was first wounded. On his first leave home his sister Foy remembered that he spoke little of the war, but helped with digging potatoes at the 'Farm' across the harbour, and wished that he had some of their long-handled Cornish shovels in Flanders. By 12 December he was back in the line.

In the summer of 1916 he was in the battle of the Somme, with its appalling casualties. He led his battery into action – 'the noise is deafening day and night without even ten minutes' pause. . . . We are digging like moles. You should see me black with dust and dirt, burnt with the sun, and always hot.' That month of July he was promoted to command the 9th Battery, R.F.A. 'It will be nice having one's own show, and a very famous battery too – *vide* the First Seven Divisions.'

The Germans, professionals as they were, had far fewer casualties; the British losses at the Somme decimated Kitchener's army with no result. People at home were very despondent – no end to the war in sight. Bevil had won the M.C., and in December got a second leave home. Q. was depressed, 'recovering from the φλû. But I cheer up because my Boy has been home and imparted life to the whole situation. They have made him a Major: which, as I told him, may make all the difference.'

An interesting exchange with Hardy took place in 1916. The Hardys were reading aloud in the evenings 'the handsome book Q. had sent' – evidently *On the Art of Writing,* for 'my wife has gone ahead privately with it, and says that now at last she thinks she may become a great writer in spite of me'. This was Florence, the second wife – odd that both his wives had not only literary aspirations but a certain competitive envy of their husband. Q. did not have that to put up with: his wife contented herself with housekeeping and bridge-parties.

Hardy was preparing a patchwork of scenes from *The Dynasts*,

for our local actors to raise money for the Red Cross . . . drudgery, but a job I could not, however, refuse to do with any sort of conscience. . . . A man must have a good deal of magnanimity in him to tell the rising youth the principles of a trade – I ought to say "art" as you do, of course – which so many of us have to find out laboriously for ourselves.

He queried whether 'the sequence of vowels in Mr Yeats's poem has much to do with its beauty, or whether any great poet ever thought much about such sequences – except perhaps Gray and Tennyson'.

I suspect that here Hardy was right as against the critic: these things *happen,* to a true poet, subtly, instinctively and inexplicably. He did not go in for literary criticism, but he *knew*, better than the critics.

That December the Hardys had read aloud Q.'s poem 'The Sacred Way'. He had been looking at reviews of the Selection of his poems:

> *What a pity that there is no school or science of criticism – especially in respect of verse. I cannot find a single idea in any of them that is not obvious. . . . You might deliver an excellent series of lectures on the Vicissitudes of Poetry, as exhibited in the history of English literature – instancing such a queer phenomenon as that of Vaughan, for example, who for two centuries dropped into oblivion, and was then duly resurrected.*

He hoped that Q. was not 'too depressed by the situation in Europe'. When the war was over Hardy was 'pleasantly surprised at receiving a book of verses by poet-friends', put together in his honour, 'with a beautiful pastoral poem of yours'. He felt unworthy of such a delightful tribute, being a 'cracked old pot at the best. I wonder how dear Cornwall is looking: I don't know when I shall see it again: perhaps never, for I seldom go anywhere now.' The correspondence rounds off later with a note from the old sage about a proposed University of Wessex, and, unexpectedly, 'I never wished to be a millionaire till now, so as to set it going.' Q. has never called round this way, but Cockerell tells of 'your great success with the young barbarians at Cambridge, as M. Arnold called them.'

At Cambridge Q. had left a card on the Staff Colonel billeted at Caius, who had been at school with him at Newton Abbot. He looked in at the Fitzwilliam to see some drawings, then went along Cow Fen by the upper river – 'not very pleasant, owing to the Tommies and young women a-courting. In fact *I* felt highly embarrassed, though *they* didn't seem to mind.' He was invited to dine to meet Earl

Beauchamp, Liberal leader in the Lords. He was *very* liberal in his views, and practice, of sex, and would have been not at all embarrassed; nor would he have subscribed to Q.'s innocent, 'you are the only woman in the world that I loved or ever have'.

That autumn politics depressed him: it saw the end of Asquith's long administration and, with it, of the old Liberalism for which Q. had fought. Asquith, an educated university man with high standards, was Q.'s man; Lloyd George, who took his place, was not. Q. does not seem to have taken into account that the country needed Lloyd George to win the war, when he wrote, 'I foresee myself back in politics again and, in a corner of the world, wearing out a stupid end of life in politics, fighting a Cabinet of parvenus, prigs and Prussians. God! what an end to every hope of 1906!'

It was, in its way, the end of Liberalism: the Party which had had such an enormous majority in 1906, and produced the ablest government of the century – except for Churchill's in the Second German War, 1940–5 – would henceforth be consigned to being a diminishing minority Party, with no further influence in the country's history.

Bevil, however, remained cheerful – was rather enjoying battle, like Julian Grenfell and his brother (both of whom had already fallen). He had a stormy crossing to France, which he thoroughly enjoyed; they had difficulty in getting into harbour and, as an old hand at boats, he was able to give a helping hand with the crew. Rejoining his battery, which he spoke of with affection, he found that crew in good heart.

At home his father was writing lectures for the coming term;

> *but I am – Heaven knows why it should be in this general defection of spirit – simply boiling over with plots of novels and plays, schemes of books, etc. And I have this day sawn up about three cwt of wood on my own farm, corrected about one-third of that weight of proofs, and dined sparsely but as a Christian. The carollers have been singing in the hall, and the holly and ivy make the usual background. At 12.30 a.m. [sc. p.m.] an airship (British) came swooping low over the house. As it rounded and turned westward again its side took the loveliest shine.*

Back at Cambridge, in February 1917, Sidney Cockerell asked Q. along to see the Somme pictures and the Tanks at the Mill Road Cinema. There was a mix-up about the cinema and they missed each other; Q. 'stuck out about twenty pictures of Transport Service (I could have invented 'em better)', then left. A letter to Bevil, in May, survives. A vote would shortly be taken on the new Tripos Q. had excogitated with his supporters: 'we are threatened with an opposition sprung upon us at the last moment. But I hope it will be all right.' It was.

I am thinking you will be taken out of action, by this time, for the rest which surely you deserve. By latest reports today the push is going forward again and going strong. It will be Good to have a homely cruise on a yacht after all this. I had a great day on Thursday. Went up far beyond Byron's Pool. Had tea in a meadow which was one sheet of marsh marigolds (I brought back an armful and have a bowl full of them), and saw all manner of birds busy around us: grass warblers, sedge warblers, snipe, etc: also a fine brown owl looking down on us in a bleary-eyed way from the fork of a tree. Journey home rather exciting as we neared Cambridge. It was early closing-day, and the inhabitants of the town have taken furiously to punting – an art which they do not yet understand. Every other punt was across-stream, full of wounded soldiers, and in charge of an agitated young woman who had completely lost her head. By King's meadow we passed one who had gone overboard and was on the bank wringing herself out.

It was a perfect day for the expedition: bright, not too hot, and a gentle breeze in the evening. Got back to the boat-house just after 7: did a sprint to Jesus College, changed, then another sprint to dine with the Mills's: felt so full of life afterwards that I put in 2 hours work before getting to bed.

We have our coffee in the Fellows' Garden after dinner. The Cadets, in the University, and especially in this College, have started a Magazine, and, as the Corps includes a Punch *artist and a man who used to write the front page for* London Opinion, *the effort is well above average. . . . I may have to run up to London next week, to interview the War Office about Guy Phelps. It really is abominable that after getting a first-class recommendation from his C.O. in India, he is now required to get one from his C.O. in Mesopotamia, who is almost certainly a prisoner in Turkish hands!*

Am dining in Magdalene tonight with Benson who wants to talk to me about something: probably about Vote. Our opponents are playing a game which is quite outside the line here or (I should hope) anywhere among decent men. They absolutely shirked the public discussion in the Senate, where we had no opposition at all put up – and have kept silence for two months: and now propose to flood the place with fly-sheets just when there is no time to get the answers printed. I rather think public opinion will resent that sort of behaviour pretty heavily. I know it will after the event, however it goes. We are stupid enough up here, no doubt, but we are not "slim" that way, and we don't like the people who are. . . .

Wednesday next, they give honorary degrees here to the American ambassador and General Smuts. . . . I gather that Father Waggett is not an unmixed success at Fowey; too affable with everyone in two minutes to be quite the sort to please your Mother (always suspicious of clerics). I doubt we're a difficult lot to please; and, what's more, a too cocksure manner of pleasing at sight is not the best way.

Lady Q. *was* difficult to please; Father Waggett was a smooth, popular, *very* High Church character of a cleric. 'I hope your Mother will have managed to smuggle out a Rashleigh cake before the export of cake is forbidden. Also they are threatening to take the starch out of my shirts to feed something or somebody.' The conscientious among the Fellows were already going about in soft collars, one has ordered 3 flannel shirts: 'I hope he won't take to dining in his strips. . . . All windows open & the Close fairly humming with song birds. Best love and God bless you. Your own father.'

During this time he was writing his *Memoir of A. J. Butler* and a last collection of stories, *Mortallone and Aunt Trinidad: Tales of the Spanish Main.* May Cannan regarded 1917 as the worst year of the war for civilians – the submarine campaign at its most dangerous, shortness of rations, Russia knocked out by two Revolutions before the United States could come to the rescue. In the battle of Arras Bevil was again heavily engaged; then home on leave for 'a divine five days'. My old tutor at Christ Church, E. F. Jacob, severely wounded at this time, went down to Fowey to convalesce, and was for ever grateful for the way he was welcomed into the family at The Haven. Bevil wrote to May from the Front, 'out here I have read more books than during the rest of my life, not perhaps saying much; among the books have been several War Novels and War Poems which naturally collect in a Battery library; but there is only one which brings the war home in a unique and beautiful way.' He meant her volume of poems which she had sent out to him.

In October he was wounded again, but slightly. Q. wrote that 'after having the wound dressed he resumed command, and has not left his unit. He tried to keep it out of the lists; but the doctors had to report. . . . I am just back from the north coast here, where for a few days I have been trying to get my nerves right after finishing a novel.' This would be *Foe-Farrell*, to be published next year.

Homeward bound, Q. usually dined at the Paddington Hotel, then took a sleeper. That December, arriving at Par at 5.50 a.m.,

I found a car waiting for me under the waning moon and gave a lift to a Tommy whom I recognised as a Fowey boy. He got out at the top of Lostwithiel Street and swung down the hill, his person all hung about with parcels and haversacks – quite like a gipsy caravan. So there were two very happy home-comings at daybreak in this little place.

The great excitement was that Bevil might be home for a month's leave. 'He has now 10 guns in the Battery and it seems to have brought much honour on itself. His sub, "Scroggie", has been given the M.C. and a Sergeant and Corporal military medals. There are probably some more awards to come. But he has been having a very fierce time. . . . The new Tripos is shaping up well.'

From Q.'s letters in 1918 to Waller, correcting proofs at the Cambridge University Press, new publishers for him, we get rather a new angle.

I can't go on thanking you as you deserve or expressing the contrition I owe. Either I must have a bill-head printed and gum it to the proofs with my tears, or save it up and hand you my remorse in the end in a cut-glass tear-bottle. . . . I regularly excise, in proof, all remarks about Skeat.[1] He used to enrage me so, in the days when I took in Notes and Queries *by his discourtesies to all and sundry, that I have to write down these things and then cut them out.*

Another irascible professor, E. A. Freeman, 'used to inhabit the next staircase to mine at Trin. Coll. Oxon.'. Q. had a characteristic story of him to tell, unfortunately omitted from the letter. Next, 'Hang grammar, anyway Use-and-wont by decent fellows is the last test of

---

[1] The Revd. W. W. Skeat, 1835–1912, Professor of Anglo-Saxon at Cambridge 1878–1912.

good English to my thinking. I have little to urge against the split infinitive except the table-manners of those who use it.' He might have cited Hardy's for example.

> *'A sonnet of Milton's' is right: a double possessive. . . . As for Swinburne, I ought never to have written about him. Yes, I'll grant you those lines and scores of others: but I hate fluency in verse – and in oratory too. Swinburne is just emptiness to me as he gets older, and the more maddening as he goes on exploiting a heavenly gift. I wish he had just shut up, like Coleridge, and left us surmising wonders.*

The University had called on him to examine for the French Le Bas Prize, and he was being consulted over the project of a French professorship. He would prefer a distinguished Frenchman for the Chair, but didn't meddle with Cambridge inner politics: 'my job begins and ends with getting the Chair'. In September, correcting proofs of his *Studies in Literature*, he wished 'I had known Saintsbury inhabits 1 Royal Crescent [Bath]. What a glorious piece of architecture it is!'

In October

> *the War Office informs me that my boy was wounded again on September 24, but "remained on duty with his command". As we have received three or four letters written since that date, and he himself makes no mention of his hurt, we trust it is not serious. . . . That makes twice, and two other nasty knocks there have been, not tabulated. I wish the Hun would hurry up with that Revolution of his and get it over. But, my word! what a nice little parcel of news, today!*

It was the beginning of their break-up.

In the last year of the war people were in low spirits – low rations, not enough to eat from the intensified submarine campaign, and then the long sickness of hope deferred. Even Q. confessed that he was low – but was called upon to preach now and again in Cambridge churches to keep morale going. He was not successful as a preacher. Though his Lectures were successful both in delivery and in book form, lecturing was rather an ordeal for this shy man – hence the careful writing out of the lecture, marked for pauses, emphases, and all.

[141]

He was criticised for his remarks in these about the Germans, which were mild enough in all conscience. But there was a substratum of pro-Germanism among Cambridge intellectuals, blatant around the group of my old acquaintance, C. K. Ogden, who ran the *Cambridge Review* from his premises on King's Parade. Though most of the group were pacifists – like Lytton and James Strachey, Clive Bell, David Garnett, and Duncan Grant, the effect of their propaganda was simply pro-German.[1] Bertrand Russell was the most notorious offender, who very properly lost his Fellowship at Trinity for his outrageous pronouncements. Keynes was irresponsible in his judgment about the war, and shortly was to do untold damage by his unbalanced condemnation of the Peace. In its political arrangements, freeing the smaller nationalities of Europe, it did historic justice; what the Germans intended was revealed by the Treaty of Brest-Litovsk in 1917, which took the whole of Eastern Europe right up to the threshold of St Petersburg. Hitler simply continued long-term German aims.

Neither A. E. Housman nor Q. subscribed to the over-estimation of German scholarship prevalent in British and American universities from the later nineteenth century; and Q.'s distaste for German laying down the law about English literature in general, Shakespeare in particular, was expressed in unexceptionable terms. He did not reply. He did not engage in controversy – only once that I remember: a comic encounter with Bernard Shaw on the subject of teetotalism, which Q. could not abide. (My sympathies are with Shaw.)

The Americans were now in the war; in France Bevil was training them and had to put off his leave: 'I should love to have been home when May was staying.' It was everywhere hot and dusty, and 'I long for a sight of the sea'. That summer vacation Q. was organising squads of helpers, schoolboys and all, to help with the harvest. In September Bevil came home on leave. 'We've had a heavenly time. It wound up

---

[1] cf. the attitude of the philosopher G. E. Moore, the *guru* of all that lot. When Lytton Strachey asked him if the war had made any difference to him, he typically paused for thought and then said, 'None. Why should it?' Strachey asked whether he was not even horrified by it; Moore replied that he had never felt anything about it at all. M. Holroyd, *Lytton Strachey*, p.591. One can imagine what Q. would have thought of such inhumanity.

with our sailing him up the river here seven miles to Lostwithiel station and seeing him and his sister off. . . . Then his mother and I pulled home on the ebb in the dusk of a lovely evening: but it was very much on the ebb and very much in the dusk.'

On his return to the Front Bevil was involved in continuous fighting, now advanced along the old Hindenburg Line. At the end of September he led his battery into action over the hill at Noyelles, where they had been in August 1914. In October, 'I hope everyone at home is soberly in the best of spirits. . . . I ride up and down the great main road from Calais and Boulogne to Austerlitz, and one cannot help having wonderful visions of the Grande Armée marching E.S.E. on perhaps just such another autumn day, still, grey and perfect.' On the 26th he was wounded again, and vexed that the War Office reported it (he was to be awarded a D.S.O.). The advance was gathering momentum, the whole Belgian coast at last freed. 'We have our waggon line by a lovely barn full of hay requisitioned by the Boche.' On the night of 4/5 November his battery fired their last barrage. May was doing war-work in Paris, which had been regularly bombarded at long range by Krupps' masterpiece, Big Bertha.

On 11 November came never-to-be-forgotten Armistice Day (at home the church bells rang madly). In Paris, where Bevil was shortly to join her, May went into Notre Dame to give thanks. 'The great cathedral was in darkness save for the high altar, on which lay the flags of France and of England; but everywhere there were candles, and before every candle knelt a figure in black.' France's blood-drain had been twice that even of Britain: Germany's not so heavy proportionately – ready for another attempt twenty years later.

Bevil was on his way to Paris. Going through Amiens, a Tommy spoke the words: 'Well, sir, it's all over at last.' Bevil wrote home, 'I simply did not realise it, as I stood there with the strange Sapper in the midst of the Somme Desert. I longed to be with you all; and to be back with the Battery who are my children – to be with people that I knew, to rejoice and share that wonderful feeling of joy and thankfulness.'

At Amiens he was whirled by the crowd into the square: 'everywhere people singing and dancing, cheering or crying. It was like a wonderful dream.' Reaching Paris, he was carried on to a chariot draped in

flowers and bunting, pulled along with an American doctor, three
Chasseurs Alpins, a couple of French artillery officers, and some
poilus (Tommies). 'Thus did I enter into a strange city.' Odd that, in
all those years at the Front, he should not have spent a leave there in
the usual way: he always came home to Fowey, and anyway his were
not the ways of relaxation usual with soldiers on leave. 'The scene',
he wrote home, 'was wonderful. Peaceful, orderly, rejoicing. Families
from the country suburbs dancing and singing hand in hand. Bands;
processions, confetti, and yet never a jostle or the sign of a soul who
looked rough. This morning I crossed the Seine and called on May
Cannan.'

They had a blissful five days together, and on one of them, 'looking
down into the waters of the Seine hurrying by and having known other
wars and other lovers', May wrote, 'he asked me to marry him.' 'After
all,' he said, 'love is best.' Writing home to his father:

> It was by no means suddenly arranged on my part, and in fact dates back
> some time before the War; and the thought has helped me no end in
> carrying on through these four years. But I made a vow, May thinks
> wrongly, that if my family had to suffer because I was out here it was
> right that no more should, and it was surely right to avoid it? I also
> thought that it would help me to 'go straight' from the start and not think
> of getting home or of 'soft jobs', and God knows, it has helped.

To his mother he wrote, 'it has been the greatest and one ideal. . . . I
am so happy.'

Quite simply, the chances had been against his coming through
those four years alive. Most of his Oxford comrades had been killed
in that murderous war. As one goes into the chapels of Oxford and
Cambridge colleges one sees the memorials of hundreds, thousands,
of his generation who were lost to the country. They were the flower
of England – and grievously the country suffered for want of their
leadership in the years to come.

He had not wanted to leave May a war-widow. Now all was well.
Safe and free, he had a job arranged (appropriately, with a shipping
company). He could now afford to marry; and, an idealist like his
father, he thought of further service to his country as a Liberal in
politics.

Q. was at Cambridge when the Armistice broke upon us. We have a long letter to his 'dearest Deare' about it all.

I was sitting in the barber's chair at 11 o'clock, when a neighbour rushed in with the news. I was so overcome that I presently found myself using both hair-brushes (luckily very clean) to brush my coat with. Then, out in the street, people began cheering and running to put out flags. But apart from this everybody is extraordinarily calm. The Boy's letter, bless him!, turned up first post this morning, and now I shall be longing for his next. It all seems so wonderful, his coming through these fearful years: I can't tell even you, my love, how I feel.

I have written out two pretty elaborate plans of the new novel. . . . I must catch the 8.30 train for London tomorrow, and shall try to see Curtis Brown before going on to the Education Office. That other envelope, marked 'Urgent', was from the Editor of Everyman, wanting to print one of my Cambridge Lectures. Yesterday morning, after putting in a Chapel, I spent finishing my letter to Boy. [Tea with the Cockerells and the rather amusing crowd he collects on Sundays] . . . then home to a meatless dinner, and afterwards work until midnight, finishing synopsis of novel.

Tonight I dine with The Society in Magdalene (Gazelee's rooms) and there will be Champagne. I see that the Times *had in a short notice of my last lecture, and yesterday I had a warm letter of thanks for it from Rider Haggard. . . . I shan't be altogether sorry if it rains tonight and so prevents people from mafficking in the streets. I don't feel a bit like that. But what a smash-up in Germany! That, at any rate, I have steadily prophesied. . . . At dinner tonight I shall drink to Boy: and think of him at home with us for Christmas.*

Some years later he looked back over it all from a wider and longer perspective.

The awful strain was over at last; and to one who for four years and more had endured it, here was, not only the salvation of his country achieved at length, but release from the awful dragging anxiety for his own, the hideous terror of any telegraph boy walking towards his house. . . . Youth won the war. . . . As for us others, the strain had been too long, and anyhow we had not deserved as youth had.

Now that 'the Boy' was safe and all was well, he could write happily to May:

*My very dear Child, it is rather pleasant, you know, when two young
people conspire to fulfil what would have been man's dearest wish. . . .
This of course means, among other things, wishing myself joy; after four
and a half years of pitching one's hope no higher than that Bevil might
come through it safely and honourably, as I put it to myself; but the
honourably I really knew might be left to him.*

That December was full of happy news and plans for the future.
Oddly enough, neither Bevil's mother nor his sister, in that reticent
family, had guessed his feelings for May. Q.'s intuition was keener:
'you see, I happen to know the symptoms, and in these matters keep
pretty young for my age, I thank the Lord'. At Jesus Bevil's health was
drunk in the Combination Room in port. Nairne had been much
impressed by May's book of poems. University news was that £20,000
had been given for a Chair of Naval History; the Drapers Company
had given a Chair of French; £25,000 went to Oxford. Q. had been
closely involved in the effort to raise £65,000. These endowments
came at the time in the nature of thank-offerings. Then he was off to
Fowey and 'turned up at the Haven as dawn was breaking with the
promise of a fine but breezy day'. They all celebrated with a colossal
turkey and plum-pudding dinner.

The town of Fowey, like the whole country, was taken up with the
Khaki Election which Lloyd George's Coalition, dominated by the
Tories, forced on a stunned electorate to take advantage of the hour.
It had the effect of splitting the Liberal Party in two, and ending its
old ascendancy. Fowey was more or less solid for their local Tory,
Hanson; Vicar Purcell, allied to the Treffrys, was even 'anxious to
preside over a meeting for him'. To Q., an old-time Liberal, it was all
nothing but a 'ramp' – as indeed it was. 'The Coalition Ramp, after
securing its majority at the polls, is bound to run itself to a standstill.'
He was willing that they should carry on as they were to the Peace
Conference, but that they must 'declare for a League of Nations or
there'll be an almighty row.' Would there have been?

Bevil was making for Cologne.

*A glance at the Rhine thereabouts will dissuade you from planning an
expedition upstream by boat or canoe. It may be my Anti-German bias,
but the Rhine did not charm me. . . . A steam-boat from Cologne to*

Coblentz, or better t'other way, is good enough for it, and you can sit on deck with a book and read about its romantic castles.

'Cannan has been the first of my friends since we met', and May was Q.'s favourite among the children. 'She has an extremely sensitive and noble mind, of which it will be your dearest privilege to be very careful. So many men, after they are married, forget that a lover should be a lover always, and *show* it. But this is an exercise which sweetens the whole of life. You have made us very happy.'

At the end of Bevil's leave father and son travelled up together, having 'a cheery meal in the Boy's sleeper, aided by the bubbly. We talked away over it, just like two friends of the same age, and he was *so* open and lovable.' They parted outside the station, Q. to find Cambridge under five inches of snow. 'The town has wonderfully recovered its 'Varsity appearance. The feeding, however, has scarcely begun to improve.'

They were all planning for the future. The directors of Bevil's shipping company-to-be proposed a salary of £300 a year – little enough; but May was willing to take on work – Q. preferred housekeeping for her.

I was earning a larger income when I married your Mother; but I was certainly no better off – as I had to make (or did make) an allowance to my Mother and the others of the family, besides having a load of family debt and no capital. It delayed me from marrying for a long while, and when we did marry it was a great risk. But when it was taken our only regret was that we hadn't taken it before, when it was bigger. . . . I married at twenty-five, to wish that I had married two years earlier.

Cambridge was under snow. His first post-war lecture was to an 'audience even larger than the old bumper ones of 1914 – rows of undergraduates *standing* it out'. Then to Nottingham in bitter weather: at the University some 600 packed the hall and 'the lecture went with a bang'. A terrible journey back – trains late – hardly any food at the stations: he has a comic description of it all. Now a coal-shortage owing to strikes; he has had in some hundredweights of wood, though it is still cold in his rooms. 'It is good news that you won't be sent abroad at once.' In the intervals of anxiety for four-and-a half years, he has wanted to see Bevil safely married. 'A good deal of my latent, so-to-say personal spite against the whole business was that it might shut you for an indefinite time out of the luck I had at your age.' Now all was set for the wedding.

Bevil's unit, the Royal IXth, were among those chosen to march into Germany – 'a great honour', he said. And then, as the Germans opened the doors and let their prisoners out: 'these poor people', who did not yet know the desolation of the battlefields where once had been their homes, the devastation the Huns had wrought all down northern and eastern France. 'Sometimes,' he wrote to Q., 'I felt like you, when I saw an old man and his wife weeping before the statue of Strasbourg; and when an old lady of eighty-four fell on my neck in Maubeuge and wept.' He arrived in an undamaged Germany, posted in a big Schloss, 'set in well-timbered grounds, with central heating and every form of luxury'.

Q. and I were agreed about the manic people who had ruined the old Europe, and were still in condition to renew their attempt. He viewed the future with foreboding.

In January Bevil got leave and took May down to Fowey – the wedding was planned for June: 'Darling, we have come home.'

We helped a little in the orchard garden that they called the 'Farm', rowing over in the old Red Boat; and sailed out to sea in 'True Tilda', and met a small gale. We walked in Cornish headland, and he showed me Menabilly, which he said he would like; and Kilmarth, which I said I would like because it was smaller and you could see, over the lift of a hayfield, the dazzle that was his sea. We went to a party where he was surrounded by people who loved him. We dined in the 'Haven' of an evening, and there was silver, and wine in tall glasses and candlelight. And then it was over. [He was to go back to duty.] *I said goodbye to him, and went back to the quiet drawing room and lamplight and the sound of the sea washing the rocks below the garden wall.*

When he got back to Dürren (where it happened that my brother was stationed in the Army of Occupation) the weather was bitter, snowing and freezing hard, and Bevil fell ill. 'When we lived in holes in the ground we never caught chills, which seems silly. It has been freezing here without a break for fourteen days.'

He was to have returned home, demobilised, at the end of the month. In a few days he was dead.

Post-War:
High Tide

Q. and May Cannan went up to London but could not get permission to go to Germany for Bevil's funeral. He had a great send-off – some hundreds from his beloved battery, his 'children', from other formations he had known, many friends. His subaltern wrote of his kindness and care for others, his complete disregard of his own safety, his devotion to his mare, Peggy, which had come through so many dangers with him.

His father and girl came back to a sad Fowey, grey sea and sky. The town mourned him: they had all known him from 'a small boy rowing his dinghy about the harbour, going fishing with Grose the boatman, sailing with his sister and his Oxford friends. He had a smile and a greeting for everyone.' One old hard-bitten sea-captain, who had watched him grow up and had no children of his own, greeted May; neither of them could speak, then at length he broke silence: 'You know, I loved him too.'

Q. himself was so stricken by the blow that he thought of giving up, retiring to Fowey so that he could be with the boy's mother. Her grief was quite as great, her courage greater – he was the one who needed consoling, though nothing ever did so. 'My time at Cambridge is not likely to be long; the household is so badly broken up that my duty seems to lie at home. I shall be sorry indeed to leave Cambridge; but there it is.'

In the event he realised that his duty was to carry on. He came to the opposite resolution – to work harder than ever, if only to kill pain. He had always been a steady worker, with plenty of out-door exercise; he now began to overwork, both at Cambridge in term and at his manifold chores in Cornwall in vacation – he took on more in both places. No more fiction writing – after *Foe-Farrell*, which came out in 1918, he left his last novel, *Castle Dore*, unfinished.

I have been rather heavily overworking – at Cambridge and, later, at Oxford – on examination work. It deadens pain. But I begin to see that it were better – and braver – to face the pain and 'have it out': for by shirking it one's whole mind gets deadened. Really I don't care, half my time, what happens in a world that has killed my dearest and most natural hope.

That was unlike the former Q., never depressed, with cheerfulness ever breaking in. Here was the liability attending such exceptional family devotion: he had made his home a cell of love – to an unwonted degree, and now he suffered doubly in consequence.

Silence descended upon the stricken household for some months. Then Q. takes up in a letter to his sister Lilian, that they had taken a house on Dartmoor to be right away from the Peace celebrations.

June 3 was to have been dear Boy's wedding day, and we always celebrated 'days' in the old time. (If a man thought himself important enough to be the sport of the Gods, I might have felt worse than I did – and it was bad enough – to pick up the paper yesterday morning, of all days, and read Boy's D.S.O. in the Birthday List.) For me, I have a wild desire to get home and plunge into writing a book. Up here I just work all the time and go to bed dog-tired. I find I have it all my own way here – now that I don't care. The new Tripos is an established success. It will double its numbers in 1920 and should double them again in 1921. So my little job is done, if I can get the PM to let me have a say about my successor.

Peggy is for the present at livery at Withers, opposite the Marble Arch. Whether or no she detected something familiar in my footstep, when I went into the loose box, she was waiting for me. Took no notice of the stableman, but came straight to me, snuffed me all over the chest, and then bent down her neck like 'Royal Egypt'. While I stroked her, she nuzzled my wrist and back of my other hand, as if kissing it over and over: and when I turned about to speak to the Manager, her nose came pushing through between my arm and body, kind of insisting that I hadn't made enough love to her. It sounds silly, but it seemed as if the creature really did know something and was trying to say it.

To Foy, away in Warwickshire ('I love every yard of Avon'), he wrote that he was making arrangements to bring Peggy down to Cornwall as soon as possible. 'Boy's portrait arrived yesterday afternoon: Grose and I hung it after tea.' Fowey news was that Sir Charles Hanson had been run over by a car in Piccadilly: Q. as usual had to step into the gap and speak to the Fowey Brotherhood. Then to St Austell to present the shield to winners in the Elementary School Football Competition. On Whit Monday the crowds were out *en fête* on Polmear Hill, while on Wednesday

> *all the nobility and gentry being off to Truro to see the Prince of Wales and the Royal Cornwall Show, I trudged off in the heat to Tywardreath and took Petty Sessions, inflicting a few small fines. . . . On Tuesday I go to Truro – combining Education business with a little ceremony in the Cathedral, at which the King's colours granted to the D.C.L.I. will be deposited. I shall find a place somewhere at the back, and think. . . . Well, anyway, that Battalion has justified the pains we took in raising it.*

At the end of the month two days in London on this Education Commission (which produced the Hadow Report on the teaching of English in schools). After that, he expected to leave Cambridge, and to be 'home for good'.

In Truro cathedral

> *Sir Courtenay Vyvyan gave an address, telling the history of the Battalion [10th Duke of Cornwall's Light Infantry], how it was raised and its services: according to the GOC of the 2nd Division 'the finest battalion of Pioneers in the British Army', and, as such, specially selected to go to Germany and receive this flag. So that's that. . . . I am sending up for Peggy. Harry Graham has got a pasture for her at 5 shillings a week: I have arranged to go half shares with him in a groom, and stabling is to be arranged. But for the present it should do her good to be out in a field.*

So Bevil's Peggy lived out her life well cared for at Fowey.

Cambridge was crowded with young men back from the war, more women than ever, and a new generation up from the schools. Q., hating lecturing, had to face enormous audiences, his classes were crowded, his staircase besieged with young people wanting help, advice, instruction.

At the beginning of the new academic year, 1919–20, he wrote to Foy ('my dearest Babe'): 'I've been working double tides to make my conscience easier over taking ten days off in the middle of term. . . . I got off my first lecture yesterday. My! There was a crush! I should say about 150 above previous records: heaps of extra chairs, men sitting in the gangways, and a whole crowd standing.'

From Fowey he received official report of a row between the Harbour Master and Pilots and a Dungeness pilot who

> to do *Ernie Dunn* out of his fee, charged in with an American at a rate estimated by the Pilots at 9 knots, refused Ernie a rope, pretty nearly swamped him, and promptly stuck his vessel on the mud off Brazen Island after just missing the fluke of an anchor mooring laid down there for the new Coal Company. I am sending the papers on to Trinity House with comments. The Dungeness man – one Laity [a Cornish name!] told our Harbourmaster, 'That's all right. I've been reported before, and the last man that reported me lost his job.'

Such were the joys of being Chairman of the Harbour Commissioners – that side of his many-sided activities.

For twenty-one years Q. served as Chairman of the Harbour Commissioners, resigning only in 1925 in the post-war years when he was hard-driven with work at Cambridge. Sub-commissioner also for Trinity House Pilotage, he took the job as no sinecure, but gave the whole shipping community there guidance and was able to speak up for it when necessary, put the case before the public.

In a long letter to the *Times*, 16 January 1920, he described the effects of the war on the harbour's condition. During the war cargo-vessels had been instructed to bring home the fuel-oil so urgently needed in place of water for ballast. When skippers disobeyed orders the docks got contaminated. 'Land-locked Fowey, where shipping pays dues on 300,000 tons a year, suffered from stench, slime and pollution for miles of foreshore. Concurrently, the fish deserted the Fowey estuary, at a time when food was scarce.'

Representations had been made to government departments again and again, but in vain: bureaucracy provided its usual 'revelation of official blunder, dilatoriness and evasion. So the Great War is over, but this government department [the wartime Ministry of Shipping] still runs on; and so, at frequent intervals, does the flood of filth into our poor little harbour.' This public blast at length spurred action. It turned out an advantage to have had a writer as Chairman of the Harbour Commissioners.

To Waller at the Cambridge University Press he explained the nautical terms in *The Tempest*.

The Master is master: he has a helmsman who does the actual work at the wheel or tiller. The Master stands by this man in any such a gale as we open with, conning the helm, the weather, the canvas etc, and giving orders in emergency. 'To leave the helm' or to 'go back to the helm' doesn't convey for a moment to any sea-faring man that the wheel or tiller has been left to its own sweet will. 'The helm' not only connotes but means the chap working it.

Of course one could say 'goes back to con the helm' or 'to the helmsman': but neither would be nautical. So, e.g. he might hail 'Fore-top ahoy!' and this would mean his summoning not the actual fore-top, but the crew of the fore-top. So from this garden I should hail 'lugger ahoy!', or 'schooner, ahoy!' In nautical parlance the thing includes the man or men working it. So the whole forecastle may suffer from belly-ache, or the lower deck want its wages raised. So (too rarely) I return to the Cambridge University Press *but Waller has been there all the time. Oh, get along with you!*

No one was such a draw at Cambridge; he was at the height of his popularity, beset with invitations to lecture or give addresses on various occasions all over the country. He felt the irony that, having worked hard all his life to gain a modest readership, he now had a vast audience he had hardly sought, and certainly never expected when he became a Professor. It was really a new Q. that a new public saw; he took it in his stride, responded gallantly, and redoubled his efforts.

Circumstances propelled him into being a grand educator for the country at large. Ernest Rhys, always a good friend at Dent's, got him to take on the editorship of a big new series of English classics, *The King's Treasuries of Literature*, intended for children in schools. Pretty little books – Q.'s taste for bright colours in evidence, blood-red and gold – over 250 were published eventually: hardly a school in the country where Q.'s name was not known. All this affected the sales of his beautifully produced volumes of Cambridge Lectures, which went into edition after edition. And now the University Press weighed in with a big task – to edit the Cambridge Shakespeare, with Dover

Wilson as co-editor: a separate volume for each play with Introduction and Notes.

These were the years in which Q.'s concern with Shakespeare was at its busiest. In 1918 came out *Shakespeare's Workmanship*, in which he seeks to discover 'just what Shakespeare was trying to do as a playwright'. All along Q. emphasised that the proper approach was that of the stage – for which the plays were written; other investigations were also rewarding, always remembering the perspective of the Elizabethan age and its theatre. In a new edition he has a flout at the disintegrators of the canon by pedants who thought that they could pick out bits by Kyd or Marlowe, Greene, Chapman or whoever. 'To be frank, I must, after examination, deny that they can do it.' Q.'s common sense was right; but it is extraordinary to think, among the loads of rubbish written about Shakespeare, how much energy used to be wasted, how many useless books have been devoted, to this deviation. Q. was too polite to say that most people were not qualified to hold an opinion on the subject; in a society without standards it has to be said.

The Tempest was Q.'s favourite play: Mr Brittain considered the three lectures on that play the best he ever gave; I am mainly struck in them by the perception of stage-craft. He analyses in detail the previous play in the canon, *The Winter's Tale*, and shows how the playwright improves in handling similar situations. Shakespeare often repeats plots and situations, but the practical man of the theatre is continually improving in conditions and with material as to which we are imperfectly informed. Q. shows a marked theatrical sense; from early days he had been devoted to the theatre: perhaps he *could* have made a dramatist, if he had not had so many other things to occupy him.

'We may all approach Shakespeare in our several ways,' he says genially – even modernising the text, as in some respects we must and practically all editions do, in spelling and punctuating at least. Q. provided the dramatic and literary criticism, Dover Wilson the text, during the first phase of the partnership, which produced fourteen of the plays, when Q. dropped out and his partner took over the rest. We learn Q.'s view of his partner from a letter to Waller, while it also throws a light upon himself.

D. W. has sent me his Introduction to Tempest. *Quite good in substance: but he and I must come to an understanding about his way of putting things. However sure a man may be of a discovery or of a conjectural emendation, he should put it modestly. It comes with tenfold persuasiveness, so – D. W. being young, talks to the world like an uncle or – still worse – a preceptor. He's a good fellow and will stand my talking. But I cannot have dogmatic talk when hypothesis is being presented: 'abundantly proves', 'leaves us in no doubt', and the like about uncertain points. 'It isn't so much the thing he sez' – that is always intelligent – 'but the nawsty way he sez it. . . .'*

'My poor old father – who was a doctor – used to say that he would hesitate to make any positive statement about therapeutics, except that in three weeks sulphur ointment would cure the itch, unless God saw otherwise.' Waller was bringing George Sampson – a scholar with a line of his own in gipsy lore – to lunch with Q., and 'I must collect Okey', another character, the Professor of Italian who had been for years a basket-maker in the East End. 'The really sporting feat would be to invite that teetotalling Public Orator [that was the Baptist T.R. Glover] and make him so drunk he could only hiccough "Samp-sonn, Sampsonn" like the man in Chaucer.'

Now he has to write a Foreword for 'young Bullett's book. God forgive these poets!' Gerald Bullett was only one among his students whom he encouraged to write. He was now 'hungering for Dover Wilson's general textual Introduction', and wanted a proof to check readings, particularly the wording of stage directions (on which Dover Wilson rather fancied himself and let himself go). 'You can't think how much it would help D.W.'s emendations if his own writing was decipherable.' Q.'s own was unusually distinguished, fine but legible. 'On the numeration question *I* give way but most reluctantly: because I think it will hamper sales among the earnest of mind.' He goes on to discuss questions of imprint, style of binding etc. with both professionalism and taste.

It is good to hear that someone is still able to re-discover and read Old Fires and Profitable Ghosts. *I have endured enough, in these last 18 months, to make me feel one or two of those stories even more sharply than I did when I wrote 'em and only felt them in anticipation. . . . Thursday and Friday may be spent in holding my old enemies of the*

English Association at bay. They are still working hard to defeat the
English Tripos.

In August 1922 Wilson came down to Fowey 'to spend three days
slogging through text of *Love's Labour's Lost* and mapping out my
Introduction to that *most* difficult play – concerning which, as yet I
only know that nobody has ever put up a rational explanation of it'.
Neither he nor Dover Wilson was an historian, and neither had a clue.
The play needs an Elizabethan historian, with a knowledge of the
circumstances and the biographical background, to explain it. An
authority on Spanish history of that period, Martin Hume, gave a clue
which everybody had missed, in pointing out that Don Armado was a
caricature of the tiresome Don Antonio Pérez, Philip II's ex-Secretary
of State, who was staying with Essex at the time at Essex House, only
too well known to all the Southampton circle, a figure of fun. The
play is a skit on Southampton's notorious refusal to marry, the
characters Berowne and Rosaline easily recognisable as Shakespeare
and his mistress of the Sonnets, Emilia Lanier.

No one had ever had a clue to *The Two Gentlemen of Verona*, which
had no known source – naturally not, for it was entirely autobiographical and dealt with the rivalry of the two friends, the poet and his
patron, for the favours of that same woman. Q. and Dover Wilson
could make no sense of these early plays because they missed, as
everybody did, the obvious clue that the dedicatee of the Sonnets, Mr
W.H., was not Shakespeare's man but Thorp's, the publisher who
wrote the dedication.

Dover Wilson, who did most of the textual work, was an engaging
enthusiast; he was himself as sympathetic as Q. to the theatre-
approach to the plays, was often perceptive, but notoriously erratic.
He wrote, candidly enough, that once Q. perceived that 'he was
launched on a south sea of discovery with a hare-brained mate on
board, he threw himself into the enterprise in the spirit of a true
Cornishman. Any other captain, seeing the direction of the ship,
would have put back to port or at least ordered the mate to keep the
stipulated course; this one bade clap on all sail and run before the
wind.' The upshot of all this is that the Cambridge Shakespeare was
defective, and it puts Dover Wilson's edition of the Sonnets in
particular completely out of court – along with others. Q. practised

what he preached, and in 1921 took the lead in forming a branch of the British Empire Shakespeare Society for Cambridge. Its object was to spread greater familiarity with the works, 'particuarly from the point of view of dramatic representation', for although he 'has been given the first place in the Study he wrote primarily for the Stage . . . and in order to be realised he must be visualised'. Q. was President, the Master of Jesus Treasurer, in whose Lodge readings took place; occasionally there were public readings in the Guildhall, and each summer a play was performed in the Master's garden.

For some eight years Q. presided over the Village Drama Society, and spoke about the countryside on its behalf. Master of Cornish dialect as he was, with Devon thrown in, he encouraged speakers not to be afraid to speak up in their own natural speech, or again to choose melodrama if they liked. 'Melodrama is based on poetic justice. Village people are taught that vice is punished and virtue rewarded, and that the inequalities of this world are put right in the next.' Then – pure Q. – 'it is not surprising that for once they should like to see them put right in this world'.

His university lectures were so crowded out that he found them a burden; it was rather a 'fetish', especially for women, to attend. Caricatures of the mobbed scenes appeared in the papers. Q. fancied that now, 'with a little money in hand I can hire a few "spot" lecturers and confine my voice for a while to *Poetics* and other classes. . . . Tell yourself that Q. doesn't want these audiences. He *does* want, weakly or not, to be remembered for a hand in making the English Tripos.'

Nevertheless he still had some opposition to put up with – as who has not from the obtuse and pedantic?

The weary dons at the Women's Colleges (philologers all) are trying to discourage their students from taking English. But the girls at Newnham have kicked right over the traces, and Girton will have to come in all of a sweat: which will be a nuisance for me, as I shall have to repeat a lot of teaching. But it's great fun doing Aristotle's Poetics with a class all like hounds in full cry. I have 'em in my rooms, no silly manuals to bother about, just put a pipe in my mouth and walk up and down, starting 'em on furious discussions and getting out the idea of the new School as I go.

This lets us see that philological pedants (so like women dons) were the opponents. This also seems to have been the line of the English Association.

Sir Israel Gollancz has been going for me. I judge (a) that the assault is in Yiddish, and (b) not formidable. When the Members of the English Association watched their flocks by night/All seated on the ground/The Angel of the Lord came down/And demanded to know (with some asperity) what language the English Association thought it was talking.

While working on Shakespeare he found that Mrs Stopes had no sense of humour: she took the *Gesta Grayorum* in earnest, whereas they were a mock-heroical account of a feast-day 'rag'. True enough: it was an account of the revels at Grays' Inn one Christmas, and this was the kind of thing he would understand, women pedagogues not.

> *The Lord has marred my many hopes,*
> *Made many plans miscarry:*
> *But He spared me marry either Stopes,*
> *Charlotte Carmichael and Marie.*

As for D.W., he was ready enough to adopt suggestions, but

> *The 'fells' are Dover Wilson's every line,*
> *For God's sake, reader, take them not for mine!*

He was now constantly pressed with invitations to lecture all over the country. He found apple-gathering at the 'Farm' more engaging than coping with correspondence to tell people that

I cannot and will not lecture at West Ham, Kettering, Tonbridge, Hull, Manchester; no, nor at Glasgow, Aberdeen, Dumfries, St Andrews, nor yet in Edinburgh. This ridiculous demand does really and truly vex me. All my life I've been writing stuff which I've tried to make sound, and people won't read it: and then all of a sudden I get this reputation which I feel to be largely a fraud.

Of course, it wasn't; it was a different reputation with a new public. He may not have realised that, since he was a pre-1914 man, really in heart and mind a Victorian. Nor would he go to America, where he had a public, and from which he received invitations. One or two he did accept, for special occasions, like the opening of the Keats House at Hampstead, for the Morrab Library at Penzance ('a Library in a garden by the sea'), or a Sir Walter Scott dinner even as far afield as Edinburgh. But he didn't like uprooting himself from Cornwall or Cambridge, which came to mean more to him since it had not such sad memories.

He flung himself even more into the social life of the University. He took on the presidency of the Cambridge Cruising Club. In addition to the Ad Eundem he was a member of The Society, a purely Cambridge dining club, where he made a friend of the naval historian, Admiral Sir Herbert Richmond, Master of Downing. When Q. was host he took particular care with the menu: 'I am preparing a Spanish ham with trimmings. You boil it slowly in Chablis, and the intelligent animal tells you when it is cooked in perfection by quietly turning upside down. And yet people question the intelligence of our dumb companions.'

He made a friend of Nairne, the somewhat eccentric cleric who occupied the rooms above him. Nairne became 'very fond of Q. and read nearly everything that he ever wrote. He enjoyed good company and knew how to order a meal; but, being an ascetic, he hardly touched the carefully chosen fare that he provided for his guests, his own usual meal being a stale bun and a cup of coffee.' A more unusual academic was Okey, the Professor of Italian – 'Okey is a daisy' – the former basket-maker. When elected professor, he was so terrified by the thought of lecturing that he nearly declined – until comforted by a letter from Q. He never forgot this kindness, and once more made a waste-paper basket – for Q.

Q. always hated lecturing, [he wrote] *and I often heard him exclaim in the Arts Theatre, where we met before our turns came, 'Okey, why do we do it? Why do we do it?' in the most tragic voice as if about to be executed. Q. was the first to hold out a human hand of welcome and to give me heart and courage. I shall never forget the letter he wrote to me out of pure helpfulness.*

Writing to Mabel in June 1920 – the conventional black-edged writing paper keeping his grief in mind – he had a pile of Oxford Examination papers beside him. He found to his unholy delight that Raleigh's youngsters were no better than his own children at Cambridge –

*rioting now, in balls and fêtes which I don't attend. I did lunch at
Trinity yesterday, though, to meet the crew of politicians and the one or
two decent men who had just been given honorary degrees. But I wished
I'd stayed away. The lady on my left hand had lost her only son: and
two away from me sat Mrs Sorley* [mother of Christopher Sorley, the
young wartime poet who had been killed]. *In the middle of the
Lloyd-Georgian eloquence I pushed back my chair gently: looked up after
a moment and found she was watching me and – well, I suppose my face
told what I thought of it all: for her eyes, poor soul, sort-of-signalled,
'Ah, but we know.' But Bergson was there, and Beatty, and old Doughty,
to make the high table respectable here and there, in spots.*

A College feast at Jesus:

*I sat in flannels, with the windows open, and worked at Shakespeare.
The courts lit with hundreds of fairy lights – the night very dark and
velvety, and the young couples walking about on the turf or sitting out
between dances – oh, as pretty as paint it was. I didn't get to bed much
before 2 a.m. The revellers were photographed at 6 a.m. in a group at the
foot of this staircase. The Marlowe Society have asked me to recommend
'em a play for next term.*

How about the two Friars Bacon and Bungay?[1] 'I shall hate going to
Oxford this time. You see, I took the job last Oxford at Cannan's
request: the idea being that I'd stay with him: and it seemed rather a
plum, as I wanted to know what Oxford was doing.' Now Cannan had
died. So there would be two ghosts to haunt him there.

At the New Year, it was 'I am wae, wae, and all out of sorts. The
latter end of life is a dreary pilgrimage.' In the May term he was at
work on the Oxford Schools papers, and then the Cambridge ones
came pouring in. He was invited to make merry at several functions to
meet the Prince of Wales. To Foy, who shared her father's interest in
such things: 'Trinity Coll. Oxon made a bump on Thursday and
almost made another yesterday. The second boat has made two bumps
and should continue its ascent almost every evening.' In July he was
to open the St Austell Flower Show. She was to be careful, on her
river trip, of Thames weirs and lashers and of batheing. Her mother

[1]   By Robert Greene.

was worried after two Christ Church men had been drowned below Sandford.

One of them was young Llewelyn Davies, the boy whom Barrie adopted, and a really charming boy too. He made the third at table when I dined with Barrie last winter.

Jesus College here has won the Pairs in great style, and should keep Head of the River. I have the better hope because they are more modest this time. My improvements in the College garden are applauded by all. I sat out there with old Watt under the big plane tree after dinner last night.

Everybody said, himself included, that he was a poor correspondent. This was not true. Every letter, when written, was either a gem in itself or contained a gem. He did not write except to some purpose: he did not indite pointless letters, like so many eighteenth-century correspondents, Pope or Young, for example, with their eye on publication.

From November 1921 we have a delightful letter to Mabel, beginning 'you all have a lot to forgive'. Q. continued to have twinges of conscience at how ill things had worked out for her, while he had had all the luck (hard work even more than good luck, as we have seen). That autumn they had decided that they deserved a holiday and went back to his childhood scenes in Devon – Newton Abbot and Lustleigh, Abbotskerswell which neither his wife nor daughter had seen. The novelist in him took command.

They walked up through Bradley Woods where, we remember, he had had a quasi-mystical experience as a boy.

The next day we took a car and went out to Haytor and down through Bovey to Lustleigh: left the car, and climbed up with our lunch to the Cleave. It was a perfect day, though precious hot: and somehow the Cleave was lovelier even than – Good Lord, how long ago! We spent the evening wandering about Woolborough: the old School grounds.

Abbotskerswell was the cream of all. A fly this time: and the old horse picked his way down past Partridge's gate (as used to be) to the wall inside Butcher Palk's (as used to be) doing a sort of egg-dance among strewn apples. The trees were drowned in apples. . . . At Abbotskerswell (wistaria gone and front garden untended, but orchard across the road much as ever – and *Sally Emmett's cottage*, and *Rose Cottage, on the bank).* I knocked and was answered by a very courteous Californian (I should say, something of a gentleman down on his luck, but cheerful and of most hospitable manners). When he heard that I had known the place so long ago, he was all over us. They were just caretakers and yearly tenants, under Henley, who runs a cider factory up the hill.

We had met a couple of waggons on our way, piled with pomace – heavenly smell! I didn't much care to face the interior of the house (may be pluckier, perhaps, next time): but the back of the buildings are just as of old: not a window altered: the farmyard there, but clean and empty: the upper line of outhouses from cider press along to stables just the same, thatch and all: but on the lower side alas! the cowhouses gone, razed to the ground, with just a strip of apple trees in their place, running to the wall of the lane (now a grass-grown track): and the garden – the old walled garden, you know – all ruinous. The walls standing, but the wall plants gone, the filbert tree cut down, even the stream diverted to the orchard side of the lower hedge. No raspberry canes: only (pathetic sight) the old summer house bravely hanging together somehow, up in the far top corner.

Foy drank it all in, and the orchards beyond: they were still lovely, the trees almost breaking with fruit. And my host asked question upon question: and really I was quite good with my answers, telling him where this had stood and where that. But all the time I was thinking of – well you know – of 'A Pair of Red Polls'. Which between you and me is one of my best books (only I can only read it now and then).

Then we took a farewell of our guide and went down through the village to the Manor Farm and the Church, which was open, with a couple of women clearing out the remnants of a Harvest Thanksgiving. The Church rather stupidly restored – gallery and big pews swept away, of course – and all the character with it. But on the whole (though they've done away with the triangle of Village Green and the elms) the place was marvellously the same. So we went on to the hayfields, and got into our fly again at the gates of The Grange.

So that's the report. It didn't seem sad somehow: I think very largely because Foy thought it was the loveliest village she had ever seen: and she never says what she doesn't think or feel. As the old lady said, 'Wild horses couldn't bribe her.'

As for me, I hope to be a decent brother again in a month or two. But at the end of last year I was knocked out by losing a very large sum of money indeed (for me) through a publisher and a film company. The Authors' Society said it was a vile shame, but was afraid to do what they exist for: and I had to choose between losing very many hundreds and

*running an endless litigation. This, coming upon Bevil's death, has made
me just turn my face from everybody till the last ounce is paid: which will
soon be. It was rotten of me – but since Bevil was taken I just go on
living. I can't speak to people yet, not even to those I love. But I do love.*

It is clear from this that he felt it his duty to go on helping the girls,
particularly Mabel, who had no resources of her own, since those
desperate days of the family break-up at Bodmin.

At home in Cornwall he was as active as ever. When peace came the
County Council called upon him to draft an appropriate resolution,
which was inscribed in stone as a memorial in the County Hall. It
recorded with gratitude the services of all who had helped in the long
ordeal and commended 'to the remembrance of their countrymen all
those who by payment of their lives have redeemed their country'. All
members rose and stood to thank God 'for delivering our nation forth
from the late protracted war; for sustenance through toil and fear,
agonies and most instant perils; for the issue awarded upon His
eternal judgement; and for the restored blessings of peace'.

Q. was a religious man. It reads with bitter irony now. They thought
that it had been 'a war to end war' – and look round the world since!
The historian sees that 1914 initiated a century of war.

On the Education Committee he was busier than he had been for a
long time; for the Chairman was ailing, and Q. had to take his place
when the post-war schemes of reconstruction and large measures of
expansion came into being. In July 1922,

*all the back-end of the week is filled up with the sort of committee work
(local) that makes up an alleged vacation. All yesterday I spent at Truro
on a School Building and Furnishing Committee. This morning I spent
on agenda of full Education Committee, at which I must take the chair
tomorrow; and this afternoon I've (1) presided at Harbour Commission,
and (2) attended meeting for winding up accounts of local War Memorial.*

Why did he take it all on? Neither Kipling nor Hardy, Henry James
nor E. M. Forster would have done. But this was Q., nurtured and
immersed in public spirit. His writing gained something from it, but
perhaps lost more.

Later that month:

*I am a bad man, not to have written before. But I warned you that dull
business was taking me to Oxford and London; and on my return I had
to run in double harness (a) a sweating conclusion of* Much Ado, *(b)
some work for Exeter University College, and (c) finally there overtook me
yesterday the fearful job of pounding through reports and getting up a
brief to carry our Education Committee through County Council today. It
went off all right, but I reached my happy home tonight feeling like a
wrung rag.*

One of the small items he was to get through the full County
Council regarded my winning the one and only university scholarship
provided by the generous county in those days – the munificent sum
of £80 a year. I had been infected with Left-Wing views at school, by
J. G. Crowther from Cambridge and his friend Ralph Fox from
Oxford. While Q. was reporting on my behalf a note was passed up to
him by an informed local busybody, 'Do you know this boy is a
Bolshevik?' Q. tore it up and went on with his speech. What I should
have done without that start I cannot think – fallen by the wayside, I
suppose. Still there were two more scholarships to win before I could
get to Oxford. (And yet students today are continually complaining,
when everything is done for them!)

In August 'I spent Monday making magistrates, on Advisory
Committee. We are seven, and the freak of it is that the Labour
representative is the most anxious of us "not to lower the status on the
Bench."' (If that particular county councillor could have understood
the scholarship boy he might have guessed that under the Left-Wing
surface of youth there lurked a Johnsonian Tory. But *he* might never
have heard of Dr Johnson.)

August in Cornwall is for visitors.

*They all pour in just as if life here was a perpetual holiday, and would
all feel so dreadfully hurt if we didn't mix cider-cups and put up
luncheon-baskets, and sail down the bay and tell them where to search for
cowries, or, like Caliban, get 'em 'young scammels from the rocks'. And
they multiply and bring their children, and 'it's always so jolly' –
whereas it's wae-wae! for me to be led out to play in these haunted spots –
these very brach[1]-pools.'*

[1] A Shakespearean word meaning young hounds.

Towards the end of August, he was as usual organising Fowey Regatta, in sailing kit, cap and all.

Didn't know that I was a Commodore, didn't you? Marry, yes: and one that hath two gowns and everything handsome about him – though they do say that the Cambridge one is the more becoming. Time was when I used to enjoy this sort of thing – firing guns and starting yacht races. Once on a day I, being laden and accoutered with two guns, stop-watch, megaphone, cartridge bag, and what not, was asked by a very rich man, 'Do you really enjoy this sort of thing?'. . .

That man made a good end. His yacht foundered in the Bay of Biscay, and all took to the boats in bitter weather, and made the land somehow. But he was dead, frozen stiff, having shed his oilskin coat to wrap up his small child. He was the lucky fellow after all. He could save his boy.

So I don't much enjoy starting yacht-races nowadays.

A week later he cheered up to report that the Regatta

went off in grand weather, the sea like champagne – such a gelasma, *and* O litus vita mihi dulcius, *etc. . . . . I got away fifteen boats in one of the prettiest starts ever seen. After which my wife and I received the rank and fashion on the Club terrace to the strains of the Royal Marines. . . . On Friday I started our visitors on a Channel race to Falmouth; watched them away like a flight of white moths . . . upped anchor, and returned in the tug to the perusal (combined) of* David Copperfield *and Forster's* Life of Dickens.

When Christmas came it was always

a festival of great ceremonies in this small house . . . and beautiful sunshine is pouring in here at this moment, glancing up too from the sea at our feet, and playing heaven with the chrysanthemums and with the hollies etc. on the pictures. . . . My daughter has been searching England for the works of Ouida. I hope you don't despise poor Ouida? She could be, and not seldom was, ridiculous: but was great all the same. Not a mean thought in her – would give herself away at any moment, like a prince tossing his best cloak to a beggar. So I sit here barricaded with Ouida; and the family cat is basking outside on my window ledge; and at 3 p.m. I have to lecture on Charles Dickens – which is a nuisance, but sounds Christmassy.

During the Christmas of 1920 they had received an invitation to the Fowey Hotel – up on its cliff with that magnificent view all over river and sea! – to dine with a few friends. When they arrived they found that their friends, over fifty of them, were all characters from the books. There were Admiral Buzza and Miss Limpenny, Caleb Trotter, Jack Marvel, Hetty Wesley, Miss Westcote, Captains Hocken and Hunken, and all. Henrietta Treffry of Place told me that she was Lady-Good-for-Nothing. It cannot be said that Q. was without honour in his own country.

At Cambridge he was called upon to speak in church on occasion, especially on Armistice Day in the years after the war. In 1923 at All Saints, just down the road from Jesus College:

> *There are few households in this land that this War has left without a domestic sorrow far more real, more natural, more abiding, than any exultation over victory. All the old statues of Victory have wings; but Grief has no wings. She is the unwelcome lodger that squats on the hearth-stone between us and the fire, and will not move or be dislodged.*

One sees the scene he had in mind, the friendly hearth in his study at the end of the corridor at The Haven.

Or again, when the authorities took a heavy line about undergraduate celebrations on another Armistice Day:

> *Elders and parents should, I hold, allow any amount of gladness to Armistice Day. For them, at any rate, All Souls' Day remains. Yet for most of them the pang, perhaps, will likelier start in some sudden moment when spring starts to reclothe the countryside, but never for them to colour it with the promise spring brought in 1914.*

How different a spirit from the empty light-heartedness of the Cambridge pacifists and Bloomsbury, of Lytton Strachey, Bertrand Russell and Co!

In his College rooms he kept open house to Cornish acquaintance. In November 1923 he had young David Hext, 'of the Trenarren stock, to breakfast. Cambridge is so cold, my hand can hardly steer the pen. "Like a winnard" [peewit] – but winnards don't try to write letters.' I met in his rooms a couple of Pethericks from St Austell, of one of whom I was to be the Labour opponent in our Cornish constituency, throughout the whole period of the Baldwin–Chamberlain ascendancy. Q., himself a celebrity, was constantly bidden out to dine 'with the good and great', on occasion this year with the Vice-Chancellor, the President of Harvard (famous Lawrence Lowell), three Heads of Houses, and so on.

Bevil's mare, Peggy, lived on at Fowey; when she died Q. had her photograph hung just below Bevil's in uniform, in his sitting room at Jesus. Sometimes a visitor who had not been warned would ask a question about the two photographs. Q. would answer very quietly, but after a moment would be overcome and go away into his bedroom to be alone.

Bevil's death had been a bitter blow to Cannan too, and to his daughter's happiness. At Oxford they were close friends of Sir William Osler, the great physician, Canadian-born of Cornish stock, whose only boy had been killed. (It fell to me, years after, to lecture in his Memorial Room at Johns Hopkins University – there were the boy's kit and Army uniform, fishing tackle and his books, faithfully laid up. One never forgets what we owe to the Germans.)

Q. contributed a portrait of Cannan to the booklet produced in his memory. It seems to have been a sad time for obituaries, for he wrote others, of Sir Walter Raleigh and of Lewis Foster, a leader in county affairs at home. May Cannan he adopted into the family; she regularly came down to Fowey, to ride about on Bevil's Peggy; and Q. kept regularly in touch by letter. At Oxford there was trouble about compulsory Greek. I don't suppose he was in favour of compulsory anything, but he wrote, 'I have seen a little of men in politics and affairs, and know that the men who have Greek have a power of command which those lack who haven't Greek.' Of course, not to have Greek is a terrible gap in one's education; I suspect that he here had in mind the primacy of Greats in his time at Oxford, when practically all the best brains took that school.

May found him at Fowey 'very tired. He had been lecturing to enormous audiences, driving himself to give his brilliant best – and "it killed thought a little", so he welcomed it.' Sometimes the supply of chairs gave out, and he had the young people squatting on the floor, making him feel 'like some old boy of the Middle Ages with his disciples at his feet'. At the Haymarket in London he had an audience of 800, and another 250 were turned away.

At home they rowed across the harbour among the big ships in the little red boat, to work on the 'Farm'; in the evenings he would carry May off to his study, candle-lit, eight in a row on the table by the window where he worked. 'We had two griefs now to share.' He encouraged her to publish her poems, particularly one she had omitted from her book:

> *'See,' once he wrote, 'they are bringing the mare round*
> *now.'*
> *And just sometimes I look for his letters still,*
> *Forget he is dead. Well, that's all life to me*
> *Riding alone the hill.*

Through Sir Charles Oman at All Souls she had an opportunity of reading the Regimental Diaries of the formations in which Bevil had served. 'Since he had served continuously from the first August till he died in February 1919, they make a remarkable picture of those years – some of the entries were in his own hand.' She made a copy for Q. He himself took pride in the letters he received from Bevil's Battery,

> *telling how he would walk up from his dug-out at night and quietly pace*
> *out, under a barrage, and measure the distances where shells had just*
> *exploded, with others playing round. Yes, and we've a letter-card from his*
> *C.O., in the early days of the 1914 Retreat telling how 'Quiller', having*
> *been sent out with a line of empty waggons to recover dropped clothing,*
> *rifles, accoutrements, etc., was lost for three days behind the enemy's line,*
> *and rode in at the end with his waggons full, and 'nothing on him but*
> *his breeches and a smile.'*

On the first Armistice Day he was 'standing all alone in the Catalogue Room [at the University Library] and had a catalogue open before me at "Tristan and Iseult"'. We know how interested he was in the 'Tristan' stone from Castle Dore (about which he was to write his last novel). 'So that was how it found me, quite without premeditation, strayed back to the thing I stray back to more and more . . . too late to write on it: at the perfect love story of the world. So you weren't very distant from my thoughts, Child.'

May got a job cataloguing the fine library at the Athenaeum in London, rather overwhelmed by the grand staircase, at the foot of which Dickens and Thackeray made up their quarrel; upstairs the long drawing-room where irascible Trollope overheard two members say that it was time he killed off Mrs Proudie, and announced to them that he would go home and do it; the window overlooking Waterloo Place where Matthew Arnold wrote his letters – the vast room that reminded Kipling of a cathedral between services.

Kipling was frequently there, for he was writing the History of the Irish Guards in which his boy had been killed, and used the library a great deal. Q., who was not a member – he said he had no use for a place where he could not take his wife – came to take May out to dinner: 'I suppose I can have a kiss even in the Athenaeum?' He was recognised by Charles Graves of *Punch*, Robert Graves's father; May said, 'If it had not been for the War he would have been my father-in-law.' 'So the bond holds,' he said.

He invited her over to Cambridge, to show her the beauties of the place, the unsurpassed chapel of King's, the long gallery of St John's – nothing like it at Oxford, the bustle of Petty Cury, 'which he said was like a scene in Verona'. In the Fellows' Garden at Jesus the rose he had brought up from Cornwall, a René André, had grown all over the wall. That evening, when he hoped for a quiet talk, there was a clatter on his staircase: 'Dear, do you think you could send them away?' 'They came, I knew, at all hours, bringing him their work, the things they had written, their troubles, and he kept for them an open door – but this evening was mine.' Next day they went on to the Sorleys'; Q. said simply, 'This is May.' They gave her a special welcome, no words needing to be said.

In the course of encouraging her work he confessed that poetry had given up on him. 'For years and indeed almost since poetry dried up in me I've started a poem called "Paradise", beginning:

> *In Paradise there is a lake,*
> *Hart and roe with gentle eyes*
> *Haunt to it at eve to slake*
> *Their thirst, in Paradise.'*

[169]

Somehow, he could never get on with it: Paradise was no more for him.

One night down at The Haven, by the library fire, he asked – with that shy delicacy of feeling so true to him: 'Dear, isn't there anyone?' May said, 'All that – it's just gone.'

Later on, she did create a new life for herself. But when Foy brought her, not long before her death, to see me at All Souls, she was still regretting that Bevil, too considerate for her – had not asked her to share the hazards of wartime.

The Professor

In the post-war period, when Q.'s *réclame* was at its height, he developed something like a new persona to meet it: a persona as professor. One would never have expected this from his earlier career. The essential man and his qualities remained unchanged, but these took a new development and projected themselves not only across Cambridge – where he was by far the best known public figure among the humanists – but across the nation at large. His message reached a far wider public through the medium of his Lectures, published in successive volumes and reprinted year after year, but also through addresses delivered on special occasions in London and around the nation.

In one of his Prefaces he evokes

> *the latter days of the War, when few of us felt able to hope that our then deserted colleges would fill again in our time; when some of us prophesied an end for ourselves of sad retirement in the shade of libraries; when none of us anticipated what was to come upon us, as it were in a tidal wave – the amazing, portentous, refluence of youth into the universities . . . It came; and it was such that we could scarcely have coped with it, even if prepared.*

This was by way of apology for having to revert to personal discourse, 'if the hungry generations were not to tread me down. I must offer my apologies to the reader for the result, but my thanks to Heaven for the cause.'

A touch of his unfailing tact again; no apology needed: we thank Heaven for the result, rather than the cause. He could not in any case have produced a dull academic 'study' – of which there are all too many; far better the familiar, *personal* discourse, in which the reader feels that he is in touch with the writer. His Lectures have the singular value of his practical experience of writing and the ways of writers – a width of experience no other professor could offer. In *On the Art of Reading*, 1920, 'I propose to discuss on what ground and through what faculties an Author and his Reader meet; to inquire if, or to what extent, Reading of the best Literature can be taught' – and, if so, can be examined upon. But that is subsidiary.

These personal touches bring the writers, their characteristics and opinions, before us. Q.'s early patron, Raper of Trinity, had once asked Swinburne, at Jowett's dinner table, which of the English poets had the best ear. He gave it serious thought: 'Shakespeare without doubt; then Milton; then Shelley; then, I do not know what other people would do, but I should put myself.' In Q.'s day at Cassell's he was much amused by the indignation Charles Reade's name aroused: he had affronted the readers of *Cassell's Magazine* with a tale, *A Terrible Temptation*, which Victorians regarded as immoral. Q. gives a just critical estimate of this writer, with pronounced qualities both good and bad, so difficult to appreciate today.

He himself had been privileged to converse with some of these figures who had already passed into history; 'or rather to listen and drink in admiration – of John Bright's exquisite voice softly repeating bad poetry by the fireplace of the Reform Club smoking-room; of Meredith, at his own board, dragging spoons and forks towards him to illustrate the disposition of Napoleon's force at Austerlitz'. One would not have known the spell that John Bright cast upon Victorians, otherwise unaccountable to us, except for the beauty of his voice.

Of Matthew Arnold, 'those of us who engage in the work of English education ... still toil in the wake of his ideals'. Q. recognised the epoch-making Act of 1902, establishing nation-wide secondary education, as the fruit of Arnold's life-long campaign. In all these discourses we find him treating his students with good fellowship, placing himself on the same level with them. One need not do too much reading to achieve good standards of culture – this must have appealed to undergraduates harassed by the thought of examinations; it was a question of selection, of selecting the best. This was his constant message – and what better guide? The students recognised it. In February 1922 he sends home two parcels of tea, a present from a man 'returned to Ceylon, who asserts that I was kind to him up here'. The young women were pestering him about a Shakespeare

Society 'of which I seem to be President. . . . They have re-papered and upholstered the Junior Common [*sic*, the Oxford, not Cambridge, term for it] Room at the foot of this staircase, and as nearly as possible copied these rooms of mine. So Education spreads.'

A man of taste, he was sending his wife, for her birthday in 1924, a bit of Coalport, 'a lovely ware, from a specimen I saw yesterday'; Worcester itself was now keen on recovering old patterns. After dinner he had had his usual Wednesday class in the Divinity School, 'several boys staying afterwards with questions and with their young mouths open'. Today the young women at 5 p.m., then a quiet evening for work on his final Thackeray lecture. Oxford had won the hockey match. As for Cambridge,

> this is never home, and I feel all the time like a changeling who has happened out of the country where he would be and to which he belongs. I suppose all men enjoy a certain sense of power, even when they don't seek it; and one gets that here all the time. But it's a poor consolation for one's own home. . . . Lift a glass of Pol Roger to yourself, as I shall drink to you – and think of your own lover always.

We have to recognise the percipience of his critical judgments. In his day Trollope had for more than a generation been in the doldrums, disconsidered; Q. was sure that he would come back into favour. With the Romantic poets on top in the nineteenth century, Crabbe had a poor press – 'a Pope in worsted stockings'; Q. knew better. He had a high estimation of Byron's *Don Juan*, when it was not the fashion; there was a case for regarding it as the second of English epics. (What a pity John Murray and the Guiccioli discouraged Byron from going on with it!) Q. even has a passage in praise of the beauty of Paddington Station – a generation before Betjeman opened our eyes to it.

He was lecturing at the height of the reaction against the Victorians, given the lead by Lytton Strachey, who had an easy success in poking fun at them, including the Queen who gave her name to the age. Q. began by warning 'the cleverer of you against thinking in periods, to *despise* this, that, or the other' – a warning disregarded by Leavis and his disciples. Q. belonged to the generation that used to lift their hats as they saw the indomitable old lady drive down the Park 'with her scarlet outriders before and her Scots gillies on the rumble behind her'. Indomitable, for in the last year of the Boer War she had gone to Dublin to thank the Irish people for their help, spending three weeks there driving through the streets without escort. (Could that be done today?) 'That was the Queen Victoria we knew.'

He had no difficulty in putting Strachey in his place, though appreciating the fun – he selected the virtuoso piece that concludes Strachey's biography for inclusion in *The Oxford Book of English Prose*. But, like a good historian – which Strachey was not – he reckoned up the positive achievements of the age.

> *Read Charles Dickens, if you would understand how these Victorians reformed the horrible old 'poor-house'; read Elizabeth Barrett Browning's* Cry of the Children *or Hood's* Song of the Shirt *if you would divine what they did against the factories and sweated labour; ponder on Charles Reade's* It Is Never Too Late to Mend, *or that awful documented story, Marcus Clarke's* For the Term of His Natural Life, *if you would learn how they fought the old penal system.*

And he cites a dozen works of Kingsley and Ruskin, the whole life of William Morris, to see 'how these men battled for mere humanity'.

'Do you deride their art? – their painting, for example?' He apparently felt it necessary to apologise for Frith's *Derby Day*, then held up to ridicule 'as if that were representative'. No need to apologise for it today, when the Victorian painters have come back into their own. He was able to cite the later works of Turner, the early work of Millais and all the Pre-Raphaelites – and a whole galaxy of artists remain unmentioned. Where today, for example, would one find a sculptor as fine as Thomas Woolner? Or that late Victorian, Alfred Gilbert, whom experts compare with Cellini?

As for the sense of security – the lack of which is the dominant feature of our own sombre time – 'I should guess that a man born in England in 1844, and passing out of it in the early part of 1914, probably enjoyed the most comfortably expanding time in the whole range of human history.'

We shall never enjoy the security or confidence, the essence of happiness, of that age again. As for creativity, Q. has only to recite the roll-call of famous names among novelists and poets alone. For all his tact he could speak out when necessary, deliver a punch when called for. He quotes a fatuous over-estimation of Charles Reade by (popular) Sir Walter Besant: 'all of which is skimble-skamble thought in slipshod language; a confusion of platitude, falsity, and nonsense stark but inarticulate'. Besant: 'One can only say that this great writer paints women as they are, men as they are, things as they are.' Q.: 'That was just what Reade could not learn to do for any length of time. . . . He wrecked *Griffith Gaunt*, which was coming near to be his best novel, as Shakespeare wrecked *The Two Gentlemen of Verona*, by making his hero for purely stage purposes suddenly renounce his nature and behave like a quite incredible cad.'

Several times Q. tilted against the improbable ending of *The Two Gentlemen*, when one of the two friends simply hands over his beloved to his rival who has behaved badly and betrayed him: 'All that was mine in Silvia I give thee.'

His first volume of *Studies in Literature* I received as a school prize at his hands. The lectures on 'Patriotism in Literature' got him into trouble with the pro-Germans. He thought that 'Germanic ways of thought' had had too much influence in the universities 'of late years'. This was a mild way of putting it, when one considers the ascendancy that German philosophy established in the universities in the later nineteenth century, not only in Europe but in the United States.

All that he says about German intellectual arrogance is this.

> *Now the general good manners of Europe have been vexed for a generation by a people, raw in character and uncouth of speech, which has prospered by dint of bravery to a very high degree. Having prospered beyond hope by this pugnacious self-assertion, it has set itself since 1870 not only to philosophise its primitive instincts but to impose that philosophy upon the civilised nations.*

Progressing a few decades further, we see that philosophy adapted by the genius of Hitler to the mass-conditions of demotic society – of the Germans at least, with extensions elsewhere.

He did not seek to disparage the scholarly work done by Germans, but his gospel was that English should be treated as a living literature. He had campaigned against 'a bad system of teaching', when a student confessed to him that in all his schooldays he had never been set to write one English essay, nor taught to arrange two sentences together.

[175]

This was a student of classics from a public school who had come to ask Q. how English should be written, 'though it will be no good for me in the Classical Tripos'.

He noted the difficulty any foreigner has in penetrating the subtlety of another language. He confessed that, much as he admired French poetry, he would not claim to have an inner ear for the subtleties of Leconte de Lisle or Hérédia. Consistently with his emphasis on studying English, both language and literature, as living and continuous, he succeeded in bringing the syllabus for the Tripos down 'to our own times'. That meant then to Meredith and Hardy – on whose poetry this volume included lectures.

On his birthday in 1923 he reported home to his wife that he had had 'an absolutely bumper audience' at his lecture. 'Your letter made me cry a little for joy. Bless you, my own sweetheart, for hinting that I have made your own life a bit happy.' He had been keeping monstrous hours of late, and received many presents. 'Most touching of all was Mrs Mitchley coming in with a curtsy this morning after breakfast and begging me to accept "a little something that you ought to have, sir": which, being unwrapped, proved to be a silver jam-spoon! I really felt quite "chokey" when the old soul "hoped I wouldn't take it as a liberty"'.

In the political confusion consequent upon the break-up of Lloyd George's Coalition there were General Elections in each of those years 1922, 1923, and 1924. After the last the country settled for virtually fifteen years of Tory rule, with Baldwin and Chamberlain as its dominating figures, which allowed Germany to recover a position from which to wreck peace and civilisation yet again. Q. was an old-time Liberal of 1906, but he did not support Isaac Foot, who was another, as candidate in their old constituency, because he disliked his ardent Prohibitionism. Again in 1923 he refused to sign Foot's nomination paper. On the other hand, 'I can't see myself ever voting for a Protectionist; but if I were to vote at home I should not vote for Foot. So that's that.'

As professor he could draw too on his practical work for schools over the years. A few of his students might become writers, but far more would become teachers. In the Preface to *On the Art of Reading* he says, 'the real battle for English lies in our Elementary [today

Primary] Schools, and in the training of our Elementary Teachers'. He had written these Lectures 'amid the dust of skirmishing with opponents and with practical difficulties'. Often his thoughts had strayed away 'to remote rural class rooms where the hungry sheep look up and are not fed; to piteous groups of urchins standing at attention and chanting "The Wreck of the Hesperus" in unison'. In my elementary schooldays we used to have periods of 'silent reading'. We owed those to his thoughtfulness, for there were many working-class homes in which there was little quiet in which to read.

His conception of a liberal education was a democratic one, 'not an appendage to be purchased by a few. Humanism is a *quality*, which can and should condition all our teaching.' Only a few days before the Armistice he declared:

> *Every child born in these Islands is born into a democracy which, apart from home affairs, stands committed to a high responsibility for the future welfare and good government of Europe.*
> *This War will leave us bound to Europe as we never have been; and no less inextricably bound to foe than to friend. Therefore it has become important, and in a far higher degree than it ever was before the War, that our countrymen grow up with a sense of what I may call the soul of Europe. And nowhere but in literature (which is 'memorable speech') – or, at any rate, so well as in literature – can they find this sense.*

Here we have Q.'s high idealism.

How was it answered? At home by the mean-minded isolationism of Bonar Law and Baldwin: a government, as was said, 'of hard-faced men who looked as if they had done well out of the War'. Q. expressly distrusted a government of business men. His hope was to lead his listeners 'to reflect that beyond our present passions, and beyond this War, in a common sanity Europe (and America with her) will have to discover that common soul again'.

And what happened? America withdrew from such responsibility into a more remote isolation than ever – leaving Europe to be betrayed, soul and body, yet again by the Germans. What a noble-souled idealism Q.'s was! Yet an historian cannot but think that the pessimism of a Gibbon about human affairs is more in keeping with the facts. Q. would not have approved: one of the reasons for his distaste for

Carlyle was his 'sick despair'; I suspect another was that Carlyle had the manners of a peasant (he also had a peasant's lack of illusions).

Q. had hopes of America – 'a country with no comparable separate tradition of literature'. I remember from elementary schooldays that our poetry reading was dominated by Longfellow; my brother's passion was for James Fenimore Cooper, while mine was for Hawthorne. Q. took heart of grace from the fact that, in his time, the United States sent as ambassadors here such men of letters as the historian Motley, the poet James Russell Lowell, Hay and Page, and 'has for her President a man of letters, and a Professor at that!'. He might have added to the list among other such diplomatic and consular represen- tatives, Charles Francis Adams, Hawthorne and (I think) Melville. Could one imagine America represented abroad today by such figures as Hemingway or Scott Fitzgerald, Saul Bellow or Norman Mailer?

He had earlier paid a tribute to the high standards in the teaching of English literature in the American universities in those days. He enforced his teaching with a famous passage from Lamb on the plays of Shakespeare as 'enrichers of the fancy, strengtheners of virtue, a withdrawing from all selfish and mercenary thoughts, a lesson of all sweet and honourable thoughts and actions, to teach you courtesy, benignity, generosity, humanity'.

This is a flight too high for me; but I should add that, in all my experience of universities, I have never known a professor who exerted so high and noble, or so wide, an influence for good. In one of these Lectures he declared his belief. 'I believe that while it may grow with increase of learning, the grace of a liberal education – like the grace of Christianity – is so catholic a thing that the humblest child may claim it by indefeasible right, having a soul.'

He carried his belief into practice by helping to draw up a syllabus of religious teaching for Cambridgeshire schools. For this he co- operated with Nairne and Glover to make two anthologies, *The Children's Bible* and *The Little Children's Bible* for use along with the syllabus. Glover was a rigid Nonconformist who would sometimes address the Anglican Nairne 'with clenched teeth'. Q. told him that he regarded himself as 'the pure white leaf in the Bible separating the Old and New Testaments'. This calmed Glover down; then privately: 'I wonder which Dispensation he supposed me to be assigning to him.' Q. was at his old game, well practised in Cornwall, of keeping the peace between Church and Chapel.

Q., who had fancied bright colours all his life, transferred this interest to the bindings of his books. The sedate Syndics of the Cambridge Press must have been amused to receive a postcard from Fowey, with his inveterate addiction to light verse:

> *The Children's Bible*
> *In this climate is li'ble*
> *In 'Cloth Limp'*
> *To be damp as a shrimp.*
> *'Cloth Boards'*
> *No protection affords*
> *Against water spilt.*
> *Even less 'Cloth Gilt'. . .*

And so he went on to the conclusion:

> *'Polished Leather'*
> *Defies every weather.*

That he had no liking for Puritans is clear from his admirable Lectures on Milton, greatest of them, in the second volume of *Studies*.

A Puritanical religion – that is, a religion which, hating art of all kinds that solace life and, preluding with a fast, assures an infernal hereafter upon decent merry folk here who crave no future bliss if it involve a bigot's company – strikes first upon the theatre as inevitably as it will continue, if successful, to bludgeon anything and everything calculated to make glad the heart of man.

He quotes Masson: 'the unlawfulness of dramatic entertainments had always been a tenet of those stricter English Puritans with whom Milton felt a political sympathy'. Here, by the way, he has a good word for Masson's rendering of Milton's autobiographical poem *Ad Patrem* into English hexameters.

For years Milton had intended his grand poetic effort to be a tragedy – highest of literary forms according to Aristotle. Why did he turn to epic for *Paradise Lost*? Q. suggests that it may have been due to the Puritan closing down of the theatre, which Milton wished to reform (along with everything else). It may not have been as simple as that; but 'years after, when those doors had been re-opened as sluices to admit the mud and garbage of Restoration drama, the old man gallantly accinged himself to his old task and wrote *Samson Agonistes*'.

Here we come upon one of Q.'s marked limitations – he could not bear Restoration drama, not even the fun; not a good word for Wycherley, Etherege or Congreve, let alone the scape-grace Roches-ter. I do not think he appreciated satire either: Pope's *Dunciad* is 'a pretty wearisome heap of bad breeding' – but it is a masterpiece for all that. I suspect that he had no inner sympathy for the 'mighty Jonathan', Swift; he preferred Burke to Dr Johnson.

He could not bear a cad. Yet not a few writers of genius have been cads: one of the greatest of novelists, Dostoievsky, for example. D'Annunzio was a cad to beat all cads. There was something of one in Benjamin Constant and Sainte-Beuve; in Byron, certainly in the way he treated his wife. (Similarly with Shelley and his first wife, Harriet.) Yet Q. lets them both off lightly – I suspect on account of Radical sympathies. He accepts the condemnation of Castlereagh by the Left intellectuals: rather a great man, wickedly maligned by them. And he shared G. M. Trevelyan's disapprobation of Pitt's repressive legislation after the French Revolution: 'Billy Pitt, damn his eyes!', Trevelyan would say to me. It did not win my assent; after all, one has to keep order in the nursery. My views agree with Shakespeare's, not with the perpetual adolescent Shelley's; one sees all too well today what anarchy leads to.

Q. convincingly lays stress on Milton's *loneliness* of spirit – almost a solipsist. Never was there such an aristocrat as in this Puritan revolutionary with his contempt for ordinary humanity.

We may note what looks like an unresolved contradiction when Q. regrets that 'our literature has ever tended to be so aristocratic, to be written for the elect'. He thought that it need not have been – witness the popular appeal of the Bible or Shakespeare, Bunyan or Dickens. An historian realises that most of our literature was naturally written for the reading classes. Q. later explained that he was 'not preaching red Radicalism: I am not telling you that Jack is as good as his master'. Experience told him that learning Greek 'makes a distressingly small difference to most boys' appreciation of Homer. Still it does make a vast difference to some, and should make a vast difference to all.' (*That* it never could.)

We may reconcile his liberal views on education and his own elect spirit by marking the distinction between education and culture. By all means give the masses the chance of a liberal education; it will not reach any significant level, except with a few (as Q. saw in the case of Greek), for culture is essentially for the elect. New Year news from Fowey in 1924 was that bad weather had swept Readymoney beach (of such a memory for Q.)

> *bare as after Harbour Commissioners' dredging. The Pilots came through their test with colours flying. One Mevagissey man couldn't manage smaller type – others fairly rattled it off, and were equally good at the colour tests. It took a weight off my chest. As for the Mevagissey man, Captain Bate was inclined to the view that 'eyesight, one way or another, wouldn't help he to pick up much' – which I thought rather ungrateful.*

This year saw the beginning of his friendship with the Tory leader, Stanley Baldwin. This seems surprising in the former Radical, but Q. was not alone in falling for Baldwin's charm: G. M. Trevelyan, who had been no less of a Radical, fell equally under the spell. It is understandable on the personal score. Baldwin was a university man, a Cambridge man, with cultivated standards. Lloyd George was neither a university man, nor a cultivated one; he was in fact a cad, and neither Q. nor Trevelyan could stand him. Churchill was not a university man, and in fact rather a bounder: neither Trevelyan nor Q. cared for him. But the fact remains that Lloyd George and Churchill were men of genius, and the country was essentially bereft of their services while Baldwin and Chamberlain ruled.[1] I have no doubt of Q.'s favourable judgment of Baldwin as a man: he was kindly and public-spirited, of good moral standards, with a vein of idealism. But that was not enough for the country's leader, in the full possession of power, during the critical Thirties when everything went wrong in Europe, and Baldwin paid little attention to it. His own excuse later,

---

[1] Baldwin did make Churchill Chancellor of the Exchequer 1924–9, an office which kept him out of (a) foreign affairs, (b) defence.

to his friend Warden Pember at All Souls, was that he was holding down a job he was physically incapable of fulfilling; Trevelyan's excuse for him, to me, was that it is difficult for a politician to be good at both home and foreign affairs. But the situation in Europe, the obvious renewed threat from Germany, was critical for Britain and undermined her future. My historical judgment of Baldwin remains unchanged.

Stanley Baldwin was a loyal Trinity man and, coming down to Cambridge speechifying early in 1924, Q. was to entertain him. Q. took his usual care in thinking out a special dinner – oysters, sole cooked with mussels and oysters, a Virginia ham boiled in Chablis, etc. Baldwin responded gracefully: 'it is a tremendous act of faith on your part to ask an unknown man to more than one meal. Froude once asked an old schoolfellow to spend the day with him, and in spite of the bond of common memories of half-a-century before, he fainted dead away within the first hour.' (Lloyd George would not have known who Froude was, and I doubt if Churchill had any clear idea.) After the event, Baldwin wrote, 'nothing but an aposiopesis meets the case. It was a crowded hour of glorious life, and I feel years younger and pounds better.' One sees that he was irresistible as a person, though he failed his country as a leader. The Tories kept him in power, and Lloyd George, who knew better how to exercise it, out.

In May Q. was as usual 'well up to my neck in Tripos papers'. He had finished lectures, 'got off the last for the term yesterday to a full sweltering audience (poor dears), and was chased up the stairs afterwards by an American, Secretary of the Lowell Institute, with a fresh invitation to go and talk in USA'. He would never go, on account of Prohibition – which he strongly disapproved of – in these years. That autumn his eyesight failed him – after years of smoking and drinking. Invited to lecture for the Keats Memorial at Hampstead, 'forgive a dictated letter. I am suffering from an affection of the eyes (temporarily, I hope) which makes it impossible for me to read, and almost impossible to write.' He resolved to carry on at Cambridge, with the help of the Master of Jesus, who doubled with him for readings.

Christmas at The Haven was as usual – distribution of presents,

with something for everybody. 'Turkey excellent, the pudding not only
was all right, but the rum went on burning all the time.' Foy couldn't

have given me two presents more dear to me than Handley Cross *and*
Old Kensington. *Mrs Charles Treffry came in and had tea this
afternoon. The house is looking very jolly indeed with decorations at
which I toiled from 11 to 3.15 yesterday. The holly is first class this year,
and Grose and I came home with a tremendous load of stuff, pulling
against a gale of wind, with the* Cillalaithe *so laden as to be in danger of
capsizing; and Jory* [the dog] *somewhere beneath it crying out to his gods
that this was not his notion of Christmas. He saw the crackers on the
table today, and escaped to the drawing room after dinner. I am the
richer by a handsome pipe, won by your Mother in the Rowing Club
raffle, and Grose has had a drink out of a diminutive silver cup, won by*
True Tilda *in the sailing races. We had some good carollers in last
night, from Foxhole near St Austell, and they sang a ridiculously old
favourite of mine, 'How beautiful upon the mountains'.*

He was to spend most of New Year's day at Truro in committee –
Mr Pascoe had been up to discuss a heap of things for it. (Q. did not
treat him, though Secretary for Education, as a social equal – nor was
he.) Today Q. was in the Town Hall to try a runaway German sailor;
but he 'was a good man and did extraordinary work for us, spiriting
up schools in all remote districts: but the main memory for us, of
course, is his amazing devotion to the Couch family. It was one of the
faithfullest, most unselfish, things.'

The next volume of Lectures, *Charles Dickens and Other Victorians,*
1925, has unity of subject, for it deals with novelists alone. Here again
Q. as critic had the advantage of being a practitioner of the art – as
against, what Disraeli saw, 'you know who the critics are? The men
who have failed in literature and art.' We learn that, for writers who
were young in the Nineties, their 'favourite models were French or
Russian – Balzac, Stendhal, Mérimée, Flaubert, Maupassant, Tur-
geniev, the Tolstoy of *Sebastopol* and *War and Peace'.* It is odd that he
should omit Daudet, with whom Q. had more in common. He tells us
that the principles that animated them then were an agonising search
for the right or most expressive word; and 'to keep *ourselves* out of any
given story, making the persons exhibit their characters of themselves

and by their actions. . . . Any chat by the author himself ranked as an offence against art.'

Yet this was clean contrary to the practice of the Victorian novelists, Dickens, Thackeray, Trollope, or their precursors, Fielding, Richardson, Scott. It is also contrary to what Q. himself observed as to the importance of the autobiographical in artistic creation.

> *No dramatist can create live characters save by bequeathing the best of himself to the children of his art, scattering among them a largess of his own qualities – giving to one his wit, to another his philosophic doubt, to another his love of action, to another the simplicity and constancy he finds deep in his own nature.*

I find this rather an ideal list for my own cynical part. All the same, how the autobiographical looms in the work of Michelangelo or Leonardo or Caravaggio, in Beethoven, Tchaikovsky, or Elgar – or, contrary to practically all imperceptive criticism, in Shakespeare.[1]

Q. brings home to us again the way the Victorians had of regarding their foremost writers as national institutions. (Flattering as this must have been to their egos, it cannot but have had a distorting effect upon their writing – so many things they thought which they dared not say, particularly about sex. Hardy came up against this restriction badly.) Dickens was, and regarded himself as being, a representative national institution. So, when he went to the United States, he spoke out against the absence of a copyright law which enabled publishers there to steal what they liked by publishing English books without payment. When Dickens discussed the matter with leading American authors, they all agreed with him, but 'not a man of them dared to speak out'. This was democracy. 'Then,' said Dickens, 'I shall speak out.' He did, and it created great offence. Q. thought that Dickens was wrong to have spoken his mind, 'as an English gentleman, being America's guest'. Dickens was not quite a gentleman, and was, in my opinion, entirely justified. This was all the more gentlemanly of Q. as he himself had reason to complain. Austin Purves, of Philadelphia, had fallen for Fowey through Q.'s books, became a great friend and used to come over each summer. In March 1906 he wrote, 'all these

[1]   cf. my *Shakespeare's Self-Portrait.*

piratical publishers copyright your works, i.e. the first one that gets hold of them does. . . . All, I think, of your books are published here – evidence that they are widely read in this country.'

Almost half of this book is devoted to Dickens; we need not traverse Q.'s warm appreciation, with its judicious criticism. We have seen him at home at Fowey, reading Dickens and Forster's *Life* together. He noticed that, for all his popularity, Dickens had little use for Victorian religiosity. In spite of Carlyle's disillusioned view of human nature, Dickens had 'a keener eye for sin' – naturally, for Carlyle lived blamelessly, where Dickens lived a double life. I don't know how much Q. knew about that, so much has come to light since. Nor would he have fully realised Dickens's schizophrenic nature: no wonder he knew about evil and the psychology of murder; his daughter said of him that he was half-angel, and half-devil.

We need not concern ourselves with the commonplaces of criticism – that Dickens' plots are, often, monstrous, his over-lifesize characters hardly of this world but of a world of his own, his faults of taste, etc. Q. is more original in pointing out how enormously much of the Victorian age this writer – so representative too – omitted. And again 'of political thought his world is almost as empty'. Original touches of Q.'s own are more to our purpose. Once more the soundness, even foresight, of his judgment is shown in his appreciation of the unfortunate Gissing, never more highly estimated than today. Or of Trollope – 'But we shall see Trollope reanimated. . . . His bulk is a part of his quality: it can be no more separated from the man than can Falstaff's belly from Falstaff.' A more surprising thought is that 'a stricter schooling is the bane of originality' – as true for Shakespeare as for Dickens. Q. recalled how these Victorians were read for prophets in his 'modest country household' – as I recall that, in a still more modest house, Dickens was a living, even acted, presence.[1] Q. gives us old Jonathan Couch's account of Tennyson's visit to him, when in Cornwall upon his Arthurian quest.

He deals with Thackeray fairly enough, though confessing to a 'broken sympathy'. Today we do not put Thackeray on the pedestal the Victorians did, on a comparable level with Dickens, though a more

[1]   cf. my *A Cornish Childhood.*

educated writer of prose. Q. had an original perception, in noting that Thackeray, 'a social delineator or nothing, never quite understood the roots of English life or of the classes he chose to depict. . . . He is on sure ground when he writes of Joe Sedley, a demi-nabob, but on no sure ground at all when he gets down to Queen's Crawley.'

In short Thackeray's view of our society was limited by his Anglo-Indian background: he had little understanding of the roots of English life in the countryside. Q. contrasts this with Trollope, whose experience of it, indeed of the whole of society, was fuller, more real, balanced and just, than any other Victorian novelist. Trollope had a curiously modest estimate of himself: he thought Thackeray his superior. Today this judgment is precisely reversed. For a generation Trollope's writing himself down was taken literally. It is always a mistake to be too modest: a *just* estimate is what is required, of oneself as for others. Milton made no such mistake, nor did Shakespeare, though no one has perceived that the phrase in *The Two Gentlemen* –

> *So eating love*
> *Inhabits in the finest wits of all –*

refers, if smilingly, to himself.

'We all have our knocks to bear, and some the most dreadful irremediable wounds to bind up and hide.' Thackeray made a mess of his early life, gambling away his patrimony, and thereafter living a seedy existence for some years, partly abroad, partly living by ephemeral journalism. Q. has more sympathy with that kind of thing than I have. He thought it a 'good gospel' to 'fall in love early, throw your cap over the mill; take an axe, spit on your hands; and, for someone, make the chips fly'. He sees Thackeray carrying on his work 'amid those pleasures and anxieties which only they can taste fully who earn their daily bread in mutual love on the future's chance'. The consequence for Thackeray's work – to use Q.'s own phrase – was that much of it went 'skimble-skamble'; except for *Esmond* and the first half of *Vanity Fair*, 'he never seems (to me at least) to have planned out a novel'.

The surprise of this volume is Q.'s appreciation of Disraeli as a novelist. He much preferred his novels to his politics: all Victorian

Liberals thought that Disraeli was a charlatan. Lord Salisbury, who was not at all on the same wave-length, knew better; he summed up: 'Zeal for England was the consuming passion of his life.' Then again, Q. did not like imperialism, and Disraeli was an imperialist. Q. had justice of mind, rarest of qualities, and that most essential to a good critic. He allowed that Disraeli's books were 'naturally suspected and unjustly treated by his opponents throughout his lifetime'. Disraeli himself was partly to blame; he trailed his coat outrageously, and as for being a Jew, he made a proud boast of it – as well he might – and took every opportunity of accentuating it, making a cult of Orientalism.

With *Coningsby* he invented the political novel – all Disraeli's passion for, and understanding of, politics, political intrigues and manoeuvres, characteristics and foibles of politicians, are in it. Q. gives him full credit: 'an inventor is great not only because he does a thing well, but because he could do it at all'. Trollope's political novels are different in tone and temper, good as they are: he is not so *engaged*; he sees the game from the outside, Disraeli from within. *Sybil* is no less original: he made the 'condition-of-England' question its subject, and created the concept of the Two Nations within one society, the rich and the poor. Disraeli and Karl Marx should have understood each other: they had much in common. Of all Victorian politicians Disraeli was the only one of the front rank who had an understanding of, and some sympathy, with the Chartists. His faults as a novelist are obvious: Q. specifies them, and also his qualities. He notes that the flamboyance of his style 'cried aloud for attack by critics who hated him on other scores'. Disraeli perfectly understood this – and raised the score to annoy them all the more.

I possess Q.'s copy of *Lothair*, bookplate and coat-of-arms as a knight, with his motto 'Do and Abide'. Unfortunately he did not enrich his books with marginal comments, though he marked salient passages. One comment only remarks 'the general fatuity of Lothair's conversation'. Evidently this book had less interest for him than for an historian, for it has the topical subject of the epidemic of conversions to Rome in late Victorian society. We are given a subtle portrait of ultramontane Cardinal Manning, along with others, for – like *Con-ingsby* – it is a *roman à clef*. Q. preferred *Endymion* 'in which so touchingly an old man, dejected from political office and power, seeks back with all his worldly wisdom, as one walking out into a garden in a lunar light of memory, to recapture the rose of youth'.

As a young man Disraeli had a genius for friendship, and collected a galaxy of talent, 'Young England', around him; even as an old man his appeal was to youth. So was Q.'s: 'if you hereafter remember at all, you will remember that never from this desk was preached anything but confidence in you'.

In these years, 1924–5, he was afflicted with partial blindness, a terrible affliction for someone so dependent on reading and writing, and who had always enjoyed the long sight of a seaman. He had for long been overworking. He thought that he enjoyed a leisured life; but his daughter says that he did not know what leisure was – just as I cannot believe that he was, as he claimed, a slow writer who had always found the construction of English sentences 'a confounded nuisance'. (This, to encourage undergraduates over their difficulties.) I think that, especially considering the dispersion of his efforts over so many activities, he must have had exceptional powers of concentration.

He was reading widely and miscellaneously at this time for an *Oxford Book of English Prose*; much reading for it was done in trains on his tireless journeys – not good for his eyes. It was an alarming prospect, which he faced with his usual courage: 'the thing may be curable. Anyway I've had a good time.' He took practical measures to carry on – lecturing extempore, which he detested even more than formal lecturing. He had now to call in regular secretarial assistance. Ritually sociable as ever, he would take the ladies who helped, upon occasions like Whit Monday, to picnic beside the stripling Cam, the river at Clare, or on the downs at Heydon. He always provided wine, though once when the College kitchen had packed lemonade, instead of his picked Burgundy, there was an explosion.

This last of his famous series of Oxford Books came out in November 1925: he gave me my copy at Christmas, to celebrate my All Souls Fellowship. The book is dedicated to his two colleges, Trinity at Oxford and Jesus at Cambridge, 'two houses of learning and hospitality, and to Friendship'. His Preface explained that he took the first virtue of prose to be Persuasion, whether in narrative or argument; that of Poetry to be a 'high compelling emotion'. His aim was to be representative, thus he had included all sorts, choosing often a passage quite pedestrian, and rejecting a purple patch that did not ring quite true. In practice literature 'will be found very much more on the side of the purple patch than the generality supposes'.

He conceded that, with increasing years, 'my sympathy with prose nowadays being written misses a right capacity to discriminate'. This was still more true for contemporary poetry – he could not abide Eliot's, for example. 'The newspaper press admits today a portentous amount of that Jargon, or flaccid writing to which flaccid thought instinctively resorts.' He had included a good deal of Berners' Froissart. 'Why? For two reasons: the first that it holds the core of true English gentility; the second that, in the matter of technique, our prose learnt its grace of our dear enemy, France.' This is true Q.

The book begins with the Cornishman John Trevisa: not only out of loyalty, for he was one of the first to write English prose and to teach school in French rather than Latin. The book ends with Rupert Brooke – Q. must have attached some significance to that too. For the few excerpts from the best prosaists among lawyers he applied to Sir William Holdsworth at All Souls. Altogether it offers a fair conspectus of our prose literature. Persuasive as ever, he hoped to offer 'a serviceable and portable volume which shall remind not only many stay-at-home quiet-living folk but many an Englishman on his travels and (still better) many a one in exile on far and solitary outposts of duty, of the nobility of this Island, its lineage and its language'.

With his eye trouble there were fewer publications for the next two years. At home in Cornwall

I have been spending the time (a) cutting brambles, knee-deep in such daffodils or ankle-deep in such primroses; (b) visiting schools and sitting on County Council committees; (c) writing at a novel as well as my poor eyes will allow; and (d) exploring – or rather renewing old explorations of the real scene of the Tristan and Iseult business. Is there anything else in the world jollier than happening on a little trifle of confirmatory evidence that has lain latent for hundreds of years and dodged the antiquarians? Last week when I was morally certain where King Mark's castle must have stood, the farmer's wife at the manor farm below got out some deeds and a map with the names of fields on it; and lo! the meadow exactly fitting my hypothesis was named "Mark's Gate".

He may have been put on to this by the young antiquarian, Charles Henderson, who became a close friend of mine. The collocation of names around the prehistoric camp of Castle Dore, dominating the river valley of the Fowey, would seem to point to something significant. Immediately below the camp, with its dykes and vallums, is the manor of Lantyan; in the earliest French romances Tristan appears in association with the place Lancien. Not far away is Kilmarth, 'kil' meaning grove, 'marth' for Mark? An early inscribed stone, now moved down the Fowey road from Castle Dore, reads something like *Drustagnus fili Cunomori*. Since Q.'s time the fortress has been excavated, revealing the post-holes of considerable wooden erections. What are we to make of it?

Q. found the makings of his last novel there, *Castle Dore*. It begins beautifully, with its evocation of this lovely countryside, the parish of St Sampson of Golant. St Sampson was one of the most important of the sixth-century saints, who left for Brittany where he became the patron saint of the cathedral and diocese of Dol.

Q. wove around it a strange tale of *revenants*, of characters returning from that remote past in modern guise, of queer intuitions of time reversing itself. His Cambridge student, J. B. Priestley, was to write a couple of plays on the theme. But Q. could never finish this novel so attractively begun. He dropped it midway; years later Foy had it finished by her friend Daphne du Maurier, who moved to Kilmarth from Menabilly, (the Manderley of *Rebecca*). Foy sent it to me: 'I fear your censure over this.' But, after all, Q. had been called in to complete Stevenson's *St Ives*. This may have suggested the time-reversal theme of Daphne du Maurier's ingenious *The House on the Strand*, about the medieval priory at Tywardreath[1] on the coast below Castle Dore.

This interest in the remote Celtic past produced an exchange of letters with Henry Jenner, the old bearded patriarch of Cornish scholarship. To him, along with Morton Nance, we owe the revival of the ancient language. This did not interest Q. Jenner wondered if he were not descended from William Couch of St Sampson's, a Popish

---

Ty-war-dreath means the house-on-the-sand.

Recusant of 1715, when the Jacobite Rebellion against the Hanoverians had some sympathisers down here.

Jenner had something interesting to tell Q. about Trollope. A High Church Episcopalian cleric in Scotland regularly inserted into the prayer for the Church Militant at Communion intercessions *by name* for 'those in trouble, sorrow, need, sickness or any other adversity'. At that time *The Last Chronicle of Barset* was coming out in numbers, and the cleric just pulled himself up in time from adding a prayer for Mr Crawley, then in a particularly tight spot in the novel. 'In 1873 came *The Eustace Diamonds*, and almost immediately came a slump in Trollopes, so that those who had read him and delighted in him all dropped him.' This rather ante-dates for us the decline of Trollope's popularity. Jenner thought that it would recover, and that 'the later Palliser novels were nearly as good a series as the Barset books, and ought to be reprinted'. He was right, and they have been.

Barrie was upset to hear the news of Q.'s partial blindness and came down to Cambridge to visit. The two old friends walked down to the May Races together. Barrie wrote regretting that

> *we did not have a long evening alone together, when we could have come closer to each other, as I am sure we both wanted. And how tongue-tied was I when we were going to the station, and at it! Yet I was full of affection for you then. . . . I could have made so much more of my time, but nevertheless it was to me the happiest visit I have paid anywhere for a very long time.*

Q., in addition to everything else, was a Syndic of the University Press, and now, with eyesight getting worse, felt he should retire. Suddenly, by the end of 1927, his sight completely recovered. He put it down to an oculist allowing him to smoke again, when it had been forbidden: I'll bet his having to knock it off for a year or two had been responsible for the recovery. Once more luck was with him – he had no more trouble with his eyes.

In January 1926 he was getting a lot of Press cuttings about *The Oxford Book of Prose*. The Aristotle classes continued to be a success – so was a lunch party in the Combination Room, with soles in white wine, woodcock, fruit *gâteau*, parmesan straws. 'You cannot say a man is ailing who lunches on woodcock and dines on haggis, and makes some well-chosen remarks in between.'

Boat news at Lent Races: Jesus was Head of the River.

For Ad Eundem *I have arranged for putting up Baldwin and Milford* [Head of the Oxford University Press]: chosen wines: arranged dinner: got out menus for printing, etc. The dinner runs very largely on my old tried lines. Oysters: Vesica soup: Soles Normandes (i.e. cooked with mussels, olives and oysters); hot Virginia ham and spinach: saddle Welsh mutton: woodcock: ice pudding Nesselrode: cheese and anchovy straws: dessert: and if they grumble at that, they are not fit to live.

The Bach-Brahms concert last night was first class. After supper

with my own hands I tidied everything up; and this morning finished proofs for the little Dent book. But, my own deare, as the birthdays come round, I long more and more to be with you. You and I only know what, in spite of one awful sorrow, a lovely thing life has been. You have made it a sort of song for me, deare, and to this day the sight of you coming along the street tightens my heart just as in the days when we were courting.

From 1928 onwards Dent published a collected 'Duchy' edition of his novels and tales, thirty volumes of it, each with a new, informative, Introduction. It was fortunate for him to have such a staunch backer as Ernest Rhys at Dent's, for Q.'s vogue as a writer of fiction was mostly over. He felt that, and was out of tone and temper with the new fashions prevailing, particularly for psycho-analysis, psychological deviations and abnormalities. 'My stories simply treat men and women, with their differences, as I have been allowed their acquaintance in life.' However, he held to the hope that in time public taste would turn back to better themes. Some hopes! What *would* he think of the way things have gone?

In 1927 the Cornwall County Council had celebrated the remarkable progress in education that had been made in the past quarter of a century with an Education Week. Q. described the work in the published *Handbook* as having been 'missionary' in principle: to plant missionary centres of Higher Education within access of every child capable of winning a Minor Scholarship 'to opportunities we would make his birthright'. That was how we all began; the principle was selective – the Minor Scholarships selected all, and rather more than all who were educable.

Q. and R. G. Rows (I was taken down to Helston to be approved by the old blind philosopher) were proud of their achievement. 'Those who originally fought against our setting up of Secondary Schools, and so fiercely that we had to build with the sword in one hand and the trowel in another, are now pressing us to build more.' His own intellectual authority, the respect in which they held him, had been a powerful weapon in the battle. Still university education was not provided for, with only *one* scholarship for the whole county. As a Labour candidate, I advocated modestly that it should be doubled – and was agreeably surprised when they made it four: for the whole of Cornwall!

In 1931 Q. resigned the chairmanship, though he continued for another three years as Vice-Chairman.

I had been wanting to do it for some time, and only held on because the clerical managers had come to trust me to 'see fair' – never once having voted to close a Church School while it could be kept open without harm to the children's health. Also, the mere fact of being a Churchman (however suspect) and not *a Wesleyan was always something of a help. . . . Moreover I have been considering the Income Tax, and find that I* must *work. Well, that's no hardship: and I like it ever so much better than Committee meetings.*

However, he continued his general activity for education. At Fowey he was chairman of the Workers' Educational Association, which had been largely started by Balliol men and did good work in its day, while there was a gap to fill.

He had ceased to take any political line, and was no help here, though no pro-German. Moreover he was a close friend of the family of my opponent, the Conservative MP who was a whole-hearted supporter of Chamberlain. This made it impossible for him to express any sympathy for my forlorn campaign, whatever he may have thought. He kept what is called today 'a low profile', where I was appallingly exposed, a target for everyone in those unforgivable years.

He said that all his thoughts now were given to his work at

[193]

Cambridge, but immersed himself in as many educational activities as ever. He came over to Oxford to inaugurate a University Extension Summer School with a lecture on Shakespeare, in the crowded Examination Schools. His visits to Oxford became more frequent after Trinity made him, none too soon, an Honorary Fellow. He continued his active work for the Village Drama Society, and gave lectures and addresses in various places – no need to go into the list of them.

In January he provided Stanley Baldwin with a passage from Augustine Birrell on the wealth of one-syllable words in English, which he used in one of his 'cultural' speeches. What a curious man Baldwin was, a magpie for collecting ornaments for them from others! John Buchan wrote some of the best of them; his most famous phrase, striking at Beaverbrook and Rothermere using the Press as a harlot of time, came from his cousin, Kipling.

In February Baldwin would 'roll up' with his daughter for tea with Q., then both would be dining at Trinity. Foy was coming up for the Lent Races, when

> *Jesus College may or may not stay Head of the River. Turn up for lunch, and then we can see the finishes, and my devoted taximan will be waiting – as soon as the finishing gun fires – to run us back here in time for you to pour tea for Baldwin and his daughter. Next morning I suggest we have one or two nice children for breakfast. On the Sunday evening Mr Baldwin has to dine in Pembroke and then address an audience of young gentlemen in the Guildhall: so you and I can have a little together.*

He was having a couple of his Oxford Books handsomely bound as a present for Aberdeen University, which had given him an honorary degree. He asked Lobban to check the inscription as 'I don't want my Latin to give Dugald Dalgetty a chance "in the slips"'. And could he discover where Verinder, 'the world's first cutler (who used to live at the top of Ludgate Hill) *now* plies his trade. When I tell you that Verinder made the knife which Atky gave me so "lang syne", you may guess that I desire one of like make.'

In April 1929 Baldwin was writing to him, 'it is great to be P.M. and try and govern decently and in order [this was one for Lloyd George, whom they all wanted to keep out]: but the road to it is Hell'. He had just read a little volume of poems by one Monk Gibbon.

'They are the real stuff, I think.' So much for his literary taste – third-rate, like the Shropshire novelist, Mary Webb, whose fortune he made overnight. That October, 'politics are very queer just now'. He had an important speech to make, and wanted to talk over some addresses he had to give, particularly one about Scott to be delivered in Edinburgh – picking Q.'s brains again.

In 1929 came a new volume of his Cambridge Lectures, a third volume of *Studies in Literature*. Those on 'The English Elegy' naturally brought back his own personal grief: 'the stroke of sorrow drives us beyond ourselves'. *A propos* of Dr Johnson's hostile criticism of 'Lycidas', he says, 'Johnson had no children of his own to die before him. Had such a stroke befallen him, he would have known something of that awful void with which, since it takes away hope, even the desolation of an orphan will not compare.' He then stresses that the agony of grief strikes us dumb, drives us beyond expression, and cites a rare sonnet of Browning, 'I tell you, hopeless grief is passionless', which expresses this thought. 'If it could weep, it could arise and go.' But is this so? Kipling endured as great agony over the loss of his only son, but – a greater writer – transmuted it in his unforgettable story, 'The Gardener'. Q. comes as near as he ever did when he says that, if it gave way, grief would express itself in outcries, challenges to God: 'Why should this be? What has love done to deserve this cruelty? Is it just to punish us so – us, that have walked humbly and been innocently happy?'

He avoids discussion of the much-discussed *Pearl*, 'that amazing and phenomenal English elegy of the 14th century', with a personal touch – 'as in a boat I should avoid a sharp unaccountable rock in a smoothly running channel'. It is here that he threatens 'to hate and haunt everyone who should hereafter attempt a memoir of the lecturer today addressing you'. One can only plead that he was incapable of hate, has always haunted me anyway – and was not Mr Brittain commissioned to write a memoir of him shortly after his death?

He never lectured on the subject of Autobiography, that delightful *genre* which many of the judicious prefer to the novel. What an impoverishment it would be to be without Gibbon's, John Stuart Mill's, Trollope's, Henry James's; or Renan's *Souvenirs d'Enfance et de*

Jeunesse, Stendhal's or Michelet's autobiographical works, let alone Rousseau or St Augustine. Q. has an old-fashioned prejudice against self-assertion, without allowing that it depends upon circumstances and the relevant society. In a society of angels or of the elect it would be unnecessary and out of place. But in the free-for-all of a democratic society it is *necessary* to make one's voice heard above the hubbub.

He insists that there is a certain simplicity in the appeal of great art – a salutary inflexion today, when we are given works of 'criticism', for example, on Tolstoy or Eliot, that make the subject more difficult than it was before. The prime aim of criticism should be to simplify, explain, interpret: criticism is not an end in itself.

We encounter again his curious wish not to want more knowledge of Shakespeare. 'Would you really wish – ought any of us really to wish – to know more of Shakespeare than we do?' Of course, we ought.

He is on firmer ground with his practical information about the Cambridge School of English Literature, to which he had devoted so much thought, and for which he had had to fight. His aim all along was to train *understanding*, rather than 'memorised information'. He was able to claim now that 'the Tripos had met its enemies and survived'. Now that the battle was won he could afford to laugh, with his students, and at himself. The men came to too many lectures, the women to *far* too many. For himself.

> When Autumn's leaves denude the grove,
> I seek my Lecture, where it lurks
> Mid the unpublished portion of
> My works,
>
> And ponder, while its sheets I scan,
> How many years away have slipt
> Since first I penned that ancient man-
> -uscript.

One of his most potent weapons was sheer charm: he challenged them, he charmed them, to do their best. All in all, he was – paradoxically, considering academic doubts when he came to that chair – about the best professor that I have known or heard of.

XI

Later Life and Work

As a historian I have always regarded 1931 as a fatal turning point, when all the hopes of the post-war period were betrayed, hopes of a juster society at home; hopes of establishing peace in Europe, by a system of collective security, which the League of Nations might perhaps have achieved, especially if the United States had supported it. Instead of that, she went back on it and betrayed President Wilson's hopes, retreating into a mean and morose isolationism, which left the situation among the powers dangerously unbalanced. France and Britain could hardly control the situation in Europe, with 80 million dissatisfied Germans in the middle of it. Britain proceeded to unbalance it still further, by playing resurgent Germany's game, hoping to appease the unappeasable, frustrating French policy, which was roughly right. 'Fair play' for Germany meant, in effect, enabling her to renew the attempt to dominate Europe by force.

Such was the background to Q.'s last decade. Talk of 'the hopes of 1906'! When that able government confronted Germany's challenge in 1914, we had on our side France *and* Russia, then Italy and the rest; after twenty years of Baldwin and Chamberlain, of Conservative dominance, we found ourselves in 1940 alone. Q. never said a word to me about all this – as Trevelyan did later, admitting that he had been wrong. On the other hand Q. never reproached me for my lonely stand, so unpopular with all of influence, in my native county, whom events were to prove to have been completely wrong. (After all, they were only ordinary fools, and the country in general was with them.) When the inevitable upshot came in 1940, these people were willing to come round and be friends with me. They were too late: I had turned my back on the county. Q. was saddened at the breach, but he had no idea how far it would go, how absolutely I would react. He wasn't a Celt; he had a nice English nature. He called me over to The Haven, the so familiar study, and told me a thing or two about the

proprietor of the local newspaper that had attacked *A Cornish Childhood* (as if they could get away with it with impunity: I had had too
much of that sort of thing throughout the Thirties). He then said a
wonderful thing: 'The best revenge is not to be like them.' That was
Q.: not me. I registered that he was right, and at the same moment
that I was not going to follow his gospel: I would treat these people in
the way that was appropriate to them, in the way they would
understand.

We have an odd letter from this time that exemplifies his too
generous response to an Irish fan, doubtless sincere in itself, if rather
flattering.

> *If your boys in the Royal School of Dungannon could only realise how
> delightful to the ear is the 'sweet wild twist' of an Irishman's native
> cadence in prose or poetry – in Goldsmith, or in Burke, or in Sheridan,
> Mangan, Yeats – they would surely go on practising that touch which (to
> me at any rate, the incommunicable lilt of it) makes an Irishman's
> writing in English one of the most delightful of sounds. There is, when an
> Irishman has taken the pains to practise it, a kind of melody of which
> alone he has the secret. Whatever happens between our two nations, to me
> it has always seemed a strain as recognisable, as beautiful, and as proud
> of breeding as – shall we say? – an Irish horse.*

I think this is very much a nineteenth-century inflexion – Tom
Moore's 'Irish Melodies' and all that; and it accounts for Q.'s over-
representation of Irish poets in his Oxford Books of Verse.

In 1932 his old friend, Kenneth Grahame, died. Q. sketched his
shy, recessive personality in a tribute to him, remembering the happy
pre-War days boating up the River Fowey. 'His *Wind in the Willows*
had its origin in a series of weekly letters invented to amuse the
schooltime of his only son, whose loss in undergraduate prime at
Oxford broke the parents' life.' It wasn't much of a 'prime': the boy
was driven beyond endurance by the impossible expectations placed
upon him, and laid his head on the railway line. Q. had written an
obituary of the boy, doing his best for the parents, suggesting that it
had been an accident.

In Cornwall there was trouble, from a different sort of human
foolery, over St Hilary. The vicar, Bernard Walke, was a friend of

Q.'s from former days when he was curate at Polruan. An Anglo-Catholic, he was also an artist – friend of the artists at Newlyn and St Ives – who helped to decorate his church and make it beautiful. Naturally all my sympathies were with him. The little church was famous for its miracle plays, broadcast from it. Bishop Frere, who was artist and musician, as well as scholar and a saint, was sympathetic to the good work at St Hilary; also a friend of my great friend, Charles Henderson, and friendly to me. Such was my alignment in Cornwall – we were very much in the minority.

Bernard Walke also had a sense of humour. Beautiful silver globes depended from the arches of his chancel. When asked what they were for: 'To keep witches off the high altar.' This kind of thing enraged humourless Protestants; and there was a witch in the village, a sex-disappointed spinster, who kept watch to let in a posse of Kensitites. They proceeded to wreak all the damage they could, smash images, destroy pictures, wreck altars, candlesticks, lights and lay waste in the church.

Q. was betwixt and between in the controversy that raged.

On the one hand you have the Kensit folk, bank-holiday cads to the bone and revolting all of us [?] by their obscenity. On the other my old friend Bernard Walke, who never could envisage any sort of law as not inviting defiance: and cornered, because he cannot quite say out what he really believes – that the one ultimate authority over the Church of England is the Bishop of Rome. And he'd be just as likely to obey him *as G. B. Shaw would be to abide any law laid down by a Socialist State of his own invention. Tis a pity the saints are so often* sly.

Bernard Walke was not a bit sly: it was Q. who was more cagey, in the disgraceful Thirties. When Bishop Frere left Truro, a round-robin was sent up by the Chamberlainite Lord-Lieutenant and his fellows not to send down another Anglo-Catholic socialist as bishop. Of course Frere was not a socialist: he was above and beyond party politics. So the unspeakable 'National' Government – which betrayed this country's interests to its ruin – sent down their man, one Hunkin, an ex-Wesleyan. We were desolated by the appointment. He went on his Philistine way to complete the destruction at St Hilary, removing the stone altars and emptying the church of its beauty.

[199]

That summer of 1932 was singularly lovely; Q. was busy with the regatta, 'three of the great racers here – *Candida, Astra* and *Westward*, and heaps of others – the harbour all be-jewelled of nights, and the lanterns of the pilchard fleet all drawn like a – by the way, what is a carcanet?' He was looking forward to The Society at Cambridge dining with him, planning

> *a boiled leg of Spanish hog (Don Quixote's country,* chaud-froid*), with a cheese salad of which I share the secret with three men only – (An interval. Knocking without. Several persons from Porlock enter thirstily on their way to or from the Land's End. Air, 'Old English hospitality was never known to fail', but I wish I could be certain the host won't, at this rate.)*

Next year was the malign year 1933 when Hitler came to power. I told Adam von Trott then, 'You can roll up the map of Europe.' I realised from *Mein Kampf* that Hitler would never give up, or give in. It was astonishing what he achieved – owing to the feebleness, and part collusion, of those who should have stopped him in his tracks. It would have saved the lives of millions.

In 1930 Baldwin became Chancellor of Cambridge University: we find him ready to discuss with the Vice-Chancellor some subject Q. had brought to his attention. Anything rather than foreign affairs, the European situation. In Cabinet he would say, 'Wake me up when that is over.' In the month after Hitler achieved power, it was 'while you are dining peacefully in your ancient halls, and your conversation is among the stars, I shall be addressing a crowded and sweating audience in Queen's Hall on Building.' (This hall, famous for the Promenade Concerts, was destroyed in the Blitz.) Baldwin had enjoyed the *Times* correspondence on his oration at Cambridge, the joke being that it was Rutherford's *verbatim*. 'What do I know of atoms?' (or of Europe either, for that matter).

In October he couldn't accept Q.'s invitation to Cambridge: he was spending the week-end 'at a house of a very old friend, who is however very die-hard about India. He is old but has a good deal of influence in the Lords, and it is a matter of some importance just now to keep our friendship green. I am like the priest of Nemi or like Freedom: I only exist at the price of perpetual vigilance!' This was very like Baldwin: he was a good Party manager.

'Don't you ever come to London? Breakfast is always ready for you here', i.e. at 11 Downing Street (Ramsay MacDonald was encumbering No. 10). It does not appear that Q. took advantage of the open invitation; but I do not find this friendship in keeping with the man of 1906.

That summer Q. was at home gardening.

We are wrestling with a plum and apple crop the like of which I have never known. Five afternoons have we worked in the hot sun and have gathered a quarter of the crop, if so much. Tomorrow I get a respite from manual labour – opening of a Girls' school in the afternoon, and in the evening a journey into the far country, to talk to a Women's Institute about the history of their parish.

I wonder how any man, as he nears seventy, can find – either at Cambridge or in the depths of the country – a spare hour for improving his own mind or for doing any concentrated work. I brought home Aristotle his Rhetoric *and a lot of Platonist stuff – instead of which I've been opening swimming baths, Church bazaars, regattas. And at my back I always hear Time's wingèd chariot – an apple-cart these five days – hurrying near, and get to bed tired out, with the beginnings of a beautiful lyric in my head, quite gone on awaking.*

He should have concentrated his energies, and shut people out. My breach with Cornwall would save me from all that.

His memories of Bodmin were ambivalent – a happy childhood, but shadowed by the near-crash at the end, with some consequences of which he kept silent. To the son of his old schoolmaster there he wrote of his kindness, 'talking to me seriously about books and even politics – the sort of thing that immensely flatters a raw boy'. Yet,

I seldom go over to Bodmin now – almost never except on public business, now and then to some function at the barracks. But I don't like the strange faces that stare out of doorways: in place of the old kindly ghosts. I seem to hear buglers Elford and Ough sounding at the head of Chapel Street, and want to turn and run. . . .

Of course I remember you well – almost as well as the face of Kate Simmons as she drove off (behind postillions) on her marriage with old

Colonel Edyvean. She was married from our house, and it almost broke my heart. For, at the age of seven or thereabouts, I fully understood she had promised to wait for me. I hope the world has treated you well, as I wish. It has been kind to me, barring the loss of my only son – a fine soldier (DSO etc.), who saw the War through from August 1914. . . . So I divide my time between Cambridge and here by the sea, and wince away from the bugles of Bodmin.

Family memories made him wince away even harder – more candidly to Mabel:

You had a worse time than I and your recollections must be bitterer than mine. . . . Apart from some old friends now mostly dead, I have never had a kind word or invitation – save ordinary ones to Balls, Barrack functions, etc – from that old place: which to me, when I have to go over for Grand Jury, Quarter Sessions, etc, is as if it had never been.

And as for fame – any wider fame – or what critics say or ignore, I simply don't care – a little once – but since Bevil's death not at all. For years in the intervals of County Councils here, I lunched at Truro with half-a-dozen political foes, and they all became close friends – before I went to Cambridge and cut connection with all politics. Pressing for advancement, all social striving, etc – the more you despise that sort of thing the more it comes bothering when you've learnt to have no use for it.

Then, with a return to the family crash, 'I ought to have guessed more than I did.' What was it that he was concealing? What had happened to the two unsatisfactory brothers who are never mentioned? Some few in the audience, when he was at length awarded the freedom of the borough, must have known.

News from Fowey in the summer of 1934 was that Mrs de Cressy Treffry (the family were proud of an ancestor who had fought at Crécy under the Black Prince) was laid up with a splintered kneepan. The Quiller Couches had all along been bent on keeping up with the Treffrys – and with the Robartes family at Lanhydrock. But these were Liberals. Q. had ceased to be a Party man – which helped his friendship with Baldwin, and accounts for his silence as to the unforgivable course of British policy in the Thirties. Actually the head of the Robartes family, an intelligent man, well understood that the course was fatal, and was in sympathy with my forlorn campaign. He had reasonably expected to become Lord Lieutenant; instead, 'they' saw to it that an ineffable Chamberlainite pro-Nazi was appointed.

Foy was friendly with the Robartes sisters, and was 'competing in a side-show at Lanhydrock'. (When the family came to an end there and the mansion was taken over by the National Trust, she retired to a flat in the upper house.) At The Haven the dining room had been done up, 'as somebody said of his donkey, it looks as if it belonged to Somebody'. At Cambridge he was President of the University Rowing Club: they had been representing England *v.* America and winning over there. 'At Falmouth they had swept the board in the dinghy races, with forty odd entries, and wound up with the Prince of Wales' cup.'

At Cambridge he was as sociable as ever, and as much in request; he enormously enjoyed his bachelor life there and its alternation with home life at Fowey. He was elected High Steward of the Red Herrings, the 'upper perch' of the Roosters at Jesus, and regularly attended their dinners in black skull-cap adorned with a red herring. Mr Brittain says that he was not in the least self-conscious – but in fact Q. liked dressing the part. Every year he wrote burlesque lyrics for the Roosters' Revue of the year. Hospitably he gave or attended luncheons to honour favourite booksellers – one for the head man at Heffers, whom the Master, by now senile, persisted in addressing as Mr Heffer (if he existed) throughout.

A more remarkable bookseller was David, who kept an open-air stall on Market Hill, and somehow collected remarkable books. He was a Cambridge institution, partly Jewish – I wish I had been in time to prowl round his stall. When he died Q. wrote an obituary tribute to this humorous Cambridge character. Then there was a Centenary celebration of Coleridge, a Jesus man; a bronze of him was cast by his descendant, Gilbert Coleridge, an old friend of Q.'s at Oxford. He was in demand for college feasts throughout the University.

He had now become its foremost, best-known 'character'. Mr Brittain has a detailed description of the ceremony that attended his leaving college at the end of every term. All the Roosters were present, sherry all round. When the car was announced Q. would put on his bowler hat, brown, black or grey according to the colour of his suit, handing his spare bowler to one of the company that attended him to the station. There he was joined by station-master and porters, all perambulating the platform to inspect a compartment that suited his fancy. Oddly enough, at Liverpool Street and Paddington he was singled out for similar attention; and of course at Par, junction for Fowey, a quasi-royal reception. Absurd as it sounds, and impossible today, it was a spontaneous tribute to an exceptional personality.

In July 1934 Europe was alerted to the evil nature of Hitler's *régime*, if such were necessary, by the 'Night of the Long Knives', when some 1250 – the official figure – of his fellow Germans were murdered, opponents along with old comrades. President Hindenburg, Germany's hero of the 1914–18 war, publicly approved Hitler's action. No notice of the warning was taken in England. The editor of *The Times* worked hard each night to keep out of the paper anything disagreeable to Hitler and Nazi Germany.

That autumn Q. produced his final volume of Lectures, *The Poet as Citizen*, dating its Preface sadly, 'Trafalgar Day'. He speaks up against 'the turgid German novel' which was all the fashion at the time. He preferred the racy idiosyncrasy of Somerville and Ross of *The Irish R.M.*, inviting bemused reviewers to better a sentence or improve on their artistry. In fact, *The Real Charlotte* is now recognised as a classic.

This volume of Lectures has a dominant theme – his reaction or, rather attitude (he was not a reactionary) to modern trends in literature, in poetry, biography, the novel. He makes short work of Strachey, while being at the same time fair. In fact he was extraordinarily shrewd when he said, 'I detect a man sincerely kind beneath or between the lines of his most corrosive writing.' Strachey's writing, his public persona, was corrosive; Q. did not know him, but as a private person Strachey *was* kind.

Q. took issue with Strachey's description of the Victorian age as 'an age of self-complacency'. Q. interjected 'What? – Newman or Clough', wrestling with desperation to find any certainty. He might equally well have cited Carlyle's despair, Ruskin's neurosis, or Matthew Arnold's career of doubt. Strachey hated Victorian religiosity, which was fair game; but the most Victorian of all writers, Dickens, was without it. Strachey was not a good historian, either of the Victorian age or of the

Elizabethan – Elizabethans he simply did not understand. He was at his best with the eighteenth century.

In the contemporary novel Q. reflected on the derisive, devaluing treatment of character as nothing new: 'it was habitual with Thackeray; habitual also, though not openly confessed, with George Eliot'. He deplored its current pervasiveness. He should have seen how much further it has gone – the cult of the anti-hero, the misfit, the drop-out.

As for poetry and its function in society, he did not urge any claim for 'patriotic' verse, stimulating as it may have been 'among peoples in crises of their history'. And Q. dismissed the idea – common as it was in the eighteenth century – that 'poetry *directly* inculcates any ethical doctrine'. Still less, we may say, the political propaganda of the Leftist poets of the Thirties, which produced so much bad verse.

In the Lecture on 'Tradition and Orthodoxy' he challenged T. S. Eliot, on his way to becoming a guru. In one of my letters to him I had inveighed against a society 'worm-eaten with liberalism'. I was furious at liberal-minded ineffectiveness in dealing with Hitler and Mussolini; I constantly argued against 'the Rationalist Fallacy', by which Liberals and Social Democrats assumed that the masses were rational: Hitler and Mussolini (and Stalin) knew better.

Eliot took up my phrase. Q., who was a Liberal, took Eliot to task and had the better of the argument. He argued with his junior with his usual courtesy, but no less effectively. Tradition is 'at once too various and too delicate a thing to be caught, constricted within formulas or creeds by any Church'. So too with poetry. 'Why is most religious verse so bad?', Eliot had asked; Q. replied 'precisely in so far as it has submitted to his own theory'. In his *Thoughts on Lambeth* Eliot made the ludicrous suggestion that a literary censorship should be exercised by Lambeth. Q. retorted that 'Liberalism' with Eliot meant 'anything which questions dogma: which dogma, to be right dogma, is the priestly utterance of a particular offset of a particular branch of a historically fissiparous Church'.

On the main issue Q. was surely right. 'The free operation of man's mind has been the fount and inspiration of the greatest literature bequeathed through centuries to civilized Europe.' We can see the obverse to that in what happened to German literature under Hitler,

Spanish under Franco, and to Russian literature under Stalin. In fact, 'this "Liberalism", which Mr Eliot arraigns as a worm, eating into the traditions of our society, reveals itself rather as Tradition itself throughout our literature – which is thought worth setting down and recording – the organic spirit, aerating, preserving the liberties our ancestors won and we inherit.'

Once more Q. put his money on Persuasion, 'the only intellectual process to which a free man should surrender'. But that applies only to few – those few who have anything to persuade. One could never persuade ordinary fools in the Thirties that Hitler was not a man of peace – in spite of all the evidence. The historian Lecky knew, as a historian should, that people will believe anything in spite of the evidence or contrary to the evidence, but hardly ever in accordance with the evidence.

This is where Q.'s liberal persuasiveness lost him effectiveness. Eliot did not bank on persuading people: 'in a society like ours . . . the only thing possible for a person of strong convictions is to state a point of view and leave it at that.' This is why, though Q. had the better of the argument, Eliot has been much more listened to: he laid down the law, and I agree with him about persuasion.

In these Lectures Q. treats his students as equals – '*us* learners in the Art of Criticising'. But do undergraduates qualify to criticise? What is the use of pretending that they do? – simpler and more effective to tell them. In a way he was playing a game with them, himself acting a part.

A master of dialect, he was well qualified to expound William Barnes, the poet who preferred to write in Dorset dialect. Andrew Lang, the Scot, had dismissed Barnes on the ground that, whereas Scots was a *language,* Dorset was but a debased dialect of English. Q. scored off him. Dorset and Somerset dialect is the direct descendant of the original Anglo-Saxon of Wessex, which produced the most remarkable literature among the early Teutons. Standard English is not: it is the descendant of Midlands Mercian. Whether British or American, Australian, Canadian, South African, New Zealand, or whatever, we are all speaking Mercian.

William Barnes was a learned poet, a philologist, who knew several languages; but, a theorist, he insisted on presenting his poems not only in dialect but with a whole system of accents to represent phonetic values – what Q. called hieroglyphics. This was a mistake: it put people off his poetry and encouraged them to dismiss it. Q. gave some examples of how well the poems came through for modernising them, presenting them in recognisable commonsense spelling. The same holds good for Shakespeare: one should get rid of archaisms and superfluous difficulties, not add to them.

Naturally he was sympathetic to dialect. There are two dialects of English in Cornwall, West and East (which approximates to West Devon speech). He liked the idea of people being bilingual, capable of speaking both good English and their original dialect. Q. himself could.

He had observed the early novels of Hardy as they came out, and the way they baffled people by their marked qualities and defects. Hardy's first effort, *The Poor Man and the Lady*, baffled both Meredith and John Morley. It was autobiographical; the theme of social inequality – the poor man falling for a woman of a rank above him – ran through the early novels. Hardy's first wife was a help to him in early years, rather as a patroness. Polite as ever, Q. describes her as 'a woman of remarkably strong character, difficult, straightly loyal, for years distrustful that novel-writing was not quite the occupation to which this queer wonderful husband of hers should demean himself: she herself being connected with the clergy – niece, indeed, to an Archdeacon.' Privately Q. told me what an appalling woman she was – no 'Angel in the House' (of Coventry Patmore).

Yet, when she died, Hardy went back to live again the dream of their meeting at St Juliot, on the north coast of Cornwall, Boscastle, Tintagel, Beeny Cliff and all. 'Dream' is Q.'s word for it, and out of it came the finest poems of *Moments of Vision*. Within the novelist was the poet, longing for release.

Q., so tender-hearted about women, noticed how curious Hardy's attitude really was – 'his uncanny, suspicious sense of the *other woman's* motives in loving. While he wrote anonymously he was generally accused, by female readers, of being a woman or, alternatively, of knowing too much.' That was in the early years. Of the late, 'there seems no harm in telling an innocent thing of which all who had privilege of converse with him were reverently aware – that his widowhood had constructed a pure fairy-tale of that youthful time'. He goes on to describe the scenes of it, as familiar to him as to Hardy.

With this last volume he had largely finished his work in criticism, had his full say at Cambridge. The characteristics are clear: sympathy and perception, justice of mind, an intuitive foresight in judgment. Going back to his Inaugural Lecture, he quoted again Renan's 'La Vérité consiste dans les nuances.' This spoke for him. He had tried as professor to get away from abstractions about literature, crude generalisations cutting up the flow of writing into periods and movements, revolts and reactions. The historian can hardly dispense with these aids; but it is remarkable to what an extent Q. managed to do so. He occasionally turned it to a joke, as with the heavy-footed Teuton, Georg Brandes, such an authority at the time, posting up his lists of periods and movements as on a police notice board.

In November 1935 Q. tells Lilian of his 'daily letter home – the one sacred observance kept through life, save folding up my clothes as Granny taught me'. He sends a present of silver, which 'looks Georgian but is actually mid-Victorian. The stamp proclaims it to be the work of some stout diehard who wasn't taking any truck in the taste of Albert the Good.' An 'impertinent portrait' of him by Nicholson had been painted,

> *which hangs there (but at my back). I cannot feel as old as the dates make out. . . . I sing (reprehensible habit) in my bath and I talk with the boys and plan things that will never be done; and can even laugh at the thought that almost everything I've sweated to write is now a back number. But we two (and Mabel in the end) have come into harbour out of (when we think of it) a pretty sad mess-up. My luck has really been Louie throughout and my share in two noble children.*

At home in Cornwall we had had a grievous loss of our remarkable historian, Charles Henderson, at thirty-three. For a selection of his *Essays in Cornish History* Q. wrote the Preface, concluding 'But who now can bend his bow?' We should record how generous he was in helping on other people's work with Prefaces and Introductions.

In these years 1936 and 1937 honours flowed in upon him from his native Cornwall: he was made a Freeman of Bodmin, of Truro, and of Fowey. He expressed his thanks, but 'thanks are silly, and don't count with those who understand what love is and do things just for it'. Fowey gave occasion for a typical joke: if in more than fifty years he had not taken liberties enough with Troy Town, he wondered for what unbridled conduct in his old age he was now being given a blank cheque. It *was* extraordinary that, in all that writing, he had given no offence – quite exceptional for any writer, especially one looking for material for comedy, of which there was plenty. It was in marked contrast with Dorchester, where Hardy was resented rather than admired.

Then the mayoralty of Fowey descended upon him: so now Dogberry will have 'two gowns and everything handsome about him'. The statutory mayor-choosing, followed by church parade, meant arriving at Cambridge a week late for lectures. He proposed to give two classes 'if they clamour', and was now finishing a lecture on *Troilus and Cressida*: 'a bad play . . . not even a Shakespeare can play the fool *understandingly* with classical matter in default of proper baptism'.

This shows a complete misconception through not being an historian: he is misunderstanding the play from his purely classical background. The Elizabethans had no such classical knowledge of the Greeks: they viewed them through medieval spectacles, and Shakespeare based his play on Caxton's *Recuyal of Troy*. His view of Cressida is the medieval view of her. Q., as a classic, was wanting in historical perspective, like most commentators on Shakespeare, not really familiar with the Elizabethan age, a knowledge of which is indispensable. Actually *Troilus and Cressida* contains Shakespeare's most profound reflections on society and social order.[1] These are authoritarian, in conformity with Elizabethan thought, and would not in themselves be congenial to a Liberal like Q. The play is also a disillusioned one, a satire on love and war – nor would that be congenial to him either: he was an incorrigible romantic.

In February 1937 Q. invited me over to stay with him at Jesus for a weekend. For dear Q. it must have been rather a bore, for he was a *bon vivant*, a wine-bibber, and I, ill as I was, had to be a teetotaller,

---

[1] cf. my *Prefaces to Shakespeare's Plays*.

the thought of which Q. could not contemplate. At dinner in Hall, the College wine did not come up to his standards, so he had a little cellar of his own – what would I choose? I should have been glad to choose a glass of milk – unthinkable on a Cambridge or Oxford dais in Hall; so I plodded along, gingerly drinking as little as possible, with Q.'s eye on me. Afterwards, at dessert in Combination Room there was port. In his room, before going to bed, whisky-and-soda. I confided to Mr Brittain my trouble; he filled my glass at the side-board with soda water, and went through the appropriate motions with the whisky bottle – 'he won't know'. But Q. was not satisfied: 'Have you got any whisky?'

Next morning breakfast was a magnificent spread in his guest-room, fried everything (bad for a member of the Duodenal Club), and I was offered beer. Beer for breakfast! I was horrified: I could not bear the taste of the stuff, apart from its ill effects. Fortunately there was coffee, though I should have preferred a cup of Miss Pym's 'Earl Grey'. The hospitable old boy took me to his best club for lunch, the Pitt Club – to be confronted by oysters, and whatever you drink with oysters, porter or stout. Years before, when I once tried stout, it broke through my ulcer, perforated my stomach, and gave me peritonitis. I don't remember any more about lunch – ready to pass out, I suppose; and I can't bear oysters anyway.

Altogether I must have been a sad disappointment. Longing for the simple life of All Souls, I staggered back and went straight to bed.

His news home to Fowey that month were of his own entertainment at the Garrick Club, where he had sat between Lord Plender (of the Bank of England) and 'the great and jovial Lutyens, with Garter King-at-Arms'. Arrangements were made for a Coronation dinner, with the 'Mansion House at our disposal'. He was going to see the Irish Players, in Sean O'Cassey's *Juno and the Paycock*. At the Garrick he had met Seymour Hicks, 'who said some flattering things – in the actor's way, and no doubt with the usual amount of sincerity!' Disappointment with his failure in the theatre shows through.

For his wife's birthday he was sending a couple of Dresden statuettes he had fallen in love with; since there was a small crack in one, he had got them for quite a little. 'They could go on each side of the Bodmin Casket. St Blazey seems under the impression that it has

conferred its Freedom upon me. . . .' They had sent him two appeals
for subscriptions; 'and now at the invitation of Mr Chamberlain we
shall all have to pay more Income Tax into the pockets of the
Birmingham armament firms. *What* a game it all is!' Here was the old
Radical peeping out. He does not seem to have understood the
necessity of rearmament, with Hitler's Germany working all hours for
another attempt. Actually, Chamberlain, as Chancellor of the Exchequer, had held up rearmament until almost too late, in the interest
of 'good' Budgets and keeping down income tax for the possessing
classes.

Once more he took charge of the Coronation ceremonies at Fowey.
'I shall get out a detailed programme for the D.C.L.I. Band and had
better – at the performance – stand by them and give the sign for
starting and closing each separate item. I wish we could have piano
rehearsals, especially for the children, to time the movement and end
each right on the closing bars.' One sees what a local leader he was,
what pains he took over everything, and what a perfectionist.

In his dining room I had had a chance to see Nicholson's fine
portrait of him, with its slight touch of caricature, as usual, so that his
family put him against it. This suggested to me that we ought to have
a portrait of him for Cornwall, to hang in the County Museum. David
Cecil recommended his friend, Henry Lamb, to paint it. Ill as I was, I
managed to write round to everybody and get it started. Henry Lamb
was willing, and went down to Fowey to paint it. By this time I was
out of circulation, in University College Hospital, undergoing a couple
of desperate operations, with slender hope of recovery. It took me a
whole year to regain strength. I was only just sufficiently recovered to
attend the unveiling of the portrait at the County Museum. Not a
word was mentioned of whose idea it had been, or who had launched
it. The ceremony was performed by the Chamberlainite Lord-
Lieutenant. An unmistakable frisson of Philistine disappointment was
discernible at Q. being revealed in raincoat and tweeds, bow-tie and
cap, familiar pipe, just as one saw him walking the streets of Fowey.
They would evidently have preferred something pompous, academic
scarlet and black.

The company filed out for refreshments in the hall; I remained
alone in the room with the portrait I had engineered. Foy came out to

find me, I expect her father had sent her: 'We realise that we owe all this to you.' No such word had been spoken: the score against them was mounting up.

I had thought, before going into hospital, that the County ought also to have a portrait of that other distinguished Cornish writer, Arthur Symons – in a way, Q.'s opposite number. So I got in touch with him to know if there was a portrait going – several had been painted. He told me of a good bust of him by Dora Gordine. The Museum authorities, Council of the Royal Institution of Cornwall, were not interested; I don't suppose they had even heard of Arthur Symons or knew what a distinguished writer he was. So I dropped the matter; after my experience over the Q. portrait I wasn't making any further effort.

In this year Hitler invaded Austria, turning the flank of Czecho-Slovakia, ready to make Germany master of Central Europe. Britain remained passive and inert, paralysed by the 'National' government's disregard of the nation's vital interests – its claim to be 'National' inherently false. By 1937 it was clear what was in store for us:

> *A day will come when there shall descend on them*
> *From the skies they do not observe, some stratagem*
>
> *Of fate to search and sear their flesh with fire . . .*
>
> *Liquid fire will rain down from the air,*
> *Will suddenly arrive upon them there*
>
> *And lick their bodies up and burn their bones,*
> *No one at hand to hear their mutual groans:*
>
> *For these are they who, warned of what's to come,*
> *Walk blindly on to their appointed doom.*

When that day came they would, and should, pay the price. But so did the young men, my pupils at Oxford, who were not guilty. Their parents were. Eliot published my poem; did Q. ever read it? Not a word about what was driving me to despair.

I think that there may have been something between him and the Royal Institution of Cornwall too: he was not a member, never a member of Council or lectured in it. There must have been some cause of offence. When my day came, and at last they were anxious to recruit me, I was able to tell them that they were too late by just twelve years. Third-rate people should not make these mistakes with the first-rate. 'The best revenge is not to be like them'? – No: better to treat them in language they understand – and, for the rest, to amuse oneself at their expense.

That year Q.'s old friend Barrie died.

The best of our intimacy belonged to the early days, when e.g. he spent some weeks of his honeymoon at Fowey, and I listened to his ambitions. As time went on and success came, and distance separated us, naturally the confidences grew rarer as his self-confidence grew. Also he felt that I didn't like – I never do – the people of the theatre and their company 'off the stage'. And also, again, he had an inkling that I thought the domestic crash – the blame of it – was not all on one side. He never spoke to me of it, and I never alluded to it, of course. But his pretty frequent visits to Fowey came to an end. Recollections, no doubt. For all that, our affection held, unstrained, to the end. A few months before his death he dined with us at Queen Anne's Mansions and talked away till past midnight. Loth to go then, as he told us, rather wistfully.

Q., sturdy and square, happily married, can have had little idea of what was wrong with Barrie's marriage. He made a very large fortune from the theatre: do I detect a slight *soupçon* of envy at Barrie's luck?

1938 was the year when Chamberlain betrayed Czecho-Slovakia at Munich, 'I prefer to trust Herr Hitler's word' – rather than that of its President; and when that unspeakable assembly, the House of Commons elected on a fraudulent ramp in 1935, shouted Churchill down when he described it as the greatest diplomatic defeat in our history.

Q. published hardly anything that year, though the Christmas before he had returned to his old trade and written 'Faithful Jane', a short story for *The Times*. He was working for his new heavily revised *Oxford Book of Verse*, 1939. He omitted about a hundred poems from the old volume, which had proudly held its own for close on forty years 'by favour of the Public', and added two hundred, extending its intake to Armistice Day, 1918. (That had been, indeed, only an armistice.)

He admitted that he felt his judgment 'insecure amid post-War poetry'. This was not simply a matter of crabbèd age, 'I am at a loss what to do with a fashion of morose disparagement; of sneering at things long by catholic consent accounted beautiful. . . . Be it allowed that these present times are dark. Yet what are our poets of use – what are they *for* – if they cannot hearten the crew with auspices of daylight?' Q. had always favoured cheerfulness, and what he called 'the note of valiancy': 'it is indigenous, proper to our native spirit, and it will endure.' (Will it? It lasted at any rate, for the heroic years 1940–5, when Britain's historic greatness went out in flame.)

The new Book, for all its revision, is less satisfactory, for its date and time, than the old one was. There are a hundred, if not two hundred, feeble poems I would omit from it, to include more of Yeats, Housman, Kipling, Hardy, Belloc, Chesterton, de la Mare, Edward Thomas, Ralph Hodgson, Sassoon, Wilfrid Owen, even among those he did include. Sometimes he could have answered, as he did when Hardy complained that his best were not chosen, that they were not at the time in print, or available. But fancy omitting Bridges' 'London Snow', or Arnold's 'Forsaken Merman', 'Dover Beach', and 'Stanzas from Carnac'. There is hardly anything from Tennyson's 'In Memoriam' – Q. did not like the sad or the satirical.

Among the new people he did not like was Virginia Woolf. He had come upon an article of hers, 'in the Lytton Strachey style of detraction', about Scott, 'Gas at Abbotsford', writing him down as – of all people – pompous. The Bloomsberries were a supercilious lot, too much written up today; they could not generously appreciate nobility or magnanimity when it stared them in the face. Naturally Q. was a better judge of such a man and writer.

In 1939 came the German renewal of war for the domination of Europe, begun in 1914, but now in the far more promising circumstances Hitler had brought about, through the ineptitude and virtual collusion of British policy throughout the Thirties. When war came, Q. was not down at heart. 'A German broadcast the other day announced that Fowey was in flames. Which it ain't, and hasn't been. Dr Goebbels must have heard of Troy, for the first time, and got the story mixed up.' The little port became a garrison town, with units scattered all round – R.A.F., R.F.A., R.E., some Yeomanry, 'not to mention the Navy – and myself the one handy J.P. sitting, and representing Peace in the centre of the small cyclone'.

In 1940 the unexpected fall of France occurred, the British Army had to be withdrawn, leaving all its armament and equipment behind, and most of Europe, including Holland, Denmark, Norway was overrun. The Kaiser's Germany had never accomplished what Hitler's did; and Italy now joined in for the kill. Britain was really defeated in 1940, and was saved mainly by the support of the United States and Hitler's attack on Russia, giving us an ally with whom we should have reached agreement in the growing danger to us both, in the 'locust years' before.

Q., no historian, was not dismayed by the Fall of France. In church at Fowey he was inspired at that moment to write his poem, a kind of hymn, 'Sursum Corda, 1940'.

> *Sullen against the east a cloud*
> *Darkened the church from choir to nave,*
> *O'er heads in supplication bowed,*
> *O'er hearts that whispered, 'Heart, be brave.'*
>
> *Then – framed amid Crusader shields*
> *Held in the space of one clear pane,*
> *Acre on acre shone the fields*
> *Our fathers ploughed and sowed again.*
>
> *And lo! the altar caught their shine:*
> *The cross was hilt upon a sword –*
> *'Lift up your hearts! Accept the sign.'*
> *– We lifted them unto the Lord.*

That January, on the point of leaving for Cambridge, he had slipped on the frozen ground and spent a week in bed, reading Scott – 'yards of him: not as in the hot days of youth, but with just as great though a quite different delight, and with awe, too. The stature of it all, and the catholic understanding of men and their affairs!' – not given to a *précieuse ridicule* like Virginia Woolf. He did not forget either that, if Scott had received a tenth of the money pirated on his books in the United States, he need not have killed himself with overwork to meet his burden of debt.

At Cambridge as at Oxford the colleges were mostly requisitioned for the war. Q. did all he could to ensure that what undergraduates remained there lost as little of university life as possible. When the blessed Pitt Club had to close down, he helped to found a substitute and took on the presidency. A certain number of bombs fell in the vicinity. After the first few alerts he took no further notice of them. But at Fowey he had a narrow escape that August.

We had then no defences, and all the Cornish ports were targets for planes from across the Channel. One afternoon I watched with helpless anger an attack on the shipping in Falmouth harbour. At night we constantly heard the crump of scattered bombs on neighbouring Par and Fowey – until the terrible week of concentrated attacks on Plymouth in 1941 when the whole city went up in flames. One half of the little Cornish fire-brigades were obliterated as they stood in the Square fighting the fires. One could see Plymouth burning from all over East Cornwall – 'a day will come', indeed. . . . A school friend told me, when it was all over, that he had never understood what I had meant before!

August 1940:

We are all well here, by the mercy of Heaven and no thanks to the Boche. The scoundrel dropped four heavy bombs on me the other day as I was working in my little orchard. No.1 was a close call, striking the cliff some twenty feet from me, and by the Lord's guidance sending the shards straight up, to scatter high over me as I fell on my face. No.2 tore down a cantle of cliff, blasted a couple of oaks. No.3 made a large crater, destroyed a neat brake, dispersed the shale underneath it for some fifty yards. No.4 fell harmlessly into the sea. We have had a field or two ploughed up at the back of us, a schoolhouse broken [one sees the ruin on the horizon still], *with some cottages in Polruan.*

'But we go about our business – picking a fair crop of apples and pears in the orchard, with a bumper crop of plums and bullaces. And now, to my joy, the wind is S.W. and knocking up quite a sea in the Channel. My wife – who instinctively drives at practice – suggests that if the Germans try to invade tonight they will be horribly sea-sick.' On the coast all that summer we were expecting invasion – the Channel

Islands were occupied – and with no defences. 'Providence looks after fools and drunkards.'

The Haven was crowded with relatives.

But noise *has everywhere invaded this haven – speed-boat on patrol, gun-practice, siren warnings, bombs, military cyclists hurrying . . .*
Truth, I suspect, is that although I felt no ill effects at the time of my little shock the explosions – which were really terrific – have played a bit on the aural nerves, so that I find myself jumping at any bang of a door. I must cure myself of this, but it's abominably difficult to sit down to work.

Q. had extremely sensitive hearing: the truth was that, though he made light of it, he had been badly shaken.

These regular raids continued on our little ports, every one of which was building small craft like mad – motor torpedo boats to chase submarines, even on open beaches, and all along the river opposite Fowey. Q. wrote in 1941,

the small harbour now bristles with guns and other defences. But invasion seems to be off the programme. For this I have a sneaking regret, because if the nasty fellow had attempted it – he knowing nothing of the sea – he'd have met with a disaster to make future readers of history shudder – a massacre so awful that, as a decently humane fellow, I'm rather glad he funked it.

Those were not my sentiments about the people who ruined Europe. And what about the massacres they were responsible for in Eastern Europe, of the Jews all over the Continent? Actually Churchill was convinced that they could not get across the Channel: he told me, 'we should have put *every*thing into it'. And this convinced Roosevelt to see us through.

Q. travelled back to Cambridge via Oxford, 'where quiet has reigned. My old friends at the "Randolph" found me a room, though the place is packed. Also my old College offered me quarters. Cambridge is livelier with a raid warning now and then.' He kept up his spirits, and other people's, with an occasional squib, as of old:

The remarks of Alexander of Macedon
Would have been somewhat more than sub-acid on
An enemy that used wings
To drop things.

It is odd that he kept contact with Lord Alfred Douglas. And he carpeted young Miss du Maurier for some modern-minded expressions in her second book: 'You know, Daphne, people don't talk of such things.' The young lady, just back from Paris, was able to assure him, 'But, Sir Arthur, they *do*!' At that thought he gave up. It may have been that the irrepressible Lord Alfred kept writing to him. Q. admired his sonnets, and had loyally put a couple of them into the Oxford Book. He now wrote, 'try to forgive a friend to whom letter-writing has been the very devil all through a long life. I love actual talk and can claim to be quite a good listener, but the world's worst correspondent.'

This was not true: if there were any point to be made in writing, he took up the old much-mended pen, with which he had got his Second in Schools and sworn that together they should henceforth make good. A lot of letters call for no reply – from loonies who write, as one did to me quite recently, that William Shakespeare must have been a woman; others that Queen Elizabeth I was a man, and that Richard III was as innocent as a new-born babe. When I was young, I used to keep a 'File of Fools'. It got too full in the Thirties. When Q. was told, at the beginning of the war, that Secret Service agents were opening and reading people's letters: 'They are welcome to read all mine – provided that they answer them.'

To Lord Alfred he wrote once again, to congratulate him on an address to the Royal Society of Literature: they shared old-fashioned views of poetry, Q. liking neither Hopkins nor Eliot. 'I purred over your address, and again over your news that the hearers took it with joy.' He himself was a natural wit, and could always turn a verse with a pun or a punch-line. When the premises of the Pitt Club were requisitioned for a British Restaurant for the people, with a 10d. lunch, he fired off straight away, extempore, clever old boy:

Though our Club has had notice to quit,
Yet as Britons we still claim admittance –

So our last one-and-eightpence we'll split,
And we'll feast at the Pitt for a pittance.

His last formal Lecture – to a much diminished audience now –
was a Shakespeare one, on *Timon of Athens*.

No play at all [he called it]; *I wonder why the idolaters keep considering
Shakespeare a static artist? Did ever – could ever – a really great artist
grow without a number of mistakes, bad shots, unhappy failures? I know
that I reverence all the better, and hope to understand him the better, for
separating his great work from his misfits.*

Q. understood that from his own experience as a writer; he still did
not have the historical and biographical knowledge to enlighten him
as to the real character of the play. He appreciated that it was
unfinished; but the fascination of this text is that it reveals to us *how*
William Shakespeare worked. He composed, practical man of the
theatre, as he saw a scene in his mind, not as most writers would –
going straight on from beginning to end. The result is that here we
can see the dramatist *at work*: the scenes at the beginning and the end
of the play shaped up, the middle only roughed out. More, we can see
some thoughts set down in prose, on the way to being shaped into
verse. It is like observing unfinished work by Michelangelo, the figure
shaping itself out of the stone.

He still kept up with his class on the *Poetics*, though there were few
to attend now; and he would give a talk to the Forces – one on
'Modest Ignorance' . . . 'in which, as you know, I am something of an
expert'. Returning to Cornwall for vacation, he was still 'hotly pursued
by parcels of bad verse'. He assured me that he had received from
America a thesis of some 750 pages, asking him to read it, correct it,
and find a publisher for it. Edith Sitwell knew how to deal with that
sort of thing: she used to tell such hopefuls to send it to Dr Leavis
who would love to have it.

Q.'s creation of the English School stood firm, for all the discour-
agements and some outright opposition he had had in creating it. His
work now done, it was his enduring monument. It was only natural
that the next generation should have a different inflexion and something new to contribute. F. R. Leavis and his rebarbative wife Queenie

had something new to say, but it was a thousand pities the way they said it. A minority in the School, they formed themselves into a Cave of Adullam, from which they attacked – again with unnecessary venom – all who disagreed with them. The organ they ran, *Scrutiny*, is deformed by the personal campaign they pursued in the name of literary criticism – none of Q.'s catholic sympathies and his realisation that in the realm of literature there is room for many mansions – even the Leavises.

T. C. Worsley's autobiography, *Flannelled Fool*, a Leavis pupil, provides evidence. Leavis would extract from his haversack 'a battered copy of *The Oxford Book of English Verse* and launch himself into his attack on Quiller Couch and all his works'. Quiller Couch along with Dowden and A. C. Bradley had been mentors of the English master at Marlborough, 'but they were soon lying in fragments on my floor. It was Donne and Ezra Pound, *The Sacred Wood* [Eliot] and *Practical Criticism* [I. A. Richards] who reigned in their stead.' To these he adds Queenie's indispensable *Fiction and the Reading Public*. 'I. A. Richards was the Evangelist and *Scrutiny* was to become our Epistles.'

Later, Eliot disclaimed his too sectarian propagandist, and there was an awkward breach. Leavis was the leader of a sect, and today his vogue is over in turn. But his career divided the Cambridge English School, and did more harm than good among innocent schoolteachers, in Britain and America, who swallowed his gospel.

Q. himself was above all that, probably beyond taking it seriously – himself going out.

In 1943, the war still dragging on, everyone feeling the sickness of hope deferred, with all the reverses and set-backs: 'I have been shamefully idle in writing – and in everything for that matter except in bodily toil, helping the war effort as far as an old man may, with bill-hook, saw and other implements, in clearing land and storing timber.' I fancy that his last poem foresaw – as poems will – the end: 'To an Old Leader' –

> *Rise to thy knees; grope for the bugle bent,*
> *Set it to lip, and sound the charge amain!*
>
> *So back. . . . Lace up the curtain of thy tent,*
> *And lay thee down, too manly to lament,*
> *Too careless to complain.*

When I last saw him, at Cambridge about this time, he seemed at length sad and discouraged – no one to come to his *Poetics* class now, his name no longer in the publishers' lists of forthcoming books. I consoled him: 'But, my dear Q., how many have you written? – It must be over forty!' At this he perked up; in fact it must have been considerably more. But he was not getting on with the two books on the stocks that remained unfinished. He never spoke to me about *Castle Dore*, but I used to urge him to get on with his autobiography. Set as ever, from his early days, against the directly personal, he had the utmost difficulty in getting forward with *Memories and Opinions*. Yet, when the fragment came out after his death, beautifully written, one saw that it was one of the best things he had ever done.

His mind remained clear as a bell. At this time a great deal of fuss all round the English-speaking world was aroused by C. K. Ogden's project of 'Basic English' – largely because Churchill gave it some backing. Since English was becoming a world speech the proposal was to reduce it to a skeleton of a few hundred words. The scheme was carefully thought out along with I. A. Richards at Cambridge, Ogden's co-author in *The Meaning of Meaning*.

Essentially it reduced the multiplicity of verbs to a short number of portmanteau nouns. Q.:

> It cuts out all but eighteen verbs. It amazes me that so capable a writer as Mr Ogden and so philosophical a critic as Dr Richards should ignore the plain fact that in all civilised speech the verb is the very nerve of a sentence; and for preference the active verb. Nouns and adjectives are but dead haulage, prepositions and conjunctions inert couplings, until the verb (verbum, the 'Word') comes along. Dr Richards prefers to call his small handful of verbs 'operatives', and that is just what they are. He informs us that 'the reduction of the verbs to eighteen was the key to the discovery of Basic.' Very likely.

He quoted the ingenious Basic rendering of 'Ask, and it shall be given you; seek and ye shall receive; knock, and it shall be opened unto you.' 'Make a request and it will be answered; what you are searching for you will get; give the sign and the door will be open to you.' Q. comments: '"Ask", "seek", "knock" – how the imperative sinks, the authority loses accent, the assurance fades out in the Basic version! – with the whole further debilitated by the substitution of "will" for "shall": "shall" being superior or master wherever authority speaks or a promise is affirmed.'

Today no one knows the correct use of 'shall' and 'will', 'should' and 'would'; everybody substitutes 'will' and 'would' every time. This would not matter if there were not a difference of meaning, or emphasis, involved. Irish and Scottish usage did not observe the distinction, so that Q.'s old acquaintance, Wilde, used to have his texts vetted for him to correct the confusion. One can always tell the Irish or Scottish background in a writer from their impercipient confusion of 'shall' and 'will' – Rebecca West, for instance, part Irish, part Scotch; or Louis Auchincloss, Scotch-American.

Q., a better stylist, would never perpetrate this linguistic confusion (it puts one off throughout Auchincloss's novels: Henry James or Edith Wharton would know better). But Q. was no fuddy-duddy: 'if English be chosen for our international language I should put spelling reform well ahead'. I agree: no point in retaining 'programme', as Eliot advocated, in place of shorter 'program'. And I prefer the sensible American spellings, 'color', 'humor', to 'colour', 'humour'. We might begin with a very large reduction of Q.'s own subjunctives – as with Shakespeare's, today mostly redundant.

This essay was Q.'s last writing, and how spry for a man of eighty! – no loss of intellectual vigour whatever. After he died I managed to get it published in the *Times Literary Supplement*, in those more congenial days.

He was not giving up, though the event of his eightieth birthday was rather a strain: newspaper calls, hundreds of letters, camera men. 'For two or three days it snowed a blizzard of letters and telegrams. Beneath the pile of it I felt – I the world's worst correspondent – much like an old sheep who lets the snowstorm cover her, snuggles down in the hollow and quietly sleeps her last.' But 'it strained my heart and I had to take to my bed for a bit'.

Even so he went back to Cambridge for the last time in January 1944. There he had trouble with his jaw and could no longer hold a pipe in his mouth; whether he knew it or not, after a lifetime of smoking, cancer of the mouth had at last caught up with him. When he returned to Cornwall his strength revived a little, until one day he had a fall in the street getting out of the way of an army lorry. Badly shaken up again, he still kept thinking of returning to Jesus College. Truth is, he had come to love Cambridge and his life there.

A last letter accompanied a birthday present to his wife of 'Irish plate candlesticks (silver on copper) – I have admired them for some time and couldn't resist the pattern'. Cambridge was full of tempting antique shops; but so cold that February, 'I have half a mind to shut up classes and come home early'. Someone was still badgering him to 'vet' a translation for him.

Mr Brittain gives us an amusing account of his manner of life there, the regular routine, his endearing quirks and grumps. I have a letter of his fussing about undergraduates coming with muddy boots to dinner in Hall. He had been brought up, he said, to regard dinner as the civil ceremony of the day. He regularly changed for it, in college as at home, and was put out when the dons in war-time discontinued the habit. Then there was servant trouble. Foy told me that one cook who had been engaged announced one morning that there wasn't going to be any dinner that day, sorry as she was, for 'the old gentleman so liked his dinner'. He at once marched her out of the house to the railway station, bought her ticket, and incontinently packed her off to where she came from – London, I think. At Jesus another such person, a bedmaker, had 'a way of washing her hands in invisible soap and saying, "Oh no, Sir Arthur, I can't do enough for you, Sir Arthur" – and, to do her justice, she doesn't'.

Life cannot always have been easy with such a perfectionist, such exacting standards. It must have been inhibiting for Foy, brought up in subjection to them and accepting them – she once mentioned to me the standards expected of her. She never married, but lived at home with her mother, both of them attending upon his every wish and whim – including answering letters. Then, after her father's death, Foy took on his mantle as J.P., doing her duty on the Bench in his place.

In truth he was irreplaceable; I have never felt Cornwall, in particular Fowey, to be the same without him. His last illness was short; 'on 12th May, when Fowey and the neighbourhood for miles round were packed with troops, and the harbour and its inlets with ships – all waiting in a dense silence for the signal to invade France – he died'.

Hundreds attended his funeral, many of them carrying bunches of his favourite wild flower, the valerian which grows everywhere on the cliffs, in the crevices and along the roadside: we call it 'the pride of Fowey'.

For me, when I go over there, with all the life that centred on The Haven at an end, something rare has departed – if, for me alone, years after, his spirit is still over all.

The Cornish have not been much of a literary folk – their genius has been all for mining, science and technology – and Cornwall has been mostly written about by others. But for those of us who do write, he is the head of us all.

Index

Index